D1335288

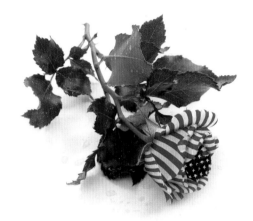

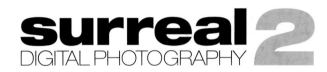

surreal 2
DIGITAL PHOTOGRAPHY

ALFORD ACADEMY
ALFORD
ABERDEENSHIRE

A+D

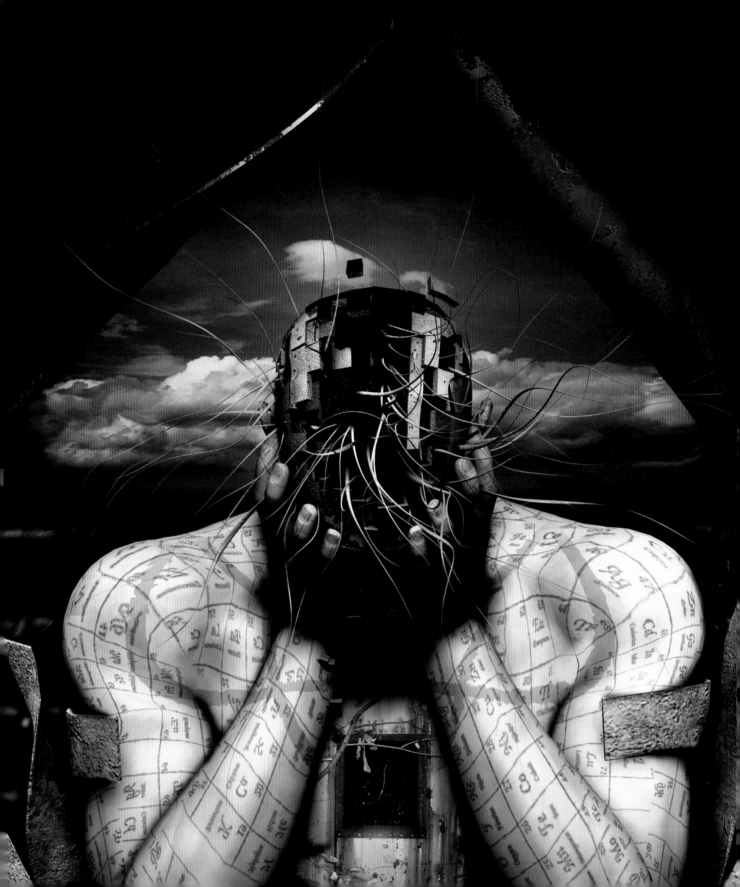

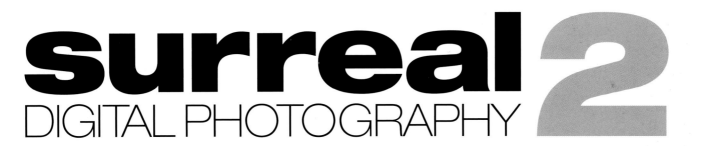

surreal DIGITAL PHOTOGRAPHY 2

General Editor: Ben Renow-Clarke

ILEX

SURREAL DIGITAL PHOTOGRAPHY 2
First published in the UK in 2007 by

I L E X

The Old Candlemakers
West Street
Lewes
East Sussex BN7 2NZ
www.ilex-press.com

Copyright © 2007 The Ilex Press Limited

Publisher: Alastair Campbell
Creative Director: Peter Bridgewater
Associate Publisher: Robin Pearson
Editorial Director: Tom Mugridge
Senior Project Editor: Ben Renow-Clarke
Art Director: Julie Weir
Designers: Tracy Staskevich & Lon Chan
Design Assistant: Kate Haynes

Any copy of this book issued by the publisher is
sold subject to the condition that it shall not by way
of trade or otherwise be lent, resold, hired out or
otherwise circulated without the publisher's prior
consent in any form of binding or cover other than
that in which it is published and without a similar
condition including these words being imposed on
a subsequent purchaser.

British Library Cataloguing-in-Publication Data
A catalogue record for this book is available from
the British Library

ISBN 10: 1-905814-07-0
ISBN 13: 978-1-905814-07-7

All rights reserved. No part of this publication
may be reproduced or used in any form, or by
any means – graphic, electronic or mechanical,
including photocopying, recording or information
storage-and-retrieval systems – without the prior
permission of the publisher.

Printed and bound in China

Vipnagorgialla font courtesy of Ray Larabie
www.larabiefonts.com

For more information about *Surreal Digital
Photography 2*, see:
www.web-linked.com/phdt2uk

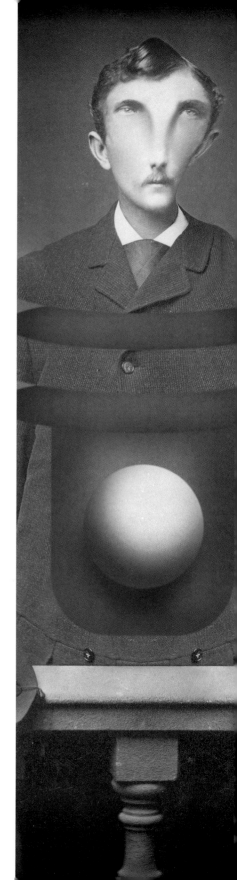

CONTENTS

INTRODUCTION

Surreal digital photography doesn't so much evolve as mutate, flowing like a Dali clock to fill every available niche as artists come up with new and even more incredible ideas. This volume presents a showcase of those new ideas. Some are so simple that you'll wonder why you've never attempted them before; others are so involved that you'll wonder why on earth anyone attempted them in the first place. All are magnificent examples of the surreal photographer's art.

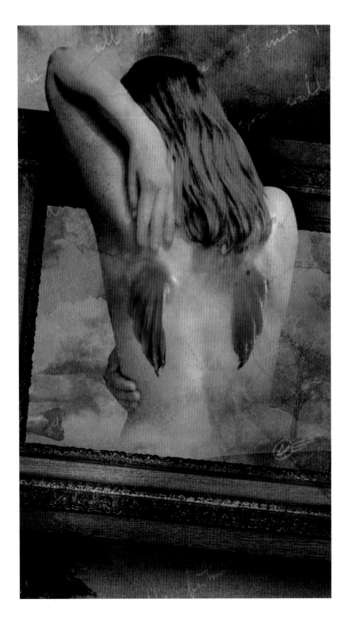

Thanks to the Internet and the ease with which digital technology allows artists to share and exhibit their work, many thriving communities of surreal artists have sprung up, with members spread across the globe. This book alone features contributors from the U.S., Great Britain, Belgium, Croatia, Latvia, Slovenia, and Sweden, and there were many more that we just couldn't squeeze in. The reason for this abundance of imagery is that people like to take a break from the norm every now and then, and just let their imagination run riot. Feel like combining a fish's face with that photo of your mother-in-law? Go right ahead (just remember to work on a copy). Want to reimagine your friend as a fairy? Feel free—Photoshop will grant your wish. Got a hankering to add flailing tendrils and an extruded checkerboard skull to a Rodinesque thinker with a migraine? Well, you may need to spend some time learning some 3D basics first, but sure, it's possible. The tools are all there waiting to be picked up and put to good use.

Left **Guardian Angel by Domen Lombergar**

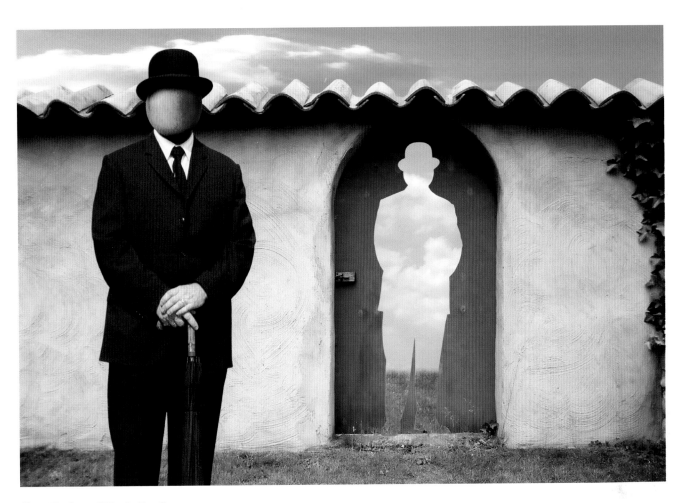

Above **The Gate of Eden by Ben Goossens**

And that's the main thing: the tools to create any image are at your disposal—all you need is the spark of an idea to set them in motion. You don't need to be a Photoshop genius to create stunning images (although, admittedly, the more complex your idea, the more technical knowledge you're likely to need to complete it); a bit of forethought and planning will help to break down the most daunting of composite images into manageable chunks. All of the source files for making these images are available to download from the Web address that you'll find on the inside cover of the book, so you can work through them for yourself and see how each of the surreal images was created from start to finish. Hopefully you'll be inspired to create even more surreal images of your own.

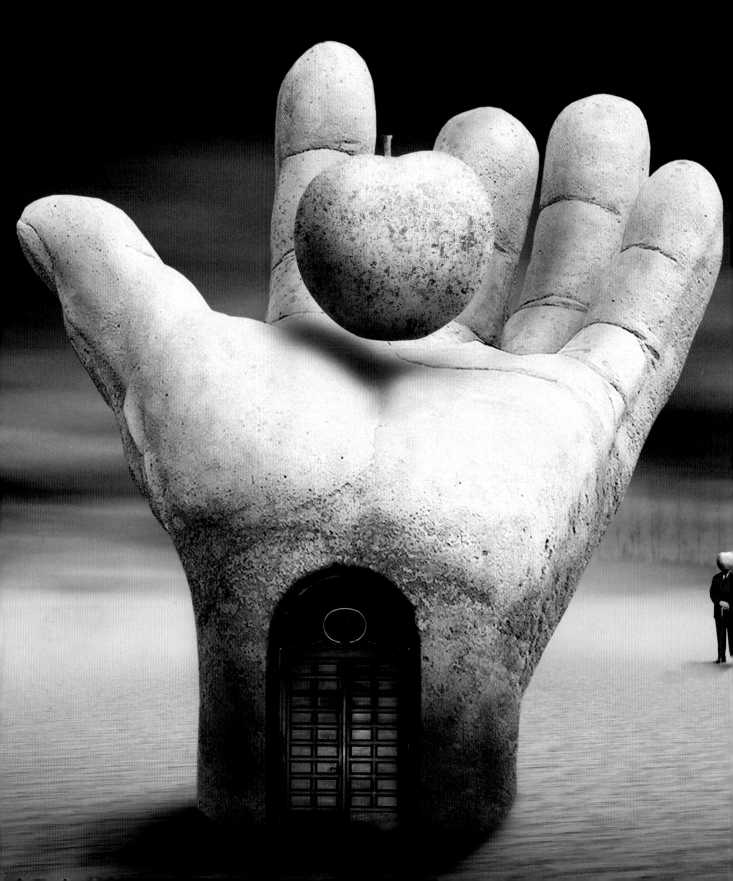

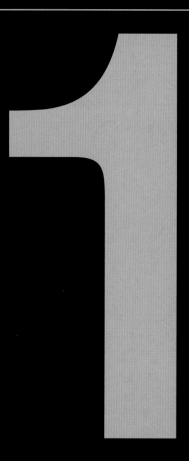

1

Naturally, before you can begin to explore the tools and techniques of the masters, you need the right equipment. Luckily, while it's possible to pour vast amounts of cash into your digital toolbox, you don't have to spend a fortune to produce images of professional quality. Follow our guide to cameras, computers, software, and peripherals, then choose equipment that fits comfortably within your budget. As pioneers such as Man Ray demonstrated, in surreal photography the equipment you use to create your images is not as important as what you choose to do with it.

the digital toolbox

The Digital Toolbox

DIGITAL CAMERAS

It's easy to become bewildered by the sheer variety of digital cameras on the market, as every manufacturer offers many variations of megapixel rating, zoom lens, and form-factor. If you intend to produce images for print, you need a camera with a high resolution, but megapixels don't tell the whole story. To produce high-quality images that can be later manipulated in an image-editing program, you need a flexible lens system and plenty of control, which often means a professional or a prosumer model.

At the low end of the digital camera spectrum are compact digital cameras. These are affordable, easy to use, and ideal for beginners or as a second camera for the serious photographer. If you wish to create images that will look professional when printed out, however, you will need to look farther up the price chain.

Prosumer Cameras

At first glance it's very difficult to spot any difference between prosumer digital cameras and professional models. Both types of camera usually have the lens mounted at the center of the camera, giving the impression that they are Single Lens Reflex (SLR) cameras, but this isn't the case. Many prosumer cameras take their pictures in a similar way to smaller compact models. The viewfinder is a separate optical system, usually situated above the lens, and what it shows doesn't always reflect what the camera will actually capture. Other cameras use an electronic viewfinder, but this may lack detail or color depth, or blur with any movement. Using the LCD screen will give you a more accurate picture, but will also drain the battery faster, and the screen might not be visible in all light conditions.

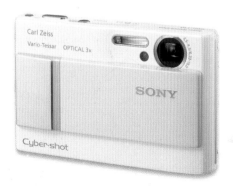

A good compact digital camera, such as Sony's DSC-T10, can produce fantastic results, thanks to high resolutions and cutting-edge lens technology, but can't match the flexibility and fine control of prosumer and digital SLR models.

Apart from this minor issue, prosumer cameras offer a range of features that rival more expensive professional models. Most prosumer digital cameras, for example, come equipped with a respectable optical zoom, enabling you to pick out detail from a distance or include depth-of-field effects in your photographs. Prosumer cameras also come equipped with a choice of automatic exposure controls to assist you when shooting in specific situations such as night-time, studio, or action shots. And most prosumer cameras also include a good built-in flash, a hot-shoe for an external flash, and a range of standard controls including automatic timer, macro function, and LCD view screen with image-editing functions. If you decide to invest in a prosumer camera, one feature is a must-have: a full manual mode that allows you to adjust exposure settings and aperture. Without this, your prosumer camera will be no more useful than a cheaper compact camera.

All of this control means that you can shoot images that are often indistinguishable from images taken with a professional camera, and recent models from Canon, Sony, Fuji, Konica-Minolta, and Nikon offer resolutions beyond 6 megapixels, meaning they are capable of producing images that will print out at sizes larger than US Letter or A4.

Professional Digital Cameras

Professional digital cameras offer all of the functions of prosumer cameras and more. The extensive range of features and build quality are reflected in the expensive price tag. As well as providing the user with full manual control over almost every aspect of the camera, professional digital cameras also offer true SLR functionality.

For the photographer this has two advantages: firstly, because you are looking through the actual lens when you shoot, you can be sure that every image you take will be exactly what you saw. Secondly, SLR cameras allow you to attach other types of lens; this means that you can purchase extra lenses, such as fish-eye or wide-angle, and fit them to the camera. This is ideal for traditional film photographers moving over to digital because it gives them the option of using their old lenses

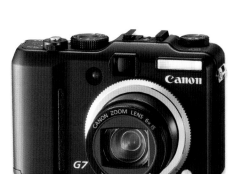

With a 10-megapixel CCD, a 6x optical zoom lens, and a comprehensive selection of features, such as 9-point autofocus and face detection technology, the Canon Powershot G7 is an advanced prosumer digital camera.

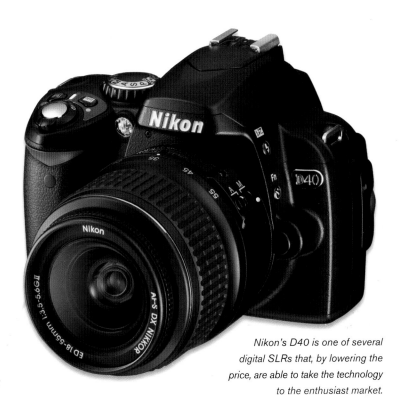

Nikon's D40 is one of several digital SLRs that, by lowering the price, are able to take the technology to the enthusiast market.

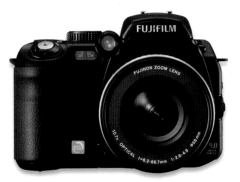

Cameras such as the Fujifilm S9100 offer professional-level features in a more convenient all-in-one form.

on their new camera—provided the mounting system is compatible. It's worth mentioning that this facility comes with a slight disadvantage. Every time you fit a new lens to a professional digital camera, its CCD sensor (the "brain" of the camera) is exposed to the elements. CCDs are susceptible to dust and this can have an impact on image quality. As such, it is wise to swap lenses under as much cover as possible, and clean the sensor regularly with a blow brush.

As mentioned earlier, professional digital cameras offer enormous capacities of up to 14 megapixels, allowing you to shoot images that can be printed out to poster size. The ability to capture such great detail is also ideal when editing images later. In addition, you should be able to save at 16 bits per channel in the high-quality RAW file format (see page 22), capturing all of the image data produced from the camera.

MEGAPIXELS

The term "megapixel" is used to measure the amount of detail that a digital camera is able to record and store when taking a photograph. While there won't seem much difference between a 4-megapixel shot and a 6-megapixel shot if printed at 8 x 10 photo size, the difference becomes more apparent during image editing. To print out an image at true photographic quality, it needs to be the size you want it printed when the resolution is set to 300 pixels per inch (300ppi). The 4-megapixel model captures enough pixels to do this at 8 x 10 photo size but, having 50% more pixels to play with, the 6-megapixel shot gives you more freedom. You can zoom in on portions of the image, expand them, or manipulate the image in other ways without having to worry about jagged digital artifacts appearing. If you're unhappy with a composition, you can crop your shot quite fiercely, knowing that you'll still have enough pixel information remaining to create a decent print.

The Digital Toolbox

SCANNERS

Not so long ago, a scanner was a major investment, particularly if you needed to scan transparencies. Nowadays, prices have fallen and perfectly acceptable scanners are available at bargain prices. If you plan to use a scanner to produce high-quality images, however, it is sensible to look at what's available at the higher end of the market.

Generally speaking, there are three types of scanner available. At the top end of the spectrum is the drum scanner, an expensive option that works by taping film on to a rotating drum and shining a narrow beam of light on to it, which is then converted to digital information. At the bottom end is the flatbed scanner, which operates by moving a CCD array across a glass plate. These can be purchased for less than $100. Most photographers, however, should opt for something more capable if they want to work with transparencies, and that could mean a specialist film scanner.

Costing more than the flatbed, the film scanner uses a row of sensors known as a linear array, moving a light source slowly across a film transparency and focusing this on to the array. Most are built to handle 35mm film, and adaptors are available for APS cartridges as well. If you are a traditional film photographer moving over to digital—or even someone who wishes to work in film and then digitize your images—a film scanner is indispensable when converting film transparencies into editable digital files. If this is not a prime consideration, however, you may decide that a less expensive flatbed scanner is ideal for your purposes. In fact, many modern flatbed scanners include transparency adapters that are capable of producing respectable results.

In either case, there are a number of features to look out for when selecting a scanner that is right for you. Probably the most important feature of a scanner is its optical resolution. This term relates to the amount of pixels that the scanner is able to capture, and is measured in dots per inch, or dpi. In general, a maximum resolution of 300dpi is more than good enough for most digital photographers. When buying a scanner, do not confuse resolution with "interpolated resolution"— this refers to a method used by some scanners to effectively "guess" the colors of extra pixels to increase resolution, which should really be avoided.

Color depth is measured in "bits," and is another important feature to be aware of. This term refers to the units of information that a computer uses to store color. Most scanners and digital cameras work in 24-bit color, with each pixel assigned 8 bits of data per red, green, and blue color channel for a total of 16.8 million colors. More high-end software such as Adobe Photoshop is able to work in 48-bit color, with 16 bits for each of the RGB color channels and billions of colors. This may seem excessive, but it actually helps keep colors accurate during manipulation. However, if your image-editing software is limited to 24 bits, there's little point in purchasing a 48-bit scanner.

Remember that a scanner is not only limited to scanning photographs and transparencies. Many photographers scan objects such as fabric for use as backgrounds in their photographs or for advanced texture mapping in a program such as Adobe Photoshop.

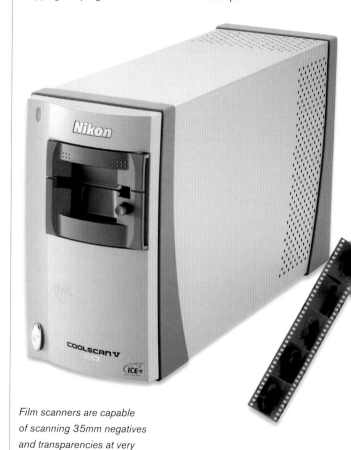

Film scanners are capable of scanning 35mm negatives and transparencies at very high resolutions.

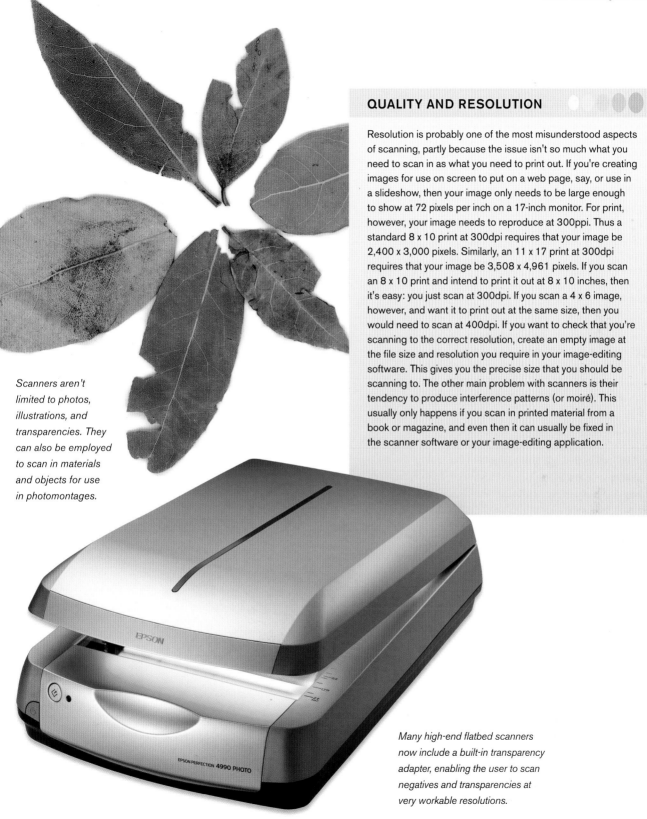

QUALITY AND RESOLUTION

Resolution is probably one of the most misunderstood aspects of scanning, partly because the issue isn't so much what you need to scan in as what you need to print out. If you're creating images for use on screen to put on a web page, say, or use in a slideshow, then your image only needs to be large enough to show at 72 pixels per inch on a 17-inch monitor. For print, however, your image needs to reproduce at 300ppi. Thus a standard 8 x 10 print at 300dpi requires that your image be 2,400 x 3,000 pixels. Similarly, an 11 x 17 print at 300dpi requires that your image be 3,508 x 4,961 pixels. If you scan an 8 x 10 print and intend to print it out at 8 x 10 inches, then it's easy: you just scan at 300dpi. If you scan a 4 x 6 image, however, and want it to print out at the same size, then you would need to scan at 400dpi. If you want to check that you're scanning to the correct resolution, create an empty image at the file size and resolution you require in your image-editing software. This gives you the precise size that you should be scanning to. The other main problem with scanners is their tendency to produce interference patterns (or moiré). This usually only happens if you scan in printed material from a book or magazine, and even then it can usually be fixed in the scanner software or your image-editing application.

Scanners aren't limited to photos, illustrations, and transparencies. They can also be employed to scan in materials and objects for use in photomontages.

Many high-end flatbed scanners now include a built-in transparency adapter, enabling the user to scan negatives and transparencies at very workable resolutions.

The Digital Toolbox

COMPUTERS

Digital image editing can be an intensive task, particularly when you're working with high-resolution digital photographs. Your computer needs a fast processor, a large hard drive, and plenty of RAM. It's also sensible to have something to back up your valuable images in case disaster strikes.

Home Computers

Many graphics professionals favor an Apple Mac computer, while others use a PC, but either is capable of producing high-quality results. PCs have an advantage in that they are more common and produced by many manufacturers in competition, which means they are cheaper and have a wider range of available software. Macs, on the other hand, feature a more attractive interface that can be easier to learn and use, and come with Apple's own suite of creative applications—iPhoto, iMovie, iTunes, and GarageBand—built in. Both PCs and Macs are able to run Photoshop, and the two versions are practically identical in use except for the keyboard shortcuts.

Nowadays, it is quite possible to purchase a home computer with everything you need for digital image editing right out of the box. You may, however, prefer a computer system that suits your own specifications. This means ensuring that the computer's processor

is fast enough to handle image manipulation, that there is enough RAM fitted to run powerful programs such as Photoshop, and that there is enough hard drive space to accommodate the enormous file sizes that digital image editing produces.

Generally speaking, an ideal configuration for a PC would comprise a 120GB hard drive, with 1GB of RAM, and a 2.5GHz Pentium processor. Macintosh users should aim for a similar configuration, with an Intel processor, as the latest version of Photoshop is designed to run natively on Intel Macs. These specifications will ensure that you are able to run almost any image-editing program without spending too much time watching activity bars edge slowly forward.

One other consideration should be the graphics card or graphics chipset used by your computer. Ten years ago these did little more than provide an interface between your computer and your monitor screen, but

Large PC manufacturers, such as Dell, produce desktop machines that are more than capable enough for photographic work. You don't need to pay out for a specialist workstation to work with digital images.

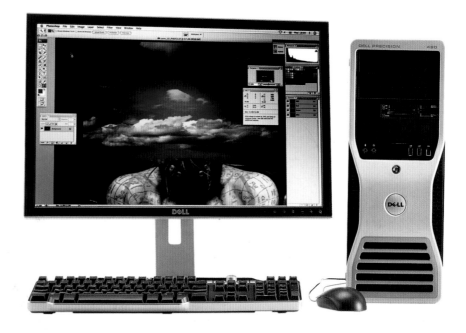

The Digital Toolbox

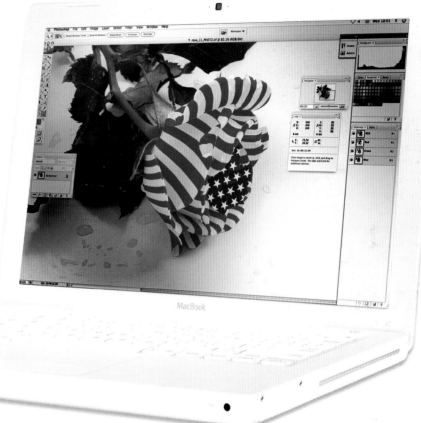

Apple's MacBooks put image-editing power in a portable package, with large screens and excellent graphics capabilities.

nowadays they include their own speedy processors that accelerate 2D and—especially—3D graphics. If you intend to use 3D applications as well as a 2D image-editor, a fast graphics card with support for OpenGL (a set of instructions for 3D graphics) is essential. Nearly any new PC or Mac will come with some form of OpenGL-supporting hardware included, but the performance can differ massively, so do your homework before buying.

Monitors

Monitors also come in two distinct types. Some still use CRT (Cathode Ray Tube) screens—a technology similar to that used in most TV sets. These offer a high-quality display at the disadvantage of being big and bulky. If you have limited desk space, you might want to look at a flat-panel monitor instead. These are more expensive than CRT monitors but take up much less room. Although there is some debate as to which of the two types of screen offers the best picture, both have advantages.

A CRT is usually brighter, but a good flat-panel offers better definition. When purchasing a monitor, try to get one with the largest screen you can afford—it will make your image-editing work that much easier.

Storage

No matter how big your hard drive is, it's likely that you'll manage to fill it up sooner or later. This—and the need to back up your precious data—is a good reason to invest in some form of external storage device. There are a number of options available to you, including external hard disks that range in capacity from 60GB all the way up to 1,000GB. An external hard drive connects to your computer and enables you to back up thousands of digital photographs. If you are on a budget, however, you might want to consider CD or DVD burners. Compact disks can store a maximum of 800MB of data, while DVDs can store 4.7GB of data. For many people this is plenty enough capacity for archiving and distribution.

The Digital Toolbox

PRINTERS

 The digital photographer's third and final piece of essential equipment is the printer. Top of the range laser printers produce consistently excellent results at high speeds, but the cost of buying one is prohibitive for nonprofessionals. Meanwhile, an inexpensive inkjet printer allows you to output prints of photographic quality, but this approach has its own hidden costs—inks and papers don't come cheap!

Inkjet Printers

Nowadays, even the cheapest inkjet printers are capable of producing prints that can pass for photo-quality, and more expensive models can produce gallery-standard output. Like digital cameras, there are dozens of different models available, and for this reason there are a few important features that you need to be aware of.

As always, resolution is a prime consideration, but once again this isn't a clear-cut issue. While an image destined for printing should have a resolution of 300ppi, most inkjets now offer a resolution of at least 1,200dpi, and sometimes up to 2,800dpi. Inkjet printers work by squirting microscopic dots of three, four, or six colors on to paper, and these colors are layered or dithered into patterns to create an impression of the other colors in the image. This makes the size of the dot a significant factor: the smaller it is, the better the image quality. Good printers use up to three-dozen dots per pixel, but. cheaper models may not even offer half this number, and print quality will inevitably suffer. For this reason, a 2,800dpi model is a wise investment if you want to hang your work on the wall.

However, resolution doesn't tell the whole story. Most inkjet printers use four different colors of ink to produce their prints—cyan, magenta, yellow, and black—while some use six colors, adding a lighter cyan and magenta. This results in more realistic-looking photo prints, but has another downside. Inkjet printers have a tendency to use up inks very quickly and replacement cartridges can be expensive—sometimes a single cartridge can cost a quarter of the price of the printer! For this reason, try to minimize your ink usage by ensuring that the printer you purchase allows you to buy replacement cartridges for each individual color. Some cheaper models demand that you replace all colors when only one color has run out—an expensive business.

Dye-Sub Printers

As an alternative, some printer and camera manufacturers now produce smaller dye-sub printers specifically for photo printing. These work by vaporizing solid dye on to paper, so producing true continuous tone images that closely match the quality of conventional photographs. Unfortunately, these printers only produce prints of a limited size (usually 6 x 4), and while larger dye-sub printers are available for professional print and graphics work, the cost of purchasing and maintaining such a system is prohibitive.

Laser Printers

A third option is the laser printer. These are becoming more affordable, and are able to produce photographic prints that easily match the quality of ink jets without using special paper or inks. For this reason, they can be a cost-effective option if you intend to output your images in the larger format, but you would have to be doing a lot of printing to really make a color laser printer a worthwhile option. As a result, only print and graphics professionals will have access to this sort of technology.

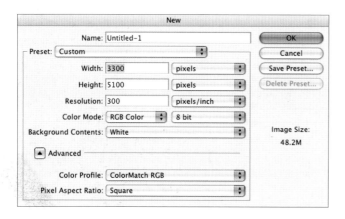

For printing purposes, the resolution of an image needs to be as close to 300ppi as possible. At 11 x 17 size, this would mean a massive 15-megapixel image—one reason why most professional photographers need all the megapixels they can get.

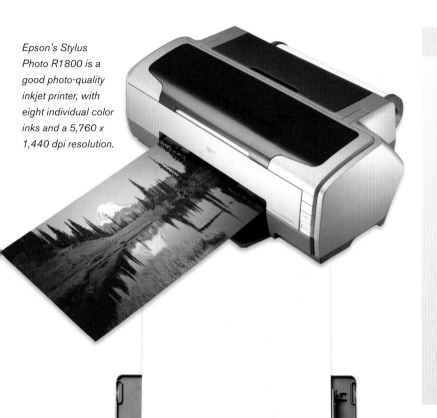

Epson's Stylus Photo R1800 is a good photo-quality inkjet printer, with eight individual color inks and a 5,760 x 1,440 dpi resolution.

PAPER PRIORITY

High-resolution inkjet technology and photo-quality inks won't produce good prints unless you're also prepared to splash out on paper. This is another hidden cost of inkjet printing. If you have ever tried to print a photo on standard copier paper, you will probably have got a poor result with dull colors and a serious lack of detail. This is because the small drops of ink hit the paper but sink into the surface and flow into the coarse grain of the sheet. Specialist photo papers use a matte or glossy coating to keep the ink on top of the paper, while a specially prepared or textured surface keeps the ink from spreading. Most inkjet manufacturers will advise you to use their own paper. On the one hand, this will be designed to work with their inks and their printer technology, but on the other hand, it's often an expensive option. In many cases, a third-party photo paper will provide excellent results.

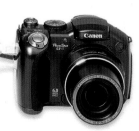

Canon's iP6700D combines a 9,600 x 2,400dpi resolution with the ability to print images direct from a memory card or camera. The LCD screen means you can review and print images without ever using a computer.

IMAGE-MANIPULATION SOFTWARE

There is an amazing wealth of software available for the digital photographer, including image-editing software, 3D landscape generators, cataloging software, and special-effects plug-ins. At the least, most digital photographers will be familiar with Adobe Photoshop or its accomplished junior version, Photoshop Elements.

Surreal digital photography is all about image manipulation. While cheap or free packages such as iPhoto, Graphic Converter, or PictureIt! offer basic correction features, manipulation requires something more heavy-duty. There are several applications that can do the job, but the big daddy of all image-editing packages is undoubtedly Adobe Photoshop. From its birth in the late 1980s, Adobe Photoshop has developed into the de facto standard in image editing on both the PC and Macintosh platforms. Now at version 10, Photoshop gives you absolute control over the photographs that you take—there is literally nothing that you cannot do with an image. Unfortunately, there are a few drawbacks to all this power. Firstly, Photoshop is not an easy piece of software to master; its learning curve is steep and has spawned a whole cottage industry of off-the-shelf manuals and tutorials to help you get to grips with it. Secondly, it has a price tag that is likely to deter all but the professional digital photographer.

Fortunately, Adobe also offers a cut-down version of Photoshop, Photoshop Elements, which offers most of the features of its elder brother at a more affordable price. For most people cutting their teeth in the world of digital imaging, Elements will provide more than enough power to get you started. Indeed, its simpler interface can provide an ideal introduction to Photoshop. By the time you have used Elements and become comfortable with its features, you will be ready to upgrade to its fully featured sibling.

On the PC, it is also worth taking a look at Paint Shop Pro. This cut-price rival to Photoshop has many of the same features and, despite a sometimes clunky interface, some extremely powerful tools all of its own.

Adobe Photoshop

Photoshop offers such an abundance of capabilities that it's difficult to know where to start, but there are some key features that you will keep returning to time and again. First among these is Photoshop's extensive color controls, including adjustments that give you control over color channels, color curves, brightness and contrast, hue and saturation, and tonal levels. These features allow you to fine-tune the colors in your images by making adjustments to the whole image or to individual color channels.

Another important feature for the digital photographer is layers. Layers are rather like pieces of translucent tracing paper laid over your image. You can select and copy elements from within your image, place them within their own layer, and work on them independently, or you can control the opacity of layers and how they interact with other layers

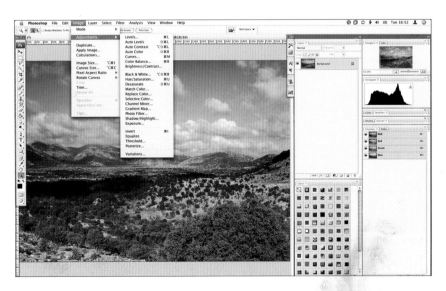

The complexity of the Photoshop interface may initially be a little off-putting. Once you use the program for a short time, however, you become accustomed to its huge range of powerful controls.

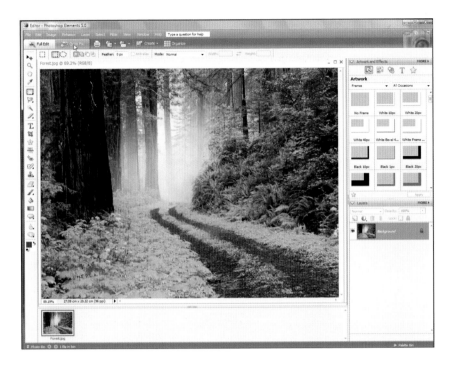

The Photoshop Elements interface shares many similarities with its elder brother, Photoshop. Elements is still a very powerful program in its own right, and a great introduction to digital image editing.

using a range of preset blending modes. You can also create adjustment layers, enabling you to control how changes to color and tone affect your image with a greater precision. When editing an image, layers give you tremendous flexibility, as you will see later on in this book.

No discussion of Photoshop is complete without mentioning its filters. There are dozens available, all offering different functions—some useful, some not so useful. Filters are used to transform the look of an image or part of an image. This can mean blurring or sharpening the focus of a picture, distorting components of the picture, or even turning it into a digital watercolor painting or chalk drawing. The possibilities are limitless. Remember: this is only the tip of the iceberg. You will be amazed by the depth of Photoshop's abilities once you start using it.

Elements

It's hard to launch Photoshop Elements without being struck by its similarity to Photoshop proper. Both programs' interfaces look more or less the same, with tools available at the sides and top of the screen, plus pull-down menu commands and floating palettes. Indeed, feature-wise there are few major differences between the two programs, and both offer extensive color adjustments, layers, and filters. The most significant difference between the two programs is that Photoshop offers more complex color adjustment features and the ability to work with CMYK

images—essential features if you're involved in professional publishing, but not so essential if you're printing to a standard inkjet printer. This makes Elements a fine image-editing package and the ideal entry-level program.

Paint Shop Pro

For PC users, Paint Shop Pro is a very commendable alternative to Photoshop. All of the standard image-editing tools are built into the program, as well as advanced batch-editing features and a useful image browser. At less than $100, it's far cheaper than Photoshop, too.

GRAPHICS TABLET

For the digital photographer, the graphics tablet is an interesting alternative to the mouse. Graphics tablets are pressure sensitive and come equipped with a special pen. They are particularly useful when using the drawing and painting tools in programs such as Photoshop or Painter. Pressing down harder with the pen on the tablet increases the flow of ink; pressing softly decreases the flow. Graphics tablets come in a variety of sizes, from 4 x 5 up to 12 x 18 inches.

IMAGE-MANIPULATION SOFTWARE

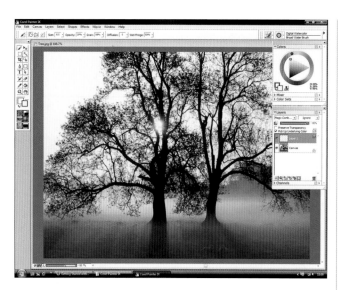

Although not a dedicated image-editing program, Corel Painter offers some interesting effects, including the ability to add textured backgrounds to your images.

Painter

Another alternative to Photoshop is Painter. Although not strictly a dedicated image-editing package, Painter offers many of the features of Photoshop—including advanced color controls, layers, and filters. Where Painter differs from Photoshop, however, is in its use of real media tools. Painter offers digital re-creations of almost any kind of painting or drawing medium, including oil, watercolor, chalk, pencil, and even Magic Markers. This is particularly useful for digital photographers who wish to add painterly effects to images.

Corel Photo-Paint

Part of Corel's CorelDRAW graphics suite, Photo-Paint offers a similar feature-set to Photoshop with a slick professional interface, plus powerful tools to extract foreground selections from backgrounds and additional creative features. Earlier versions are also available in inexpensive bundles, meaning you can pick up a professional-level photo-editing package at a bargain price.

iPhoto

Available for purchase as part of Apple's iLife 06 or bundled free with any new Macintosh computer, iPhoto offers limited image-editing features. Of more use, however, is iPhoto's image browser, which offers cataloging facilities and "smart" slideshows. Not intended as a professional editing tool, iPhoto is still an excellent means of organizing your photographs.

Plug-ins

Plug-ins are small "applets" that are added to host programs to extend their features or functionality. There is a wide range of plug-ins available for Photoshop, and most other programs, including Photoshop Elements, Paint Shop Pro, and Photo-Paint, will support Photoshop compatible plug-ins, although it's always wise to check first.

Corel KPT Collection

KPT, or Kai's Power Tools, is long established as one of the premier suites of plug-ins for Adobe Photoshop. Consisting of a set of different plug-ins that allow you to create textures, gradients, and diverse effects such as lightning and fractal patterns, the KPT Collection is aimed at the digital photographer with an equally diverse imagination. KPT has an unusual interface that many find difficult to master. In terms of what you can do to an image, however, the suite of filters has no peer. Where KPT really excels is in its ability to generate unique backgrounds and textures—ideal when working with photomontages.

Eye Candy 5

The Eye Candy suite of plug-ins is another eclectic set of effects. It's useful for adding effects such as fur, fire, shadows, and bevels to selections, and is particularly well-suited to adding special effects to type. Note that, with a little knowledge, many of Eye Candy's effects can be created using Photoshop's standard toolset.

3D Landscape Creation

Adventurous digital photographers might also consider a 3D landscape generator, such as Bryce or Vue. These allow you to create photorealistic landscapes with complete control over terrain, oceans, trees, skies, and weather. Using them takes some technical skill and practice, but they do have advantages for surrealist photography because you can create your own world, then place photographed figures or objects within it.

Bryce 6

Bryce is the most famous 3D landscape generator, and is now resurgent after a few years in the wilderness. At its highest render settings you can create 3D scenes that are scarcely discernible from the real thing. The program features a unique "organic" interface that is designed to speed up your workflow. Landscapes are created as polygons that can be edited and positioned anywhere within the picture frame. Bryce also gives you control over the weather and time of day; the program even includes a Tree Room, in which you can generate naturalistic-looking trees. You can import 3D models from other programs, or use your own photos as backdrops in the image. The results can be output to a variety of formats, including layered TIFF files that allow you to store channels and masks for use in Photoshop.

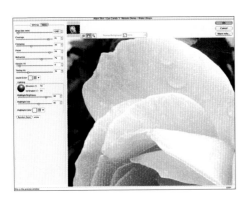

The Eye Candy plug-in offers a host of special effects, including the ability to add water drops to your photographs.

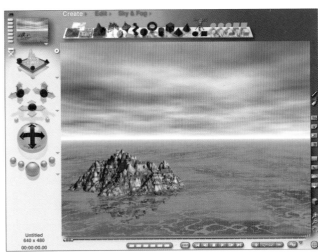

With Bryce you can "shoot" your own exotic landscapes without ever having to leave the house. You can then import the file into Photoshop and use it as an exotic background in your photomontages.

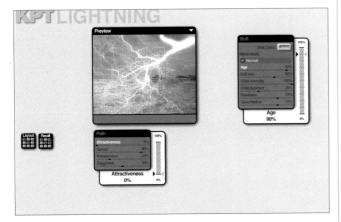

KPT's unique interface is an ideal aid to creativity. Here lightning effects are added to a seascape.

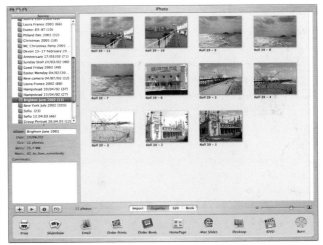

Apple's iPhoto is bundled free with every new Macintosh computer and is a very useful image-editing program. Not only does it include rudimentary brightness, contrast, red eye, and correction tools, the program is also adept at cataloging photographs.

Vue 6

Vue is available on both the PC and Macintosh platforms and is another powerful 3D landscape creator. Originally developed as a plug-in, the program is now stand-alone and shares many of the features of Bryce. Vue is currently considered top-of-the range in this field and integrates very well with Photoshop.

Cataloging Software

Although Photoshop now includes its own image browser, Bridge, it's useful to have a means of organizing and cataloging photographs. Programs such as Extensis Portfolio (available from **www.extensis.com**) and Expression Media (the latest incarnation of iView MediaPro, now owned by Microsoft; **www.microsoft.com/expression**) can help. These enable you to label, organize, archive, and search through your photos in an easy-to-understand manner.

The Digital Toolbox

COLOR MANAGEMENT

One of the best things about image-editing's move into the mainstream is that you don't really need much technical know-how to get on with it. However, if you want to do justice to your art, then you need to understand something about color management. Getting your printed color to match what you see on screen is a science, and it helps if you know a few basics.

One of the biggest problems that you will encounter when using a computer to edit photographs is the tendency for colors to appear differently on screen to how they appear when printed out. The rich blue of a sky, for example, may look perfect on screen. When printed out, however, it may lose its proper hue—the difference might be subtle, but it will have an impact on your image. This partly occurs because your monitor might not be set correctly, with the colors too dim or the contrast too high or low. To make things more complicated, the colors on a computer monitor are described in terms of how much red, green, and blue (RGB) light is present in a pixel, while colors on the printed page are described in terms of cyan, magenta, and yellow ink. Getting one to match the other isn't always as straightforward as you might think.

To combat these color discrepancies it is necessary to calibrate your screen. This isn't as difficult as it sounds—you just need to use a Color Management System or CMS for short. The easiest way to do this is to use ICC profiles. Developed by the International Color Consortium, ICC profiles change the colors on your screen so that they match the color profile of the device to which you are outputting your image.

Many output devices such as inkjet printers include software-install disks that contain an ICC color profile of the device. In the Windows or Macintosh Displays control panel, all you need to do is select your printer's ICC profile and the colors on your screen adjust to match it. For this reason, it is best to decide how you intend to output your images—if you intend to send your image to a printing bureau, ask them for a copy of their ICC profile.

Color calibration is a good idea if you're printing on an inkjet at home, but essential if you're sending images out to print elsewhere. Even if you use an ICC profile, it is good practice to test the results by comparing prints that include neutral tones such as flesh or skies with those seen on screen. This should be an ongoing process of refinement until you finally achieve printed results that you are happy with. When you do so, be sure to save a copy of your settings, which can be loaded into your image-editing software whenever you open a new image.

FILE TYPES

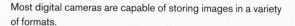

Most digital cameras are capable of storing images in a variety of formats.

JPEG
The most common format, and the standard format in most digital cameras. JPEG uses sophisticated compression methods to produce high-quality prints while keeping file sizes to a minimum. At the lowest-compression/highest-quality setting, a JPEG file can be output at photographic quality. At higher compression settings, however, detail is lost and imperfections, known as artifacts, can appear. If your camera only stores its images in JPEG format, it is advisable to convert them into the generic Photoshop (PSD) format before editing.

TIFF
Some cameras allow you to save your images as TIFF files. These are uncompressed files that support 24-bit color, allowing for very high-quality photographic output. TIFF files also include lossless LZW compression that can reduce file sizes by up to 50 percent. Use TIFF files if you want to print photo-quality images with full detail and no risk of artifacts appearing.

RAW files
High-end professional digital cameras will allow you to store files in the RAW format that acts like a "digital negative." This format stores the same level of detail as a TIFF but with more color information (RAW files can store 16 bits per channel if your camera will support it) and with extra information, such as camera focus and exposure settings, stored as part of the file. Naturally there are drawbacks: RAW files can be up to eight times the size of a JPEG file, which means that a digital camera memory card can fill up very quickly, and many image-editing programs need a special plug-in before they can open RAW images.

COLOR MANAGEMENT IN ADOBE PHOTOSHOP

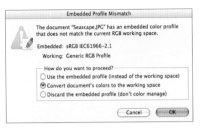

Mismatch

Opening any digital photograph in Photoshop brings up a range of options designed to assist with the color-management process.

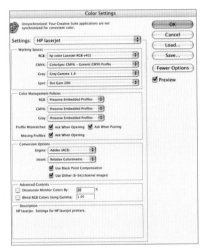

Custom Settings

A better option is to load settings that you have already fine-tuned to suit your output device. In this case, I'm using a Hewlett Packard color inkjet printer.

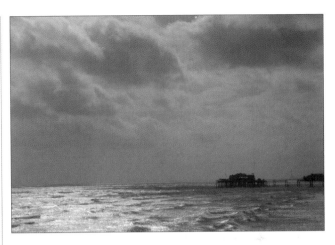

No Conversion

Selecting the *Use the embedded profile* option leaves the image with the color profile assigned to it by the digital camera that produced the image. In this case, the end results are unsatisfactory, leaving the overall colors muted and the blues in the sky washed out.

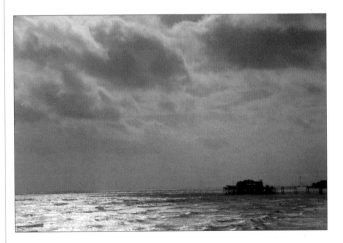

Converted

An alternative is to select the *Convert document's colors to the working space* option. This converts the file's colors to the same profile that is currently in use by Photoshop. Again, the results are far from perfect.

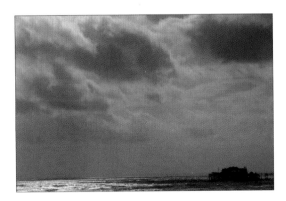

Print Settings

With these settings loaded, the image is converted to your printer's working color space. This increases the contrast and strengthens the blues in the image. More importantly, because these settings are adjusted to match your specific printer, the image will print out exactly as it appears on screen.

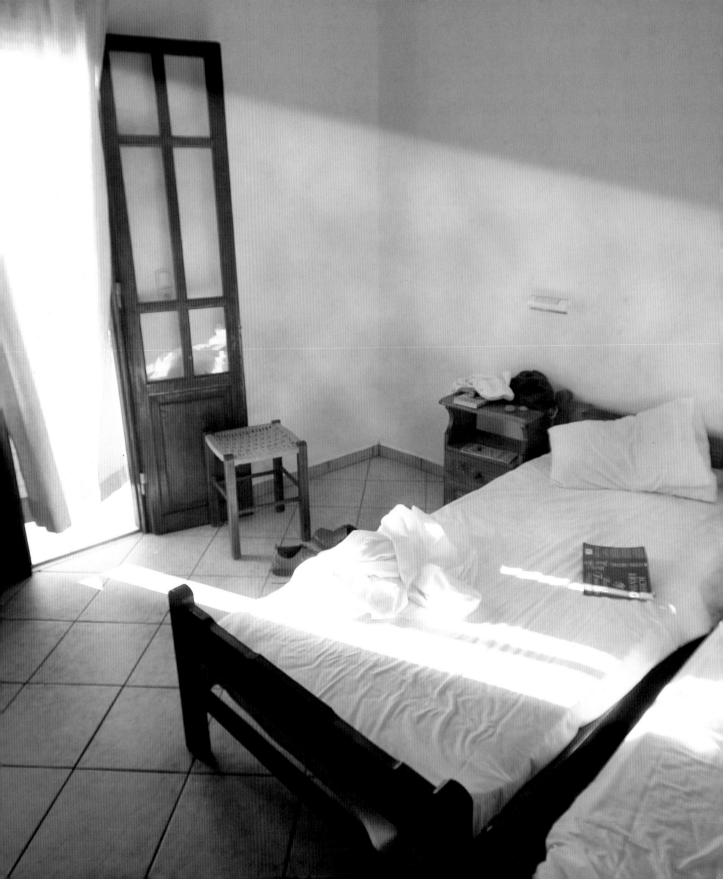

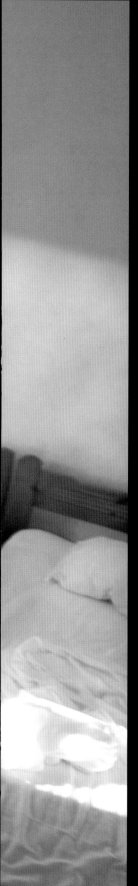

2

Whoever it was that said you need to learn the rules before you can break them was certainly onto something. To create the most effective surreal images, you first need to know the basics of image editing—making selections, adjusting colors, adding textures, using filters, and other tricks of the trade. This section will arm you with all the tools you need for creating successful surreal artwork.

special effects workshop

MAKING SELECTIONS

Compositing images is an integral part of creating surreal digital imagery—and the key to good compositing is being able to isolate elements of a digital image in such a way that when they're combined with elements from another image, it's impossible to see the join. Here, we're going to take a look at the various tools that Photoshop puts at your disposal to make accurate selections (most other image-editing packages have similar selection tools).

Marquee Tools

The *Marquee* tools are the easiest of Photoshop's selection tools to master, and as such they have a somewhat limited function. But with the right images they work just as well as more sophisticated tools.

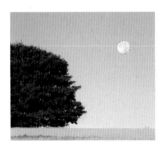

1 Here I've used the *Elliptical Marquee* tool to make a selection of the moon in this late summer evening shot. By holding down the Shift key while dragging the *Marquee* tool's cursor, a perfect circle is drawn.

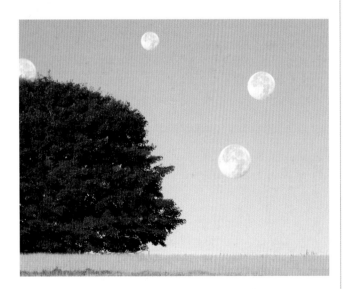

2 By going to *Select > Feather* and inputting a value of 2 pixels, the edge of the selection is softened, so that when a copy of the selection is made (Ctrl/Cmd+C), pasted (Ctrl/Cmd+V), and then moved using the *Move* tool to other areas of the image, there's no unsightly hard edge.

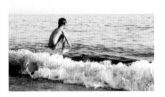

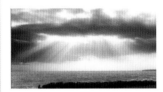

1 The *Rectangular Marquee* tool works in the same way. In this example I've made a simple rectangular selection of the sky from one image, which I've feathered slightly as before. Now I'm going to drag the selected sky onto the image of the boy jumping into the sea.

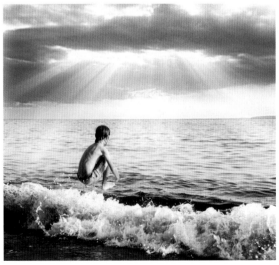

2 After positioning and resizing the sky (*Edit > Transform > Scale*) so that it filled the appropriate area on the sea image, I selected *Layer > Flatten Image*. With the image flattened I then desaturated it (Ctrl/Cmd+Shift+U) and used *Image > Adjustments > Hue/Saturation* to add a universal tone that helps bind the images together.

LASSO TOOLS

The *Lasso* tools are very useful for isolating areas of an image that you want to enhance. However, they are of limited value as "cut-out" selection tools, because they are difficult to control around complex shapes.

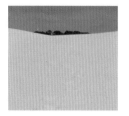 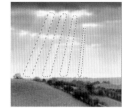

1 To enhance this image slightly, I've used the *Polygonal Lasso* tool to select the principal shafts of sunlight. The *Polygonal Lasso* tool draws a straight line between the first point you click and the next, and so on until you arrive back at the starting point, when the selection is defined. With the shafts of light selected, I used a *Feather* radius value of 20.

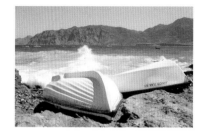

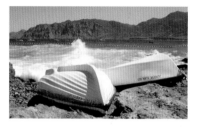

1 In this example, I'm going to use the *Lasso* tool to make a fairly rough selection of the background mountains and some of the sea in the middle distance. As a freehand tool, the *Lasso* tool is difficult to control, particularly around complex shapes, but it's ideal for isolating large areas that don't need to be defined too accurately. After making the selection I've feathered it with a value of 50.

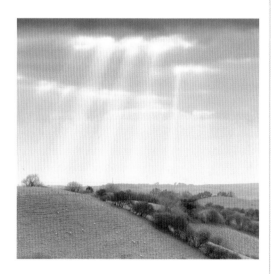

2 Now, by going to *Image > Adjustments > Levels* (Ctrl/Cmd+L), I can adjust the brightness value of the isolated beams of light so that they stand out a little more from the forbidding sky.

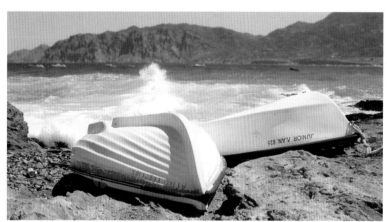

2 I can throw the background slightly out of focus by going to *Filter > Blur > Gaussian Blur* and inputting a value of between 5 and 10. This simulates depth of field and draws the viewer's attention to the boats in the foreground.

TIP

If you find that the "marching ants" selection border makes it difficult to gauge the effect of any image editing or enhancements, click Ctrl/Cmd+H to hide the selection. When you're satisfied with the enhancement, click Ctrl/Cmd+H again to reveal the border.

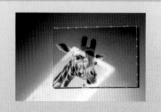

Special Effects Workshop

MORE SELECTION TOOLS

Magnetic Lasso

The *Magnetic Lasso* tool identifies the edge of an object by comparing the tonal and color values of the pixels that make up an object's edge with those of the background. Simply drag the cursor around the edge of the object and the *Magnetic Lasso* will automatically trace the edge and lay down square anchor points. If the tool goes off track, simply hit the Backspace key and the last anchor point will be deleted. The *Magnetic Lasso* is certainly a clever idea, but it can be frustrating to use and it's rarely the first choice for making selections.

Magic Wand

One of the earliest selection tools to be included in the program, Photoshop's *Magic Wand* is often the first tool people will turn to when making selections. It's quick and easy to use, and in the right circumstances provides an excellent result.

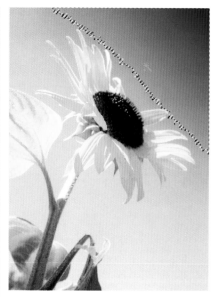

2 With the *Magic Wand* tool selected, I began by clicking in the top-right corner. Additional areas of the sky were selected by clicking with the mouse while holding down the Shift key. The *Magic Wand* works by selecting pixels of similar tone and color value—by increasing or decreasing the *Tolerance* setting in the *Tool Options* bar, the *Magic Wand* will select more or fewer pixels.

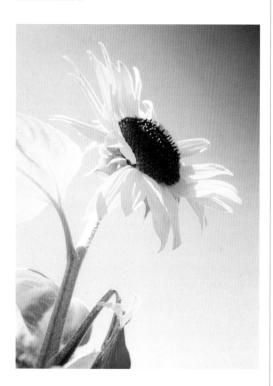

1 This photo of a sunflower is an ideal candidate for a *Magic Wand* selection. The outline of the flower sits in front of a bright uniform sky, which can easily be selected by the *Magic Wand*.

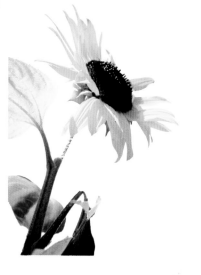

3 After less than a minute, the entire sky is selected. I feathered the selection to disguise any jagged edges, and then removed the sky, leaving a perfect cutout of the sunflower. Alternatively, by going to *Select > Inverse* you can select the flower rather than the sky.

TIP

Forward planning helps enormously when creating surreal digital imagery. For example, if you know you want to include a cutout of a particular object in your composition, photograph it against a white or uniform color that differs from the subject. That way you'll be able to use the *Magic Wand* to select the background easily and avoid having to make more complex and time-consuming masks or paths.

PATHS

For complex shapes that can't be selected with the *Magic Wand* tool (because either the background or the object is insufficiently uniform in color), Photoshop provides the *Pen* tool that can be used to create "paths" around the object. Creating paths can be difficult to master, but will provide a precise result.

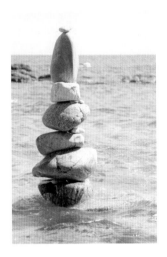

1 This pile of stones forms a highly complex shape. The irregular background cannot be selected using the *Magic Wand*, nor can the stones themselves.

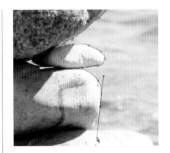

3 Within a few seconds an accurate path begins to form around the stones. It takes practice to manipulate the curve, but once mastered, creating complex paths becomes second nature.

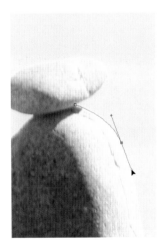

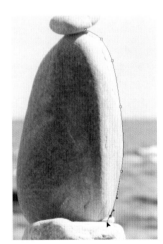

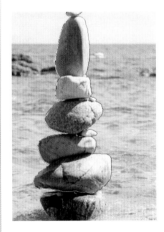

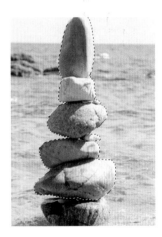

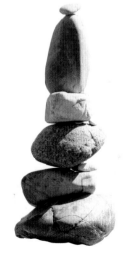

2 To complete this complex cutout, select the *Pen* tool and check that the small *Paths* icon is selected in the *Tool Options* bar. I can now click anywhere on the edge of the pile of stones to create an anchor point. When I next click on a point and hold down the mouse, a straight line running perpendicular to the point appears. Dragging this line up or down alters the curve of the path; once it fits neatly to the outline, I can release the mouse and click on another point to repeat the process.

4 With the path completed, I can fine-tune it by editing the anchor points using the *Direct Selection* tool. When I'm satisfied that it's as accurate as possible, I click the *Load path as a selection* icon in the *Paths* palette and the familiar marching ants appear around the selection, enabling me to cut out the stones or edit them in isolation. One of the main benefits of paths is that once they're created they become part of the image file, and can be reloaded whenever necessary.

COLOR RANGE

Photoshop's *Color Range* tool works in a similar way to the *Magic Wand*, but provides greater control through the use of a slider. The slider dictates the tolerance, and therefore the extent of the selection.

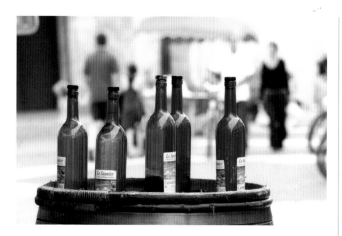

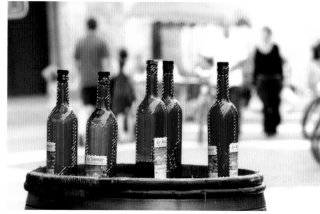

1 I want to select the blue bottles in this image in order to desaturate color from the rest of the image. I could select them using the *Magic Wand* but this would take a long time and require a lot of clicking—it will be much simpler to use the *Color Range* tool.

3 When I'm happy with the selection (I could add to it or subtract from it using the *Eyedropper* "+" and "−" icons in the *Color Range* dialog window), I click *OK*. The selection is then shown in the main window.

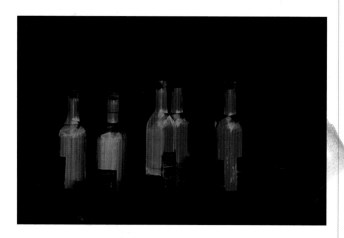

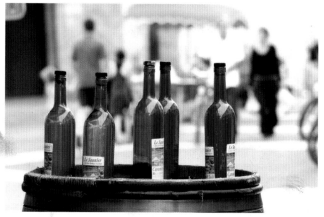

2 I begin with the *Eyedropper* tool and click on any of the blue bottles. Next I go to *Select > Color Range* to bring up the *Color Range* dialog box. As I move the *Fuzziness* slider to the right, a wider selection of blues (based on the blue selected by the *Eyedropper* tool) is incorporated. Here I've dragged the slider to 200, the maximum value.

4 Now I can simply go to *Select > Inverse* to select everything except the bottles and then desaturate the selection using *Image > Adjustments > Desaturate*.

EXTRACT

A relative newcomer in Photoshop's arsenal of selection tools, the *Extract* command can be used to isolate all sorts of objects. The tool's greatest strength probably lies in its ability to make selections of subjects with fine fur or hair—in fact, any task with which more conventional tools may struggle.

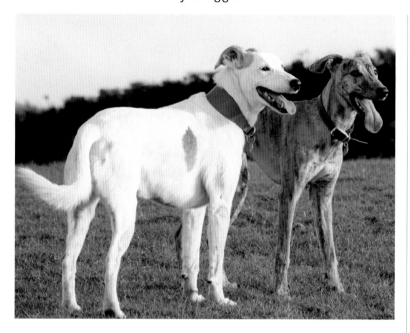

1 Let's see how the *Extract* tool copes with the challenge of isolating the white dog from both the background and the other dog. To launch the tool, go to *Filter > Extract*.

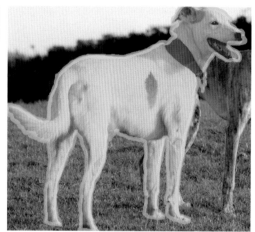

3 Once the outline is complete, all I have to do is click on the *Fill* tool to automatically "color" the area for extraction, and then hit *Preview*. This brings up a preview of the extracted area, which can be modified using the *Cleanup* and *Edge Touchup* tools. In this example I needed to tidy up the area around the dog's tail to remove some of the grass, and around those areas where the white dog overlapped the brown.

2 A dialog window appears showing the image to be worked on. The first part of the process is to draw around the outline of the subject to be extracted with the *Extract* tool's own *Highlighter*.

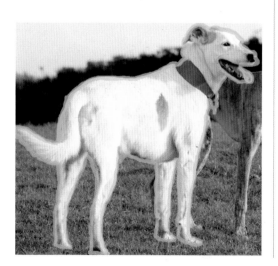

4 After tidying up the preview image, click *OK*. The subject is extracted from the background.

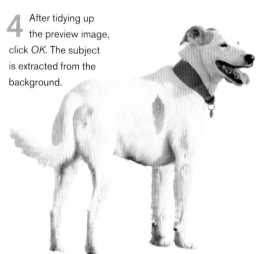

QUICK MASK

Like many selection tools in Photoshop and other image-editing software, *Quick Mask* usually works most effectively when used in conjunction with other selection tools. In the following example, I'm going to use the *Quick Mask* mode after making an initial selection with the *Magic Wand*.

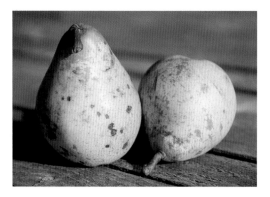 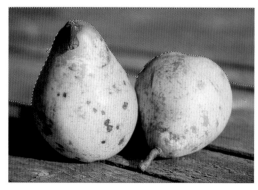

1 I'm going to start the selection of these pears by using the *Magic Wand* to select as much of the background as possible. With just a few clicks of the *Magic Wand*, most of the background is selected.

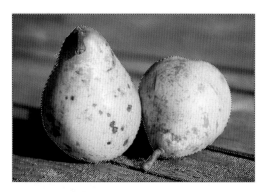

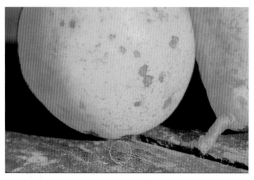

2 With a few more clicks I've managed to select a fair portion of the foreground with the *Magic Wand*, but selecting the wood texture that's in sharp focus at the very front of the image is not feasible with this tool. By clicking *Edit in Quick Mask Mode* near the bottom of the *Toolbar* (or typing Q), everything outside the marching ants selection is covered in a pink overlay, indicating those areas that are masked. Now by painting with white using a medium-sized brush I can paint out the areas of the wooden surface that I don't want to mask.

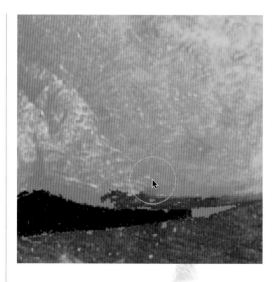

3 And here's the really clever bit. By changing the color of the brush to black, I can add to the mask and include the edges around the pears that were inadvertently included in the initial *Magic Wand* selection.

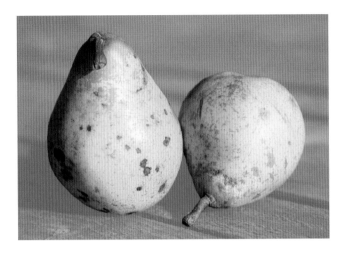

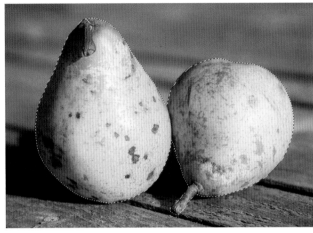

4 With the mask completed, I return to the marching ants selection by clicking the *Edit in Standard Mode* button (next to the *Quick Mask* button in the *Toolbar*), or by hitting Q again.

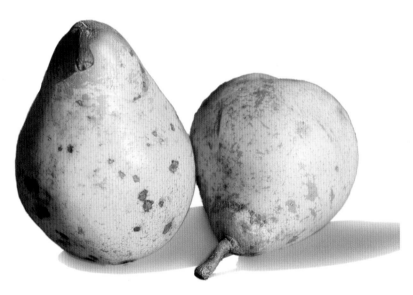

5 After feathering the selection slightly, I'm now free to complete the cutout of the pears.

TIP

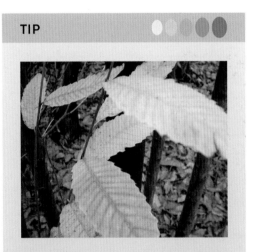

Double-clicking the *Edit in Quick Mask Mode* button in the *Toolbar* brings up the *Quick Mask Options* dialog window. Here you can adjust the color of the mask if the default pink color (the color of the material–rubylith–that was used to make masks before the days of digital imaging) is not suitable for your image; and you can also switch the mask option so that it is the selected areas that are tinted.

MASKS

Layer Masks

Layer masks are a powerful yet satisfyingly easy way to combine two or more images. Scan through any glossy magazine and you're bound to see the result of a layer mask; think of a poster for a Hollywood blockbuster and it's more than likely that it was created using a technique similar to the one shown here.

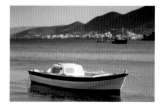
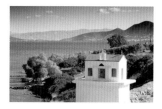
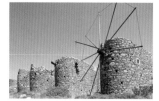
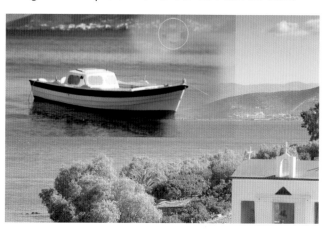

1 The first step is to select the images that I want to use in the composition. Here I've tried to select images that will give a flavor of the Greek island of Crete.

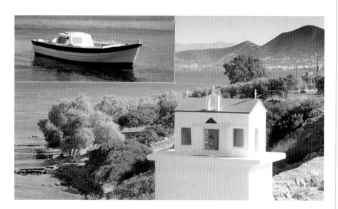

2 Next I open the image that will work best as a background. Then it's simply a case of opening one of the other images and dragging it over to the background image. Ensuring that the *Boundary Box* is ticked in the *Tool Options* bar, I can resize the image and place it in position.

TIP

Because layer masks are, as their name suggests, created on separate layers, all the blending mode options (examined in more detail on pages 44-45) can be used to affect the way the layers interact with one another. It's worth experimenting to achieve the best results.

3 To fade the new image into the background image, I go to the *Layers* palette, and with the inset image selected, click on the *Add layer mask* icon at the bottom of the *Layers* palette. By painting with black over the inset image with a soft round brush, I gently reveal the background image.

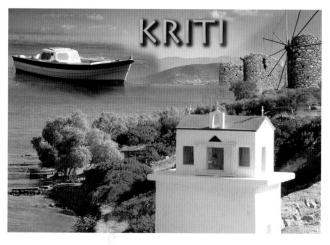

4 I repeat the same process with another image until I'm happy with the result. It's best to set the brush *Opacity* to a low value as this makes it easier to blend the images together. Here I've finished the composition with some simple typography.

Clipping Masks

Clipping masks can at first be a difficult concept to grasp, primarily because there are so many ways to implement and utilize them. Perhaps the easiest way to understand clipping masks is to think of them as a way of containing one image in a specific area when placed over another.

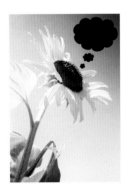

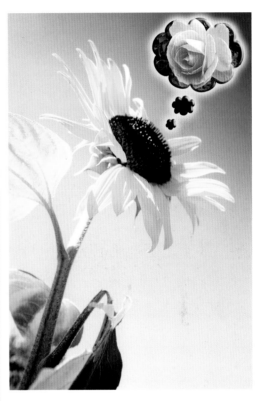

1 I'm going to begin with the sunflower image we used on page 28, and use the *Custom Shape* tool to add a "thought bubble," which in this example is going to act as the clipping mask. There's a whole array of preset shapes available in the pull-down menu in the *Tool Options* bar; select the one you want, place the cursor on the image and drag until you achieve the desired size. If you now check the *Layers* palette, you'll notice that Photoshop has automatically created a new layer (with a vector mask) for the shape.

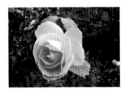

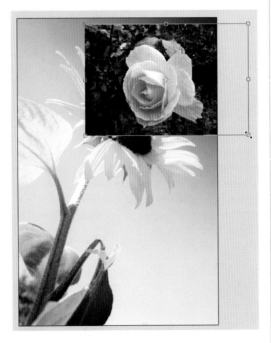

3 To fit the rose image into the thought bubble, I can either select *Layer > Create Clipping Mask*, or place the cursor between the rose layer and custom shape layer in the *Layers* palette, hold down the Alt key (the cursor will assume the clipping mask icon), and click—the rose will instantly be caught in the thought bubble. I finished this image by applying an outer glow and drop shadow to the custom shape by clicking on the *Add a layer style* icon at the bottom of the *Layers* palette.

2 Next I'm going to open the image that will be enclosed in the thought-bubble clipping mask, and drag it onto the background image. Using the boundary box corner handles (and holding down the Shift key to retain the proportions) I can resize the rose image to the size I want.

BRUSHES

Although brushes were included in the earliest versions of Photoshop, it's only in the more recent versions that they have become such sophisticated and powerful tools, packed with useful features and options. There are far too many variations to show here, so let's have a look at one or two examples, and then you can experiment with the settings for yourself.

When the *Brush* tool is selected, there are a huge number of preset brushes available, all of which are accessed via the *Brush selection* pull-down menu in the *Tool Options* bar. To change the color of the brush, simply double-click the *Foreground/Background* color box near the bottom of the *Toolbox*. The *Brush options* are accessed via *Window > Brushes* or by pressing F5.

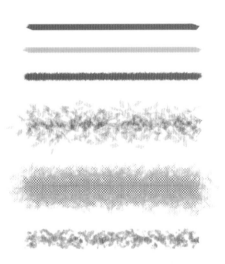

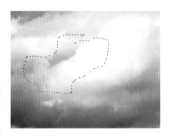

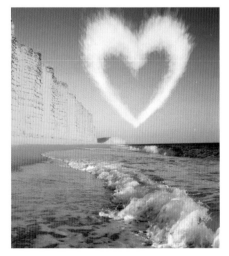

1 To show how the *Brush* options vary, the example here shows (from top to bottom) the standard *Chalk 60-pixels* brush; the same brush set at 50% *Opacity* in the *Tool Options* bar; *Chalk 60* set with *Shape Dynamics* (the various "jitter" settings control the shape of the brush edge); *Chalk 60* set with *Shape Dynamics* and *Scattering* (the settings of which "scatter" the individual brush strokes); *Chalk 60* set with *Shape Dynamics*, *Scattering*, and *Texture* (the various textures are accessed via the pull-down menu at the top of the *Textures* window; here I've selected *Optical Checkerboard*); and finally, the same brush set with *Shape Dynamics*, *Scattering*, and *Dual Brush* (which paints both the foreground and background colors). There are other options available, including *Noise* and *Wet Edges*.

2 As well as the mind-boggling number of preset brush shapes and the various settings that can be applied to them, it's also possible to create your own brush shapes. Here I've made a small selection of cloud from another picture using the *Lasso* tool and gone to *Edit > Define Brush Preset*. I've named the brush "Cloud 1," which I can then select when I next choose the *Brush* tool. Now I can use the Cloud 1 brush, combined with *Shape Dynamics* to randomize the way the brush paints, to draw cloud shapes in the sky.

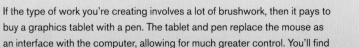

TIP

If the type of work you're creating involves a lot of brushwork, then it pays to buy a graphics tablet with a pen. The tablet and pen replace the mouse as an interface with the computer, allowing for much greater control. You'll find that certain options in the *Brush* window only become available with a tablet, providing even greater variation and control.

AIRBRUSH

The airbrush was the tool of choice for fine post-production work before the days of the computer. Today, although Photoshop and other image-editing programs offer a vast array of digital tools specifically designed to do certain jobs, the digital airbrush still has a role to play. Creating or accentuating highlights, for example, is an ideal task for Photoshop's *Airbrush*.

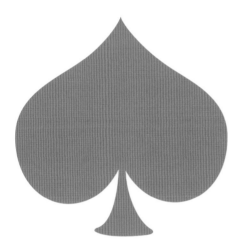

1 I'm going to use the *Airbrush* to give this flat two-dimensional Photoshop shape some body and form. I'll use the *Airbrush* to apply some black and white paint.

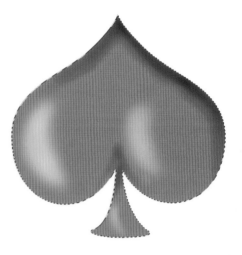

3 With the shadows completed, the next stage is to paint with white to create the highlight areas. Remember you can use the [and] keys to change the size of the brush.

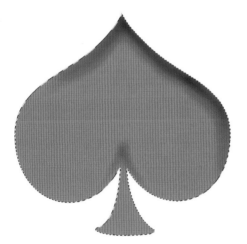

2 First I create a selection around the shape to keep the paint from the *Airbrush* from spreading into the background. Next, with the *Airbrush Opacity* and *Flow* set to around 15% in the *Tool Options* bar, I begin to paint with black on the shape to create shadows.

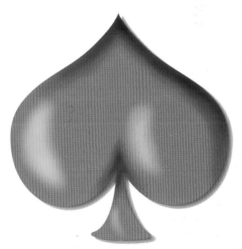

4 Now all that remains is to add a drop-shadow effect using the *Add a layer style* icon at the bottom of the *Layers* palette. By creating shadows and highlights and adding a drop shadow, the flat artwork has assumed real form.

LEVELS

The *Levels* command is one of the most important features in Photoshop. Despite its apparent simplicity, the *Levels* dialog is an extremely powerful tool that can be used to adjust color as well as an image's brightness values.

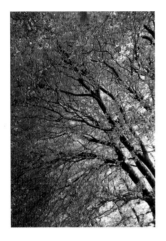

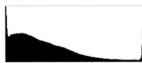

1 *Levels* can be used to effectively adjust the tonal value of any image. This photograph of trees, as the accompanying histogram indicates, is underexposed—although there is a complete range of pixels from the black point at the right to the white point at the left, there are many more pixels in the left half (black) of the histogram.

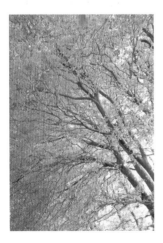

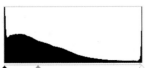

2 By moving the central gray point slider to the left, the histogram is more evenly balanced; and with more pixels falling to the right of the left-shifted gray point, the image is made brighter. You may notice that as you increase the overall brightness of the image, the colors become a little washed out. To bring back some of the lost color I increased the *Saturation* slightly in the *Hue/ Saturation* dialog window.

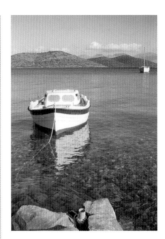

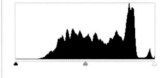

3 As well as improving an image's tonal values, the *Levels* controls can also be used to fix color casts. This photograph was deliberately taken with an inappropriate white balance setting, resulting in a strong blue cast. By selecting the *Blue* channel in the *Levels* dialog window, you can see how the pixels with a strong blue value are not spread evenly across the histogram.

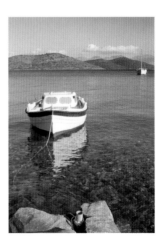

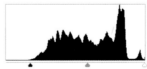

4 Moving the left slider to the right so that it sits under the end of the histogram balances the blue channel and dispenses with the blue color cast.

CURVES

While *Levels* is an excellent tool for adjusting the overall brightness of an image, what happens if you want to make more localized changes? By the far the most versatile tool for the job is *Curves*. With *Curves* it's possible to edit up to 14 different brightness points—generally, though, four or five is the most you'll need.

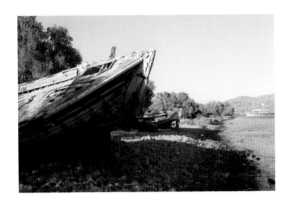

1 The foreground of this image of derelict fishing boats is badly underexposed, making it almost impossible to see any detail. We could increase the overall brightness of the image using *Levels*, but that would leave the boat in the background overexposed.

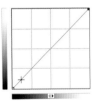

2 Go to *Image > Adjustment > Curves* to bring up the *Curves* dialog box. The first thing you'll notice is that there aren't any curves. The existing straight diagonal line reflects the tonal range of the existing image. It's this line that I'm going to curve to help bring out the detail.

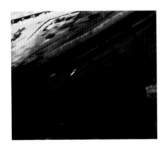
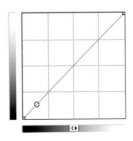

3 With the *Eyedropper* tool selected, when I go to an area of the image I want to brighten and click, the corresponding section of the image is highlighted on the *Curves* line in the form of a small circle.

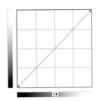
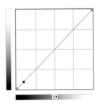

4 Now I return to the *Curves* dialog window. By clicking on the line with the cursor (now shaped as a cross), I can add points to the line for adjustment. An even easier way to add points is to hold the *Eyedropper* tool over the area of the image you want to plot, hold down the Ctrl/Cmd key and click. The same point is plotted instantly.

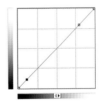

5 With the shadow area plotted, I repeat the same process with the highlight area; not necessarily because I want to adjust this but because I want it to remain in place. Unsurprisingly the highlight region is located at the other end of the line.

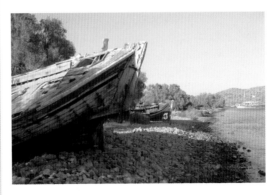

6 With both shadow and highlight areas plotted, I can now start to manipulate the brightness curve. By moving the shadow point up I can increase the brightness of the underexposed region, and by plotting additional points in the highlight and midtone areas I can ensure that those regions remain unaffected by keeping the line as straight as possible.

HUE/SATURATION

The *Hue/Saturation* command is a very easy-to-use yet powerful tool, and one that should be treated with respect. It's all too easy to oversaturate images, thinking they look bright and colorful, when in fact they simply look unrealistic. However, this can be turned to your advantage when creating surreal images, as we'll see.

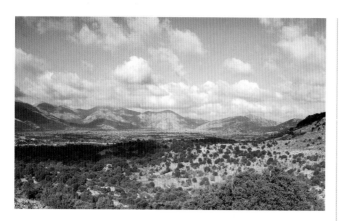

1 For most photographic purposes, the *Hue/Saturation* command is used to boost color in images that appear faded for one reason or another, such as this image of a plateau in Crete.

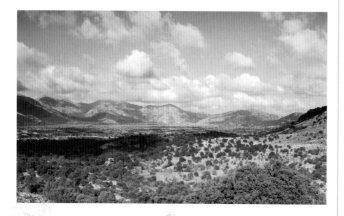

2 Going to *Image > Adjustments > Hue/Saturation* brings up the *Hue/Saturation* dialog window. To fix a faded image, slide the *Saturation* slider to the right and the colors will appear brighter. It's good practice to click on and off the *Preview* button in the window to see the adjustment you are making; this will help prevent you from going over the top.

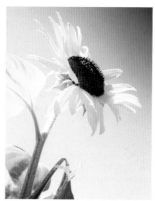

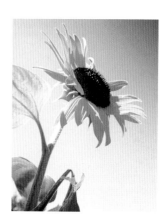

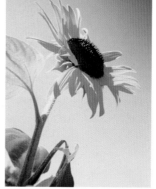

3 The *Hue/Saturation* command also features a *Colorize* button that can radically alter the colors in an image. This is a very useful feature when creating surreal imagery. Just click the *Colorize* button and adjust the *Hue* and *Saturation* to apply a color wash over any color or black and white image.

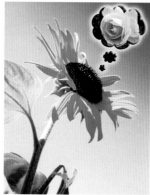

4 Here, for example, is an earlier project colorized with *Hue/Saturation*.

REPLACE COLOR

One of the quickest and easiest ways to alter the color of an object without having to make time-consuming selections is with the *Replace Color* command. This tool works best with fairly uniform colors, but the results are quick and effective.

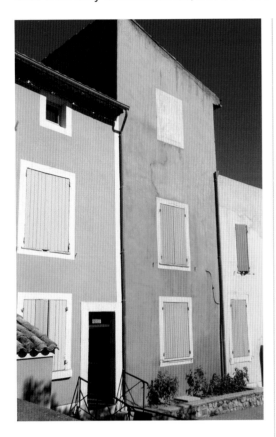

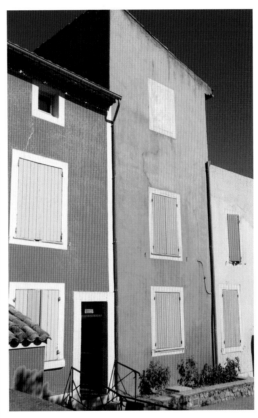

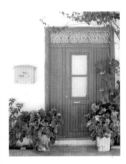

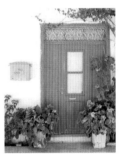

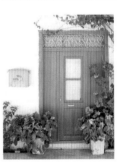

1 These colorful houses in Rousillion, southern France, can be given a new lick of paint in no time using *Replace Color*.

2 Selecting *Image > Adjustments > Replace Color* brings up the *Replace Color* dialog window. This looks similar to the *Color Range* dialog window we looked at earlier, and works in a similar way. By clicking with the *Eyedropper* tool on the main image, the *Replace Color* dialog window shows which areas have been selected in the preview screen. Using the *Fuzziness* slider increases or decreases the area selected by including or excluding similarly toned pixels. Additional areas can be added by selecting the "+" *Eyedropper* icon and clicking other areas of the image, while the opposite can be achieved using the "−" *Eyedropper* tool. In a matter of moments the colors of the houses can be altered dramatically.

3 With this simple tool, it's possible to alter the color of just about anything. This does have real-world applications as well as providing a useful creative imaging tool—particularly if you're thinking of redecorating your house or respraying your automobile.

Special Effects Workshop

ADJUSTMENT LAYERS

If you're not familiar with adjustment layers, they may at first appear to be more trouble than they're worth; however, get into the habit of using them regularly and you'll quickly realize that they can save you time and effort. Adjustment layers allow you to try out all sorts of adjustments, either to fix photos or enhance them, and they leave the original image untouched.

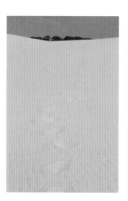

1 I like this image of footprints in the sand leading back up a hill to trees in the background, but the sand seems to be lacking texture and the footprints don't feature sufficient contrast.

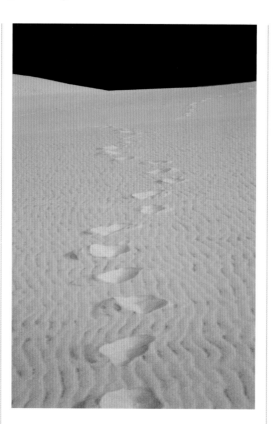

2 By clicking on *Create new fill or adjustment layer* at the bottom of the *Layers* palette, I can select a number of adjustment layers, including *Levels*, *Hue/Saturation*, *Channel Mixer*, and *Color Balance*. Here I'm going to select *Curves* and create a tonal curve that gives the sand much more punch and really brings out the footsteps.

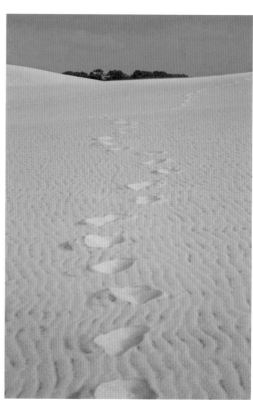

3 The *Curves* adjustment, while improving the foreground, has unfortunately rendered the background almost entirely black. However, adjustment layers automatically come with their own layer mask, and by painting with black on the image, I can reveal the sky and trees from the original image.

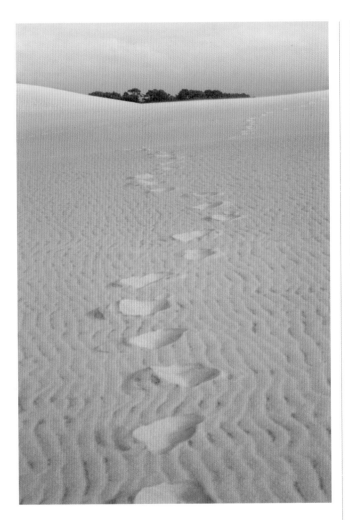

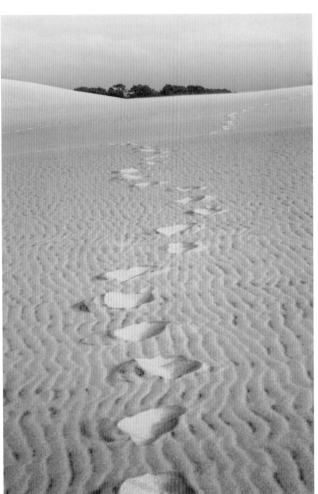

4 The original background was a bit gloomy. So by adding another adjustment layer, this time a *Gradient*, I can add a white gradient running down from the top of the image. With the *Gradient* adjustment layer's blending mode set to *Overlay*, the background becomes brighter. As the *Gradient* adjustment is on a separate layer, I can reduce the effect of the gradient by reducing the *Opacity* of the layer from 100% to 80%.

5 The beauty of adjustment layers is that you can go back and adjust the settings of any of the adjustments layers you've created at any time. Here I've returned to the *Curves* adjustment layer and used the curve to increase the contrast of the sand even more.

Special Effects Workshop

BLENDING MODES

Blending modes offer a powerful way of applying special effects between one layer and another. However, the way each blending mode causes layers to interact with one another is extremely difficult to predict, and experimenting is really the only way to discover what effects can be achieved. Here we show how the various modes affect the same two "target" layers.

The two target images were deliberately selected for their variation in color and form. The cloud image is the base and the geometric shape the blend or top layer. The *Opacity* of the blending mode is set to 100% except where stated.

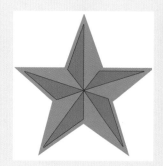
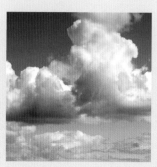

With the blending mode set to *Normal* at 100%, the blend layer sits over the base layer, and the cloud is not visible through the shape.

Reducing the *Opacity* of the blend layer to 50% makes the blend layer partly transparent, rendering the cloud partially visible.

Dissolve combines the blend layer with the base layer by removing random pixels from the blend layer. The effect only really becomes apparent when the *Opacity* of the blend layer is reduced—here it's been set to 50%, creating a speckled effect.

Darken compares the color values of both layers and displays the darker of the two.

Multiply multiplies the base and the blend pixel values and so produces a darker color.

Color Burn darkens the base color using increased contrast to reflect the blend color; the overall effect is to darken the image. As we can see here, blending with pure white creates white.

Linear Burn darkens the base color by decreasing brightness to reflect the blend color; again the overall effect is to darken the image, but in more pronounced way than *Color Burn*. Blending with white has no effect.

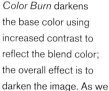

The opposite of *Darken*, *Lighten* compares the colors of both the blend and base layers and selects whichever is lighter.

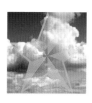

The opposite of *Multiply*, *Screen* multiplies the base color with the inverse of the blend layer; in this case, blending with black therefore leaves the color unchanged.

Color Dodge brightens the image by reducing the contrast of the base color to reflect the blend color. It is the opposite of *Color Burn*.

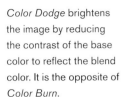

Linear Dodge, the opposite of *Linear Burn*, lightens an image by increasing the brightness of the base color to reflect the blend color.

Overlay creates a very contrasting image by multiplying when the blend color is darker than the base color, and screening when the blend color is lighter than the base color, while preserving the highlights and shadows of the base color.

Soft Light burns (darkens) or lightens (screens) the colors depending on whether the blend color is darker or lighter than 50% gray.

Similar to *Soft Light*, *Hard Light* multiplies or screens the colors depending on whether the blend color is darker or lighter than 50% gray.

Vivid Light, like *Soft Light* and *Hard Light*, uses 50% gray as a defining point. If the blend color is darker than 50% gray the color is darkened by adding contrast; if the color is lighter than 50% gray the color is lightened by reducing contrast.

Linear Light works in the same way as *Vivid Light*, but increases or decreases the blend color using brightness.

Pin Light applies a *Lighten* blend mode to blend colors lighter than 50% gray and a *Darken* blend mode to blend colors darker than 50% gray.

Hard Mix posterizes colors based on the blend colors. If the blend colors are lighter than 50% gray, the base colors are brightened; if the blend colors are darker than 50% gray then the base colors are darkened.

Difference either subtracts the blend color from the base color or vice versa, depending on whichever has the highest brightness value.

Similar to *Difference*, *Exclusion* works in the same way but applies less contrast.

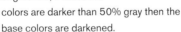

Hue retains the luminance (brightness) and saturation of the base colors but includes the hue values of the blend colors.

Saturation retains the luminance and hue of the base colors, but includes the saturation of the blend colors.

Color retains the luminance values of the base colors, but includes the hue and saturation values of the blend colors.

Luminosity retains the hue and saturation of the base colors, but includes the luminance of the blend colors.

TIP

Rather than going to the *Layers* palette and laboriously changing the blending modes by selecting them from the pull-down menu, it's much quicker to scroll through the blending options by pressing Shift-+ or Shift-− (minus).

LIGHTING EFFECTS

The *Lighting Effects* filter, as its name suggests, can replicate the effect of a huge variety of lighting sources, and can successfully be used to emulate all forms of studio lighting. However, the filter also features a *Texture Channel*, which adds another dimension to this powerful and complex tool.

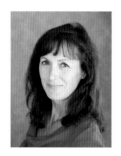

1 This portrait shot is ideal for experimenting with the wide variety of lighting styles available with the *Lighting Effects Filter*, accessed via *Filter > Render > Lighting Effects*.

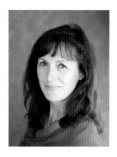

2 Here a conventional lighting setup has been recreated with the subject gently lit from bottom right with a soft spot light. The filter features a vast array of controls, including *Intensity*, *Focus*, *Exposure*, and *Ambience*, to help you achieve the effect you want.

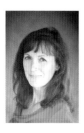 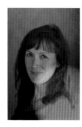 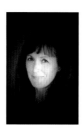

3 Here's a small selection of the kinds of effects that can be achieved; but as these examples demonstrate, some work better than others.

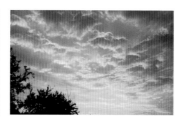

1 Some interesting effects appropriate for surreal digital imagery can be created using the *Texture Channel* in the *Lighting Effects* filter. This dramatic sunset image provides the starting point.

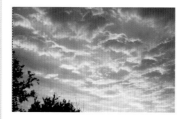

2 I now hit Ctrl/Cmd+A to select the image, copy it by selecting Ctrl/Cmd+C, and then bring up the *Channels* window, where I create a new channel by clicking the *Create new channel* icon at the bottom of the window. A small black window labelled "Alpha 1" will appear. Now I select Ctrl/Cmd+V to paste the image of the sunset into the new Alpha channel.

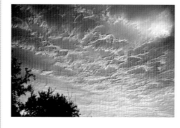 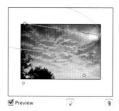

3 Now I click the *RGB* icon at the top of the *Channels* palette and go to *Filter > Render > Lighting Effects*. In the *Texture Channel* pull-down menu I select Alpha 1, which loads the alpha channel. I can now position and add lights to create an embossing effect.

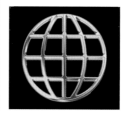

4 Similar metallic and embossing effects can easily be achieved by using some of Photoshop's preset shapes and patterns as alpha channels, applying the *Lighting Effects*, and using curves to create the chrome effect.

CLOUDS/DIFFERENCE CLOUDS

Photoshop's *Clouds* and *Difference Clouds* both create a soft, mottled texture, and are, not surprisingly, ideal for adding clouds to boring empty skies. They can be also be used in more creative ways, as shown here.

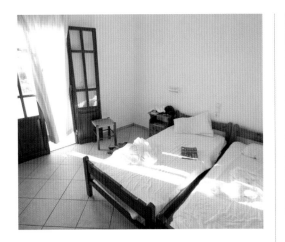

1 I'm going to apply a *Clouds* layer to this interior shot to recreate a dusty ray of sunlight.

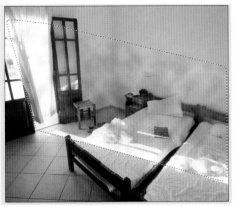

3 On the sunbeam layer, I reselect the actual beam by holding down the Ctrl/Cmd key and clicking the thumbnail. This should put a marching ants selection around the beam. I set the *Foreground/ Background* colors to default and go to *Filter > Render > Clouds* to introduce the hazy effect.

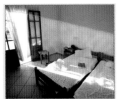

4 Next, I change the blending mode of the sunbeam layer to *Overlay* and adjust the *Opacity*. Finally I switch to the background layer, invert the selection so that everything other than the beam is selected, and use a *Levels* command to darken the rest of the room.

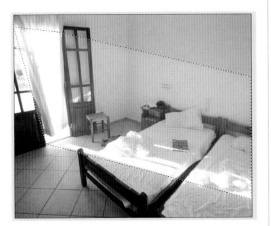

2 Before applying the *Clouds* filter, on a new layer I draw the outline of the ray of sun using the *Polygonal Lasso* tool. I fill the selection with a very light yellow color. After deselecting the sunbeam I apply a large amount of *Gaussian Blur* and fade the *Opacity* to around 20%.

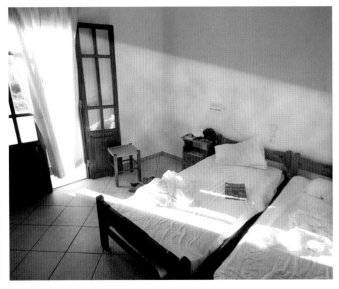

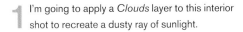

Special Effects Workshop

FILTER GALLERY

Photoshop has a huge selection of filters, and each has a variety of settings that can radically alter the overall effect of the filter's application. Some, such as *Sharpen* and *Noise*, are primarily designed to digitally improve images (and aren't covered here), while the majority are intended to enhance images by applying graphic effects, many of which may come in useful for surreal imagery. Below is a small selection of the latter; again you really need to experiment (combining filters with blending modes) to fully appreciate the effects that can be achieved.

Artistic

As their name suggests, the *Artistic* filters aim to emulate various types of painterly techniques, such as *Rough Pastels*, *Palette Knife*, and *Watercolor*, to name just three out of the 15 available.

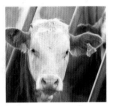

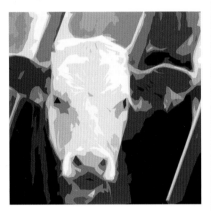

Cut Out with settings:
Number of Levels 6;
Edge Simplicity 7;
Edge Fidelity 1.

Brush Stroke

Another collection of filters that attempts to reproduce "real-world" painting effects. Although applications in surreal digital imagery might at first be hard to perceive, there's something here for everyone.

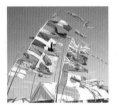

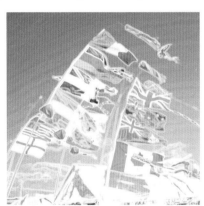

With *Edge Width*, *Edge Brightness*, and *Smoothness* set to maximum, *Accented Edges* provides an almost neon effect.

Blur

The range of *Blur* filters provides numerous ways in which images or parts of images can be blurred—sometimes to replicate a motion blur, sometimes to emulate depth of field; the possibilities are endless.

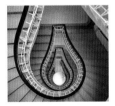

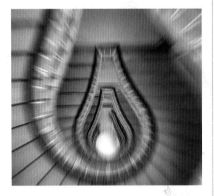

Zoom Radial Blur set at a value of 28.

Distort

With the possible exception of *Diffuse Glow*, which imbues an image with a gentle soft-focus effect, the *Distort* filters provide some of the most drastic effects.

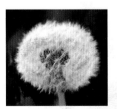

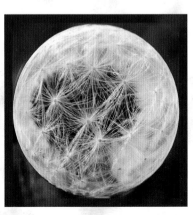

This dandelion has undergone two applications of *Spherize* set at 100%.

Pixelate

Pixelate, along with *Artistic* and *Brush*, houses a group of filters whose intention is to create special effects rather than improve images.

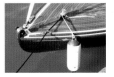

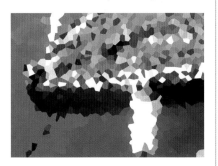

The *Crystallize* filter has been applied to the bow of this sailing boat at a value of 120.

Render

Render contains the *Clouds* and *Lighting Effects* filters, which we've already looked at, but also *Lens Flare*, which if used judiciously can add atmosphere to an image.

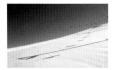

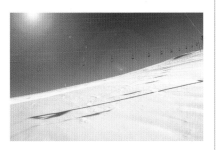

The *105mm* lens flare option provided the most naturalistic effect for this skiing photo.

Sketch

Another set of "creative" filters, the *Sketch* group certainly has something for digital surrealists, but as with most of the filters they often work better when used in conjunction with other filters and/or blending modes.

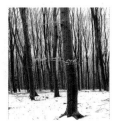

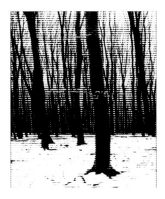

The *Line Halftone Pattern* filter has been applied to this image of trees with a *Size* value of 8 and *Contrast* of 37.

Stylize

The *Stylize* filters are a strange mix of effects, with perhaps *Find Edges* and *Glowing Edges* providing the most interest.

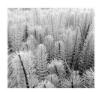

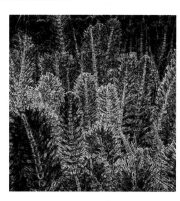

These already somewhat surreal plants are made even more surreal by using the *Glowing Edges* filter with *Edge Width* set to 3; *Edge Brightness* 11; and *Smoothness* 10.

Texture

Many of the *Texture* filters are based on old-fashioned crafts or the effect of aging—as always, some are more successful than others.

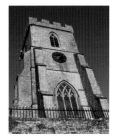

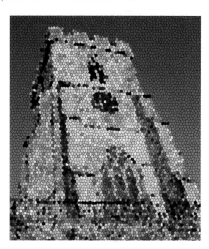

Here the *Stained Glass* filter has been applied with *Cell Size* 15; *Border Thickness* 3; *Light Intensity* 1.

Of course it's also possible to apply a texture, such as the *Brick* texture, to a selection of an image.

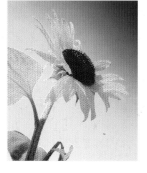

TEXTURES

It's possible to apply a number of preset textures to an image using the *Texture* filters in Photoshop, but it's also possible to create your own textures using the *Texturizer*.

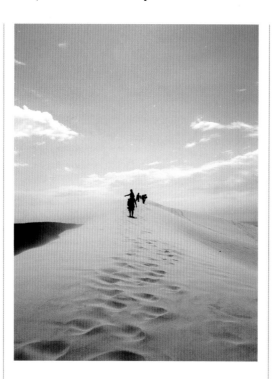

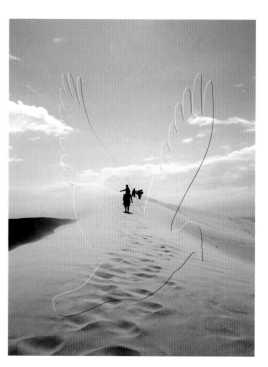

1 Here, I've created a new texture using a preset custom shape (*Bird 2*) from the *Custom Shape* picker in the *Tool Options* bar. After drawing the shape on a new white background document, I go to *Layer > Flatten Layer*. Next I click the *Create a new channel* icon at the bottom of the *Channels* palette, click at the top RGB layer, and then select and copy the bird image. Finally, I return to the new Alpha 1 channel at the bottom of the *Channels* palette and paste in the bird image, before saving this new document as a .psd file in an easily identifiable folder.

2 The next step is to open the image I want to apply the texture shape to. With the image open, go to *Filter > Texture > Texturizer*. In the resulting *Texturizer* window I click the *Load Texture* arrow next to the *Texture* menu and navigate to the newly created .psd document to select it.

3 Finally, by adjusting the *Scaling* values I can get the image to fit neatly over the image. Photoshop will automatically repeat the texture pattern if it's saved as a smaller size, and the *Scaling* slider is reduced in the *Texturizer* window.

TIP

Here I've used another shape from the *Custom Shape* tool to create an alpha channel and applied it to this image of children via the *Texturizer* command. It's an excellent way of creating your own personal watermark.

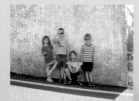

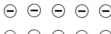
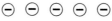
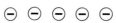
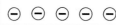

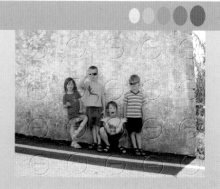

DISPLACEMENT MAPS

A displacement map is a grayscale image that is used to distort another image. They are commonly used with 3D programs for making textures, but can also be invaluable for making realistic distortions to images, whether photographs or text layers.

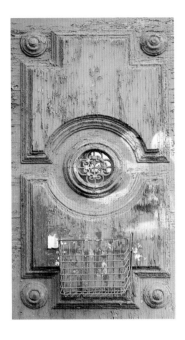

1 I'm going to use a displacement map to chisel out a sun shape on this door, making sure that it hugs the contours of the ornate moulding.

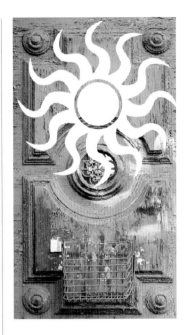

3 Now I return to the original door image, and, using the *Custom Shape* tool, draw the sun shape on the image. When I'm happy with the shape I rasterize it with *Layer > Rasterize > Shape*. To get the shape to wrap around the door moulding, with the *Shape* layer selected I go to *Filter > Distort > Displace* and select the door displacement .psd that I made earlier.

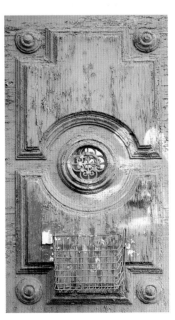

2 The first stage is to create the map. With the door image open, I select *Image > Adjustments > Desaturate* and save the grayscale version of the door as a .psd document where I can easily locate it.

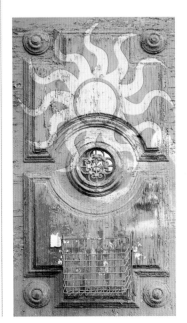

4 To make the shape more realistic, I've changed the blending mode of the shape layer to *Overlay*, duplicated it to give it more substance, adjusted the *Opacity* of both type layers and finally applied an *Inner Shadow* using the *Add a layer style* pull-down menu at the bottom of the *Layers* palette.

Special Effects Workshop

LIQUIFY

Photoshop's *Liquify* filter is an extremely powerful image-manipulation tool, capable of distorting groups of pixels into any new shape you wish. Unsurprisingly, such a powerful tool needs to be handled with care.

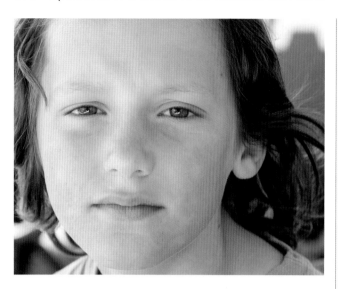

1 The *Liquify* filter has a number of individual tools with which to edit the images.

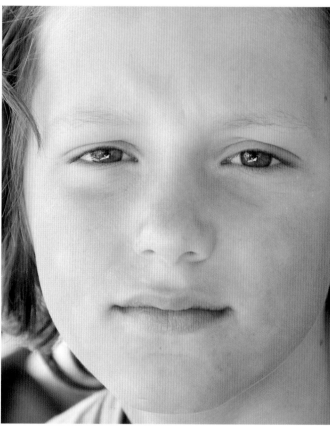

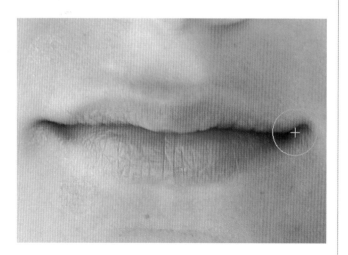

3 Only a very small adjustment is required to change the once-neutral expression to a hint of a smile.

2 Here I've used a medium-sized *Warp* tool to lift the edges of the subject's mouth very slightly.

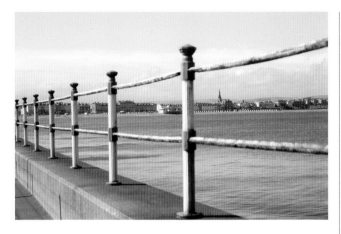

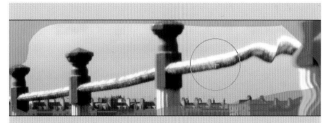

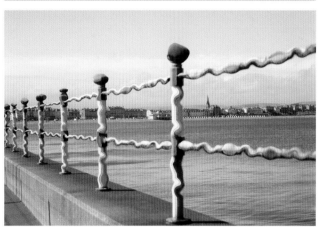

4 Of course it's not only people's faces that can be manipulated. In this example, I'm going to change this photograph into a sizzling summer painting.

5 Here I've used the *Liquify* filter's *Twirl Clockwise* tool to add twists and turns to the railings, and the *Bloat* tool to make them look as if they're blistering.

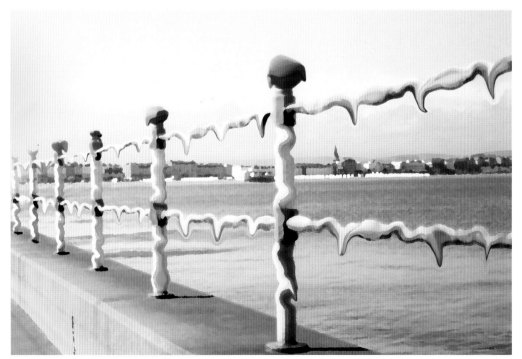

6 I finished by dragging down on sections of the railings with the *Warp* tool to make them look as if they were dripping. The addition of a glowing sun and a bright orange gradient all run through the *Palette Knife* filter completes the scorching summer artwork.

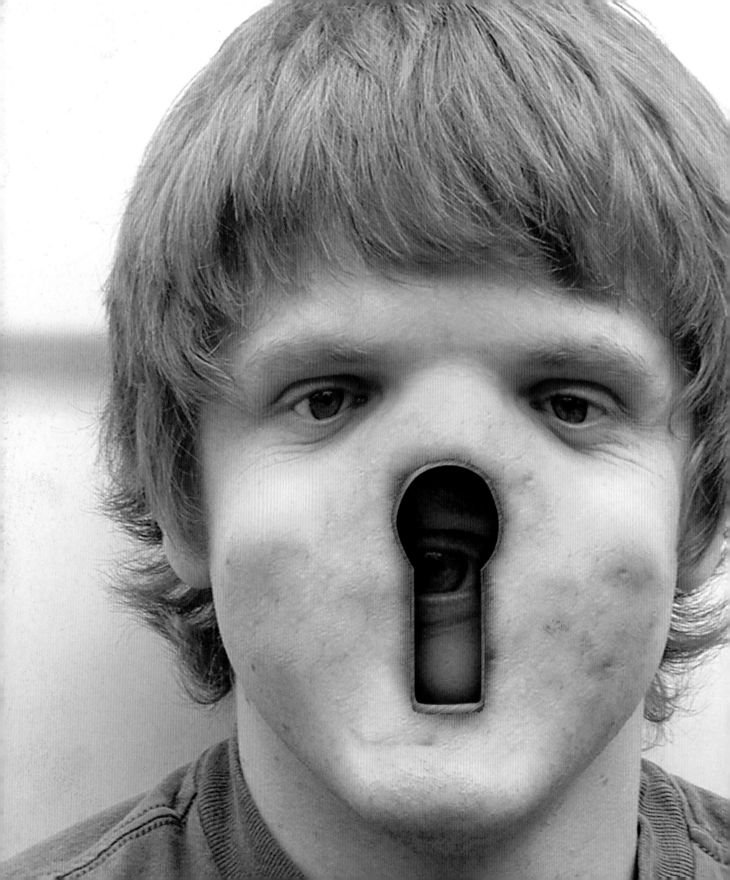

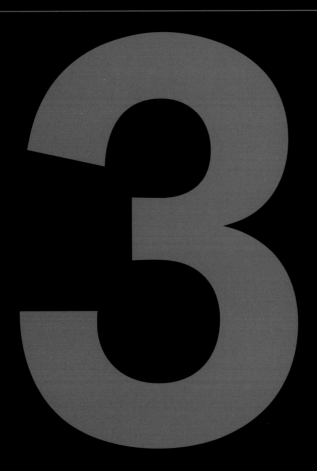

3

Humans are boring. Okay, that's not entirely true, but that friend of yours with the slightly fishy look about him would look so much more interesting if his features were mixed with those of a real fish! This section deals with exactly those kinds of situations, where the ordinary becomes the extraordinary. You'll learn how to convert old photographs into examples of Victorian surrealism, how to create ghosts from a couple of models and a large tube of stockinet, and yes, how to add fish features to your friends. Welcome to the world of the surreal portrait.

portraits

THE LEONINE HATMAN

by Jeffrey Harp

Magritte once said, "Art evokes the mystery without which the world would not exist." I like to think my work imparts some of this feeling upon the viewer. The piece we are going to be creating is a recreation of my older piece entitled The Leonine Hatman. It's a study in threes: three hats, spheres, sections, buttons... even the majority of the composition is a triangle. The techniques and tools used are basic Photoshop with no filters being applied.

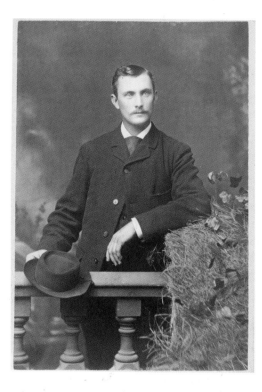

1 Open the file steps_leonine.psd. If you do not see the vertical guideline, hit Ctrl/Cmd+H to reveal it. This guideline marks the figure at the point where we will begin to mirror his body.

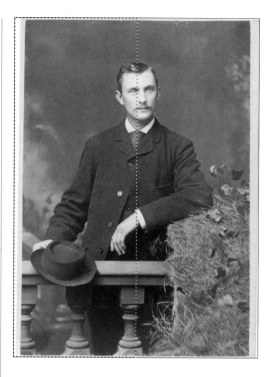

2 Select the *Rectangular Marquee* tool and draw a box over the left side. Select *Edit > Copy*, and then *Edit > Paste* to paste in the selection.

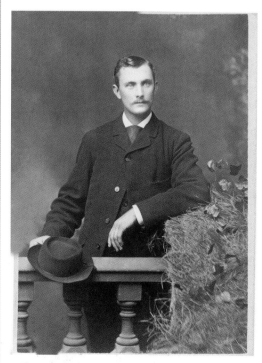

3 Next, select the *Clone Stamp* tool and use a soft brush of 150 pixels to begin cloning out the distracting white areas to the left and removing the background scenery. Continue by filling in the area between the columns, changing the size of the brush whenever necessary.

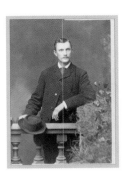

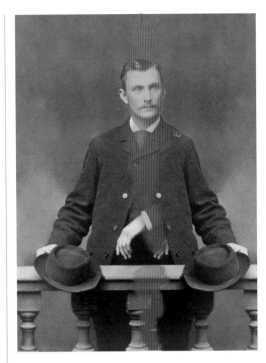

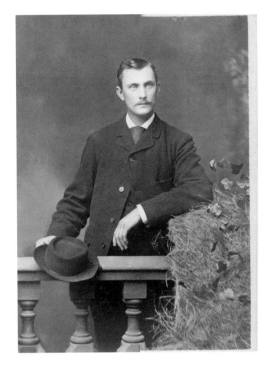

6 Select the *Rectangular Marquee* tool and draw a box around the man's left side. Select *Edit > Copy* and *Edit > Paste*. Select *Edit > Free Transform* and slide the selection to the right. Press Ctrl/Cmd+H to hide the vertical guideline, and apply a mask to the selection. Paint out the harsh edge, paying attention to the area around the shoulders and head.

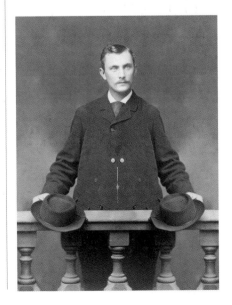

7 Press Ctrl/Cmd+A to select all, then *Edit > Copy Merged*. Select *Edit > Paste* to obtain a flattened file of all the previous steps. Using the *Rectangular Marquee* tool, draw a selection around the middle column, selecting *Free Transform* to move toward the center of the area. Clone out areas that show layers underneath. Continue transforming and cloning areas of the jacket until the body is complete.

4 Select the *Rectangular Marquee* tool and drag a box around part of the column in the lower-left corner. Select *Edit > Copy* and *Edit > Paste*. Select *Edit > Free Transform*. Right/Ctrl+click inside the selection, choose *Flip Horizontal* and slide it over to mirror the column.

5 Apply a mask and paint along the edge to get rid of the harshness. When you are happy with the result, turn off the origin layer by clicking the eye next to it, and select *Layer > Merge Visible*. Continue to clone until the left side is complete.

LEONINE HATMAN

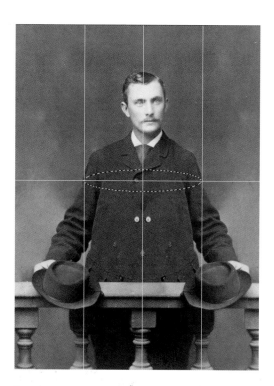

8 Define the first cut by pulling down a horizontal guideline beneath the man's shoulders. Mark this by placing two vertical guidelines at the edge of his body on the right and left sides. Select the *Elliptical Marquee* tool, and draw an oval into this area. Go to *Select > Feather* and set the radius to 2 pixels. Create a new channel of this selection. Deselect and copy the layer.

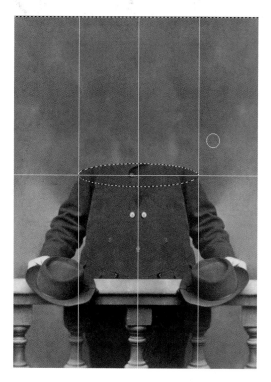

9 Activate the oval selection from the *Channels* palette by holding Ctrl/Cmd and clicking on the layer. Invert the selection and clone out the top of his body, then deselect.

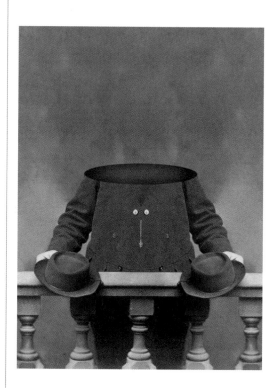

10 Activate the oval selection again, and choose an open area from the top left to copy and paste into the selection. In the *Layer Style* dialog, select *Inner Shadow* and apply these settings in the *Structure* box: *Blend Mode: Multiply*; *Opacity*: 75%; *Angle*: 120°; *Use Global Light* checked; *Distance*: 0px; *Choke*: 26%; *Size*: 185px. In the *Quality* box, use the default settings: *Contour*: *Linear*; *Anti-alias* unchecked; *Noise*: 0%. Repeat steps 7-9 to define the rest of the cuts to his body, moving the pieces slightly up each time.

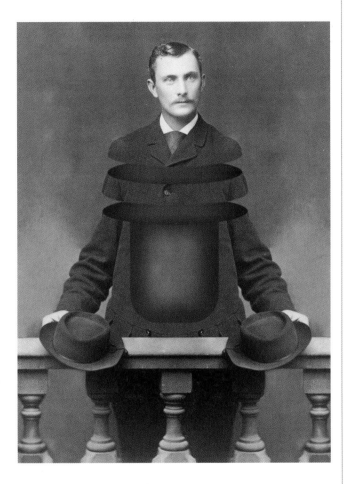

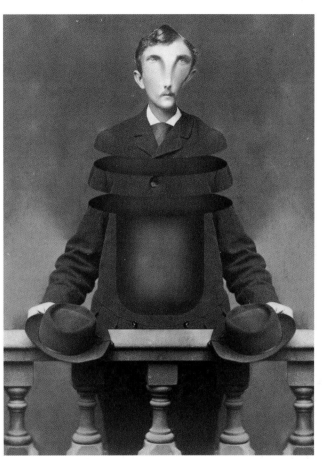

11 Select the *Rounded Rectangle* tool and set the radius to 200 pixels. Draw the rectangular part inside the man's body and Ctrl/Cmd+click the selection and delete the rectangle layer. Feather the selection by 2 pixels, and create another channel. Again, choose an open area from the top left to copy and paste into the selection. In the *Layer Style* dialog, select *Inner Shadow* and apply these settings in the *Structure* box: *Blend Mode*: *Multiply*; *Opacity*: 62%; *Angle*: 120°; *Use Global Light* checked; *Distance*: 0px; *Choke*: 50%; *Size*: 250px. In the *Quality* box, apply these settings: *Contour*: *Linear*; *Anti-alias* unchecked; *Noise*: 0%.

12 Select the *Rectangular Marquee* tool and draw a box around the man's head. Select *Edit* > *Copy Merged* and then *Edit* > *Paste*. Copy this layer. Go to *Edit* > *Free Transform*, Right/Ctrl+click, and choose *Warp*. Pull the points around until the head is distorted into a shape you like, and then clone out the areas you don't like. I cloned out the eyes completely, pasted in new ones, and burned in the bridge of the nose to give his face more definition.

Portraits

LEONINE HATMAN

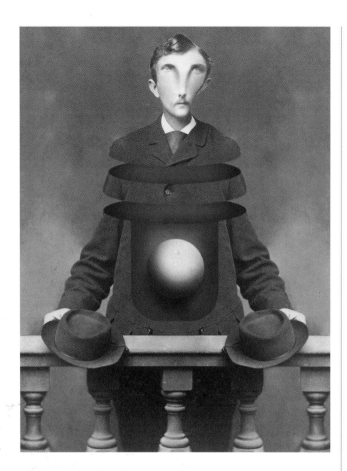

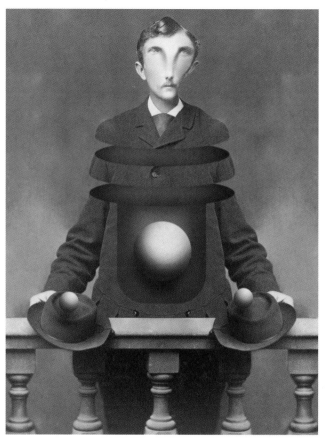

13 Using the *Elliptical Marquee* tool, choose a circular section from the top left to copy and paste into a new layer. Lighten the area slightly using the *Levels* adjustment.

Go to *Layer Style > Drop Shadow...* and apply these settings in the dialog: *Blend Mode*: *Multiply*; *Opacity*: 75%; *Angle*: 79°; *Use Global Light* unchecked; *Distance*: 97px; *Choke*: 0%; *Size*: 87px. The *Layer Knocks Out Drop Shadow* box should be checked.

In *Layer Style > Inner Shadow...* apply these settings: *Blend Mode*: *Multiply*; *Opacity*: 89%; *Angle*: -114°; *Use Global Light* unchecked; *Distance*: 81px; *Choke*: 24%; *Size*: 136px.

In *Layer Style > Inner Glow...* apply these settings: *Blend Mode*: *Screen*; *Opacity*: 75%; *Noise*: 0%; *Technique*: *Softer*; *Source*: *Edge*; *Choke*: 0%; *Size*: 57px; *Contour*: *Linear Gradient*; *Anti-aliased* unchecked; *Range*: 50%; *Jitter*: 0%.

14 Move the circle into the middle of the removed section from his body. Repeat Step 13 for the smaller two spheres, only changing the angle of the drop shadow to account for your light source.

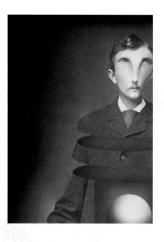

15 Hit Ctrl/Cmd+A to select all, then *Edit > Copy Merged*, *Edit > Paste*. Move the flattened file slightly downward to correct the composition, and then burn in the edges using the *Burn* tool and a large soft brush.

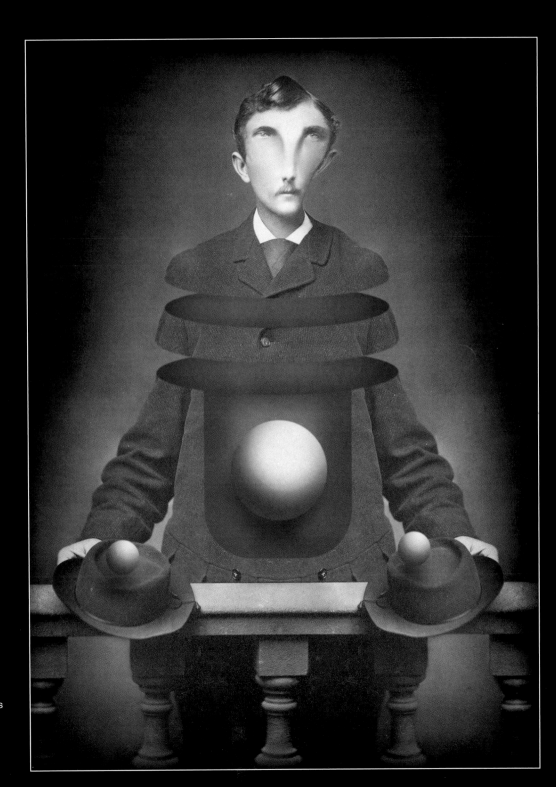

© Jeffrey Harp

Final Image

The final result has come a long way from the original black-and-white photograph. The triangular composition is important to the image and helps draw the eye through the picture.

MUSCLE MAN

by Georgia Denby

Muscle Man was created using only three images and worked together in Photoshop. My initial shot was of the model, arms crossed over his chest, taken in my studio using a black background. The wasting muscles were created using photos of sand on the beach. The background was a different sand image.

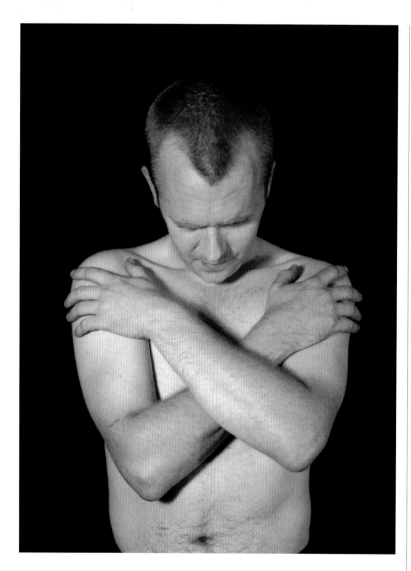

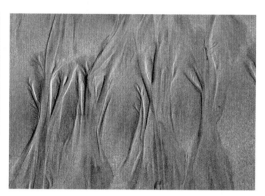

2 The second image now comes into play. The "torn muscles" look was just the texture of sand on the beach. Shots like this can sometimes be difficult to source. I found my local beach didn't create this effect at all, but noticed it on another. I located the texture in the sand near the water's edge where the tide had dragged the sand back into the sea. These patterns create wonderful abstract images in their own right, but they reminded me so much of how muscles are formed that I felt inspired by them and took many shots of the varying patterns up and down the beach. I chose one that most closely resembled muscles, and another, simpler one which will be used later as a background.

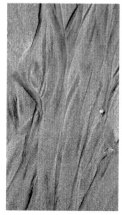

3 Open the studio shot and the main muscle sand image and place them side by side so you can see them both clearly on the screen. Convert your background layer into a usable layer and turn off the original background.

1 The studio was unlit except for a lamp on the left side of the model and another on the right. No other light source was used. This simple image of the man with arms crossed over his chest was then transferred into Photoshop and worked on at 25%, 50% or 100%. Always use an even percentage—33% or 66.7% will not give you an even and sharp image to work on. If an even percentage is too small to work on, use a higher even percentage and move the image around as you work.

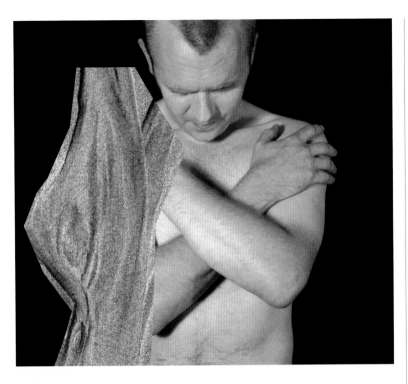

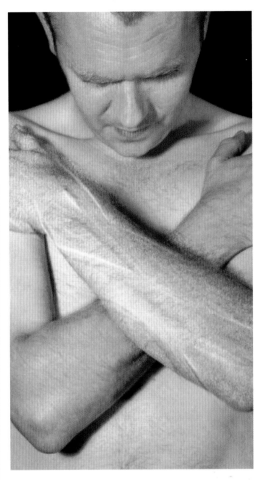

4 Using the *Polygonal Lasso* tool, choose sections of the image and pick out the muscles individually. Drag them across to the muscle man and drop them in on the picture.

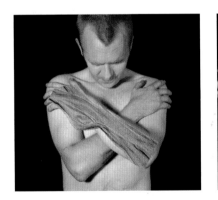

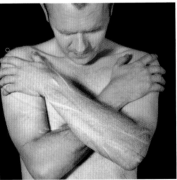

6 As you go along, use the *Eraser* tool to remove excess muscle from the body, or any muscle areas that overlap in an unrealistic way. Don't forget to change the blend mode of each layer to *Overlay*.

5 When the first muscle has been added, change the blend mode of that layer to *Overlay* and the muscle instantly looks like it's part of the flesh. To enhance that illusion further, reduce the layer's opacity to approximately 65%, or whichever percentage you feel looks best. These muscles can then be distorted, twisted, stretched, or shaped in any way you wish to fit the contours of the man's body.

MUSCLE MAN

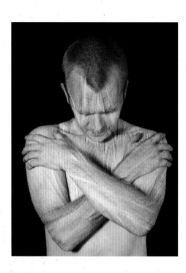

7 Continue to work with different areas of the sand image, dragging the chosen parts onto the muscle man until almost the whole body is covered, removing the excess as you go. Make sure the sand is showing through clearly in some areas as this adds texture to the skin. Leave the stomach area for now—we'll come to that in the next step.

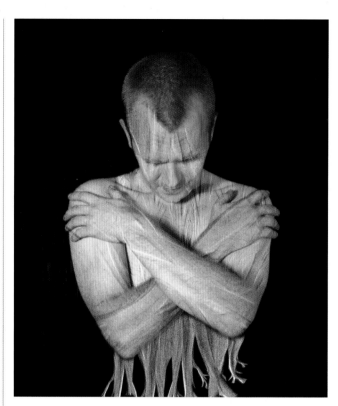

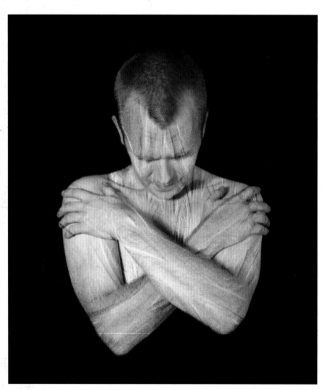

8 Now for the lower body part. Create a new layer in *Normal* mode and at 100% opacity. On that layer, remove the flesh completely from the waist down by painting over it with the same black as your background. (Use the *Eyedropper* tool to select the same color as your studio background).

9 To make the areas where the flesh has gone altogether and left only muscle tissue, create a new layer in the same way as in the previous steps, but leave it at 100% opacity (and *Normal* mode). Remove the small areas between the muscles to reveal the black background. The color may need tweaking a little on these layers to match the skin tone of the rest of the model.

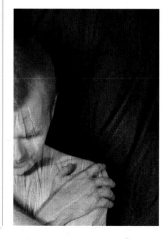

10 Finally, to add the background, create a new layer and drag the other sand image behind all the others. (At this point you can't see it, of course.) With a wide *Eraser* and opacity reduced to approximately 40% (or adjusted to your own preference), erase areas of the black studio background to reveal the sand image behind. Don't take too much away or it will detract from the main part of your picture.

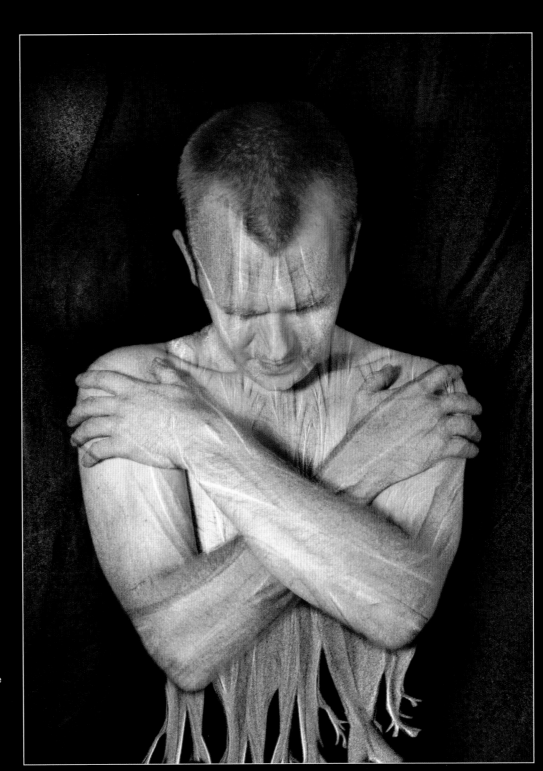

Final Image

Because the sand image was carefully overlaid so that the lines followed the natural contours of the figure, the wave-washed beach has now become convincing muscle.

© Georgia Denby

Portraits

TROLL

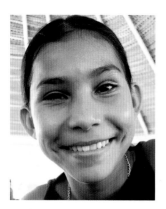

by Simon Rudd
Some people don't believe in fairies and monsters, but I'm here to tell you they do exist!
I know because I've seen them. Using the power of Photoshop—layer masks and the *Clone* tools in particular—we are going turn a photo of a boy into an evil-looking troll.

1 First, we need our photo. This boy has a nice wide smile, giving the natural lines and face shape we need. The photo also has very few shadows or highlights on the main part of the face, which makes blending easier. The model also has quite a large forehead—this will come in very handy later on when we need extra skin for cloning.

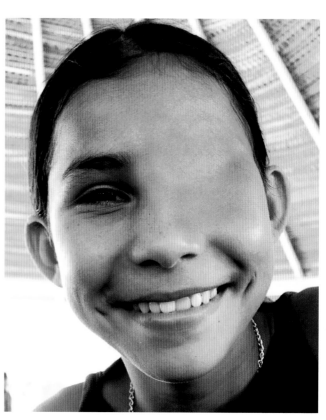

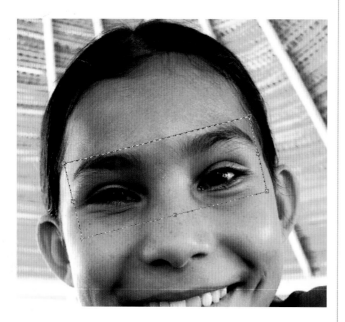

2 Choose the *Rectangular Marquee* tool, making sure that you have the *Feather* option set to 0 pixels. Draw a large box around the boy's eyes, incorporating as much of the detail as you can. I then rotated the box using *Select > Transform Selection* to produce a tighter selection. Now copy the model's eyes, paste them onto a new layer, and call it "Eyes." Hide this newly created layer for the moment; we will come back to it later.

3 We are now going to remove some detail from the boy's face (this is where his large forehead will be useful). We'll use Photoshop's *Clone Stamp* to remove everything but the boy's mouth. Set the *Clone Stamp's* opacity to between 40 and 70%. Press the Alt/Option key and click on the middle of the boy's forehead. This sets up the source for the *Clone Stamp*. Gradually clone over the features, changing opacity or resetting the stamp's source to another area if necessary.

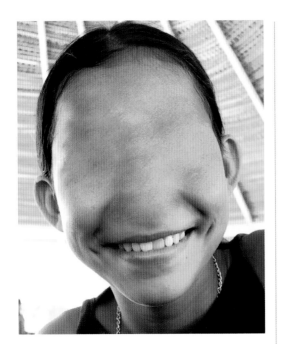

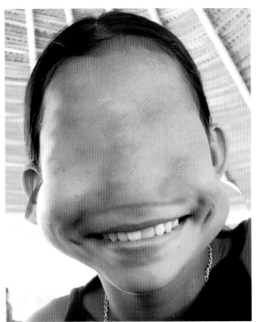

5 Next, we will begin to manipulate the structure of the face. We will use Photoshop's *Warp* function for this (if you have an early version of Photoshop, you can produce the same effect with *Liquify*. You may have to repeat steps 3 and 4 for the texture). Using the *Rectangular Marquee* tool, make a selection around the mouth and copy this to a new layer by going to *Layer > New > Layer Via Copy* or pressing Ctrl/Cmd+J. Name this layer "Smile." Go to *Edit > Transform > Warp* and pull out the two middle handles on either side, giving the boy large, protruding cheeks.

4 When using the *Clone Stamp* tool, you may notice that the picture loses a lot of its texture and starts looking unnatural. Photoshop has a very good device for combating this—the *Patch* tool, which copies texture and matches color with the underlying section. Select the *Patch* tool, set the option to *Source*, and draw around a small section of the cloned face using your mouse. When the section has been chosen you will see the marching ants. Click this selection and drag it on to an unmodified section of skin. Releasing it will copy the texture to the selected area. Repeat this procedure until you're satisfied with the overall skin texture.

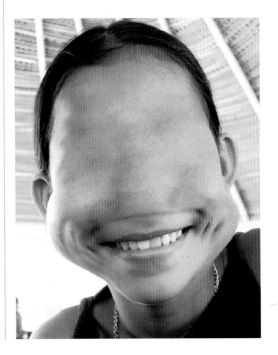

6 The next step is to mask out any unwanted background that the *Warp* command has affected. Click on the Smile layer and go to *Layer > Layer Mask > Reveal All* to add a layer mask. Painting with black on the mask will hide those parts of the layer; painting with white will reveal them. Choose a hard-edged brush with a size of around 150 pixels, making sure that the foreground color is set to black, and begin to mask away the unwanted parts of the layer.

Portraits

TROLL

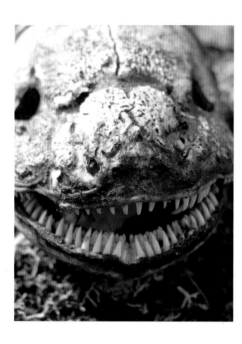

7 Now for the fun part. Open picture2.jpg, and, using the *Rectangular Marquee* tool, put a selection around the right side of the fish's mouth. Copy the selection and place it onto the mouth of the boy. Duplicate the new layer and flip it horizontally by going to *Edit > Transform > Flip Horizontal*. We now rotate the two halves until they're correctly positioned, move them together, and merge them into one layer using *Layer > Merge Layers*. The two halves don't match perfectly, so use the *Clone* tool to correct them.

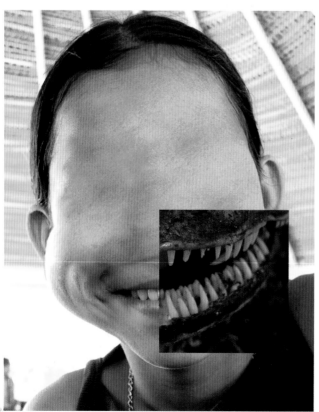

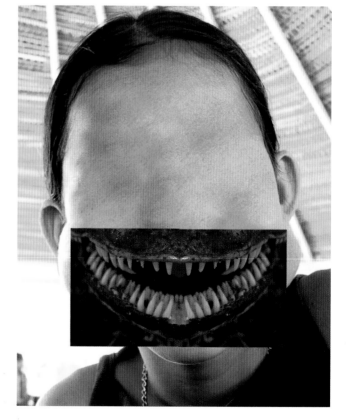

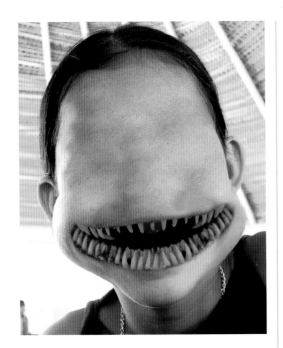

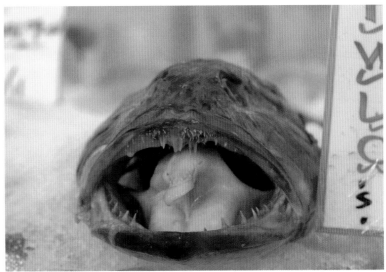

8 Name the layer "Mouth 1," and drag it below the Smile layer. Click on the Smile layer's mask, and, using a large, soft-edged brush, begin to paint away the boy's mouth, revealing the teeth. Take your time with this, changing brush sizes when you need to. When most of the teeth are visible, select the *Burn* tool. In the *Toolbar*, set the options to *Range: Highlights*; *Exposure*: 50% and darken the skin above the teeth on the Smile layer.

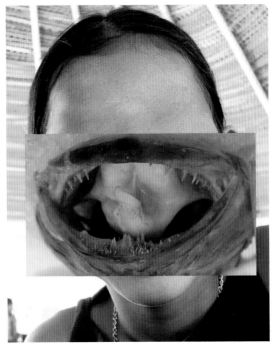

9 This mouth works very well, but we are going to add more depth by adding a second mouth. Open picture3.jpg, place a rectangular selection around the whole mouth, and copy it onto the picture. Place this new layer above the Smile layer and name it "Mouth 2." The next job is to flip the Mouth 2 layer vertically because we want the top jaw at the bottom. Go to *Edit > Transform > Flip Vertically*, and then resize the mouth so it fits over the top of the Mouth 1 and Smile layers.

TROLL

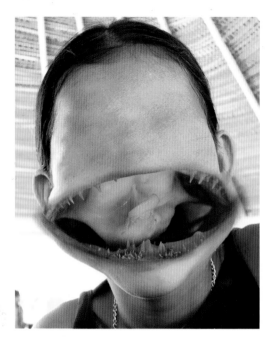

10 The mouth now needs to be masked, so go to *Layer > Layer Mask > Reveal All* to add a layer mask to the Mouth 2 layer. With a large, 150-pixel soft-edged brush, begin to paint away the mouth—all except the bottom teeth and lower outer edge. We are going to use the edge to create more depth, so the curves of the jaw must be left intact. When most of the unwanted parts of the mouth are masked, zoom in and use a smaller, hard-edged brush of around 30 pixels to remove more of the mouth, making sure that the teeth remain and look sharp.

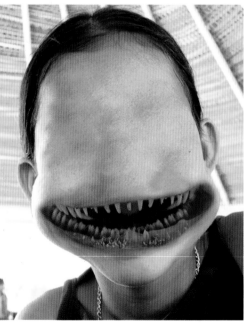

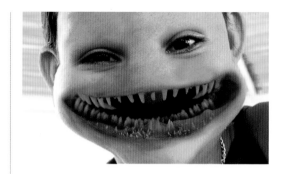

11 Back in Step 2 we took a copy of the eyes and hid them. Now we want to reveal them and reposition them on the face. Drag the Eyes layer to the top of the layer stack and move the eyes down toward the mouth using the *Move* tool. Once again we need to mask out some of the skin, this time around the eyes. Add a layer mask to the Eyes layer, and, using a soft-edged, medium-sized brush of around 70 pixels, with the foreground color set to black, paint away the skin, leaving just the eyes.

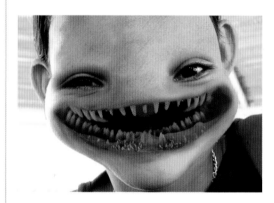

12 The final step is to reposition the eyes farther apart. Right/Ctrl+click on the Eyes layer mask and select *Apply Layer Mask*. This permanently deletes the masked pixels—so make sure you only do this when you are happy with the mask. Make a selection around one of the eyes and go to *Layer > New > Layer Via Cut*. This will put the selected eye on a new layer, leaving the original layer with only one eye on it. Rename them "Left Eye" and "Right Eye" respectively. Move the left eye slightly to the left and the right eye slightly to the right to complete the troll image.

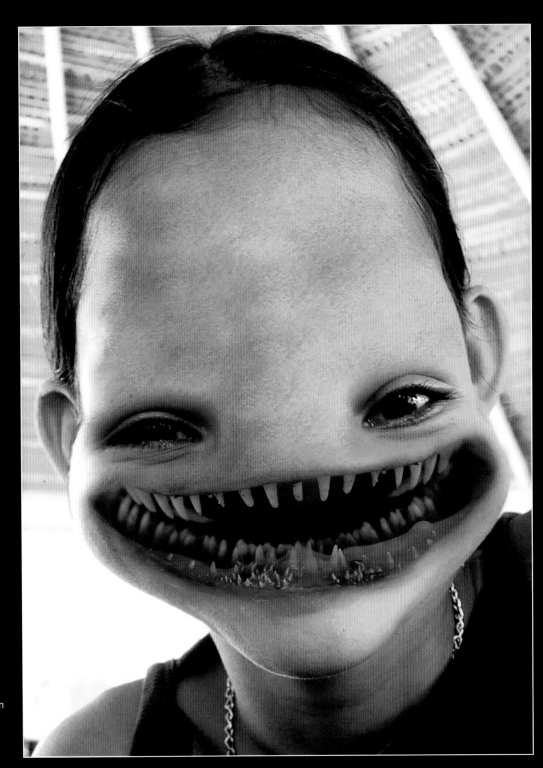

Final Image

This type of horrific, yet humorous, image can be created using any suitable animal mouth—a leisurely yawn from your pet cat can be a fearsome maw when pasted onto a person.

© Simon Rudd

Portraits

TRStapp TRAPPED

by Georgia Denby
This image was created with only one source picture and a little work in
Photoshop. It was very easy to create, and any similar photo-editing program
would give much the same result. All that's needed is a roll of stockinet, available from
bicycle and car accessories stores, and two willing models!

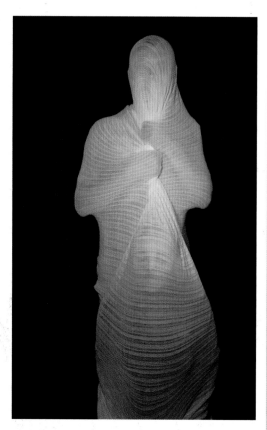

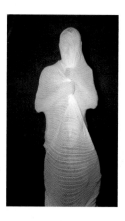

2 Open the image
in Photoshop and
convert it to Grayscale
by going to *Image >
Mode > Grayscale*.

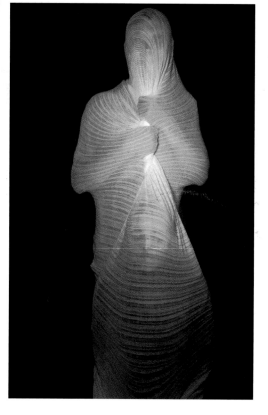

3 To make the models
more prominent,
copy the background
layer so that you have
two identical copies, one
on top of the other—your
background and your
background copy. Then
change the blending
mode of the new layer
to *Multiply*. This instantly
gives the image a more
ghostly feel.

1 Position the models as shown, with one standing
and the other kneeling in front, both facing the
camera. The stockinet is a very long, stretchable tube of
fabric and is easy for any model to get into. Take one end
and slip quite a large quantity of it over your standing
model, and then extend it to go over the head of the one
in front. Make sure the fabric is pulled quite tight over
their faces or they won't show through. Use two studio
lights, one either side, and be sure that the faces are
visible before the shot is taken. You may need to play
with the lights a little to get the effect right.

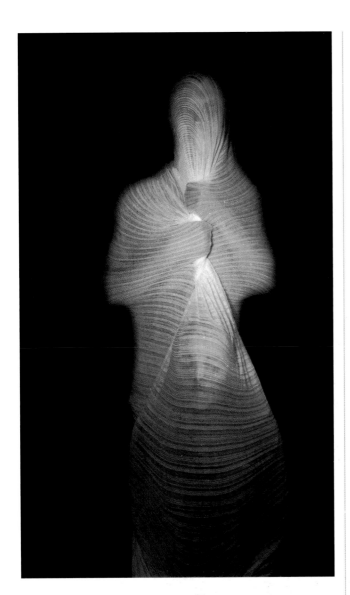

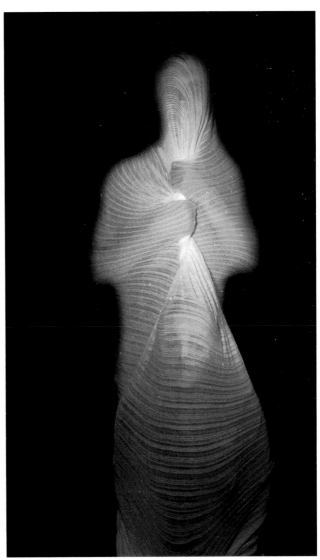

4 Next we need to soften the sharp edges around the models. To do this, choose the same black as your background using the *Eyedropper* tool and select a soft, wide brush. Reduce the brush's opacity to 70% and slowly work your way around the edges of the models. You may need to go over it a few times to get the desired result. Leave the right and left sides of the lower model intact for the moment.

5 Change the brush's opacity to 40% and go over the edges again, moving your brush farther in to soften the edges even more. You may need to increase your brush size to the get the right look. Still leave the lower model untouched for now.

TRAPPED

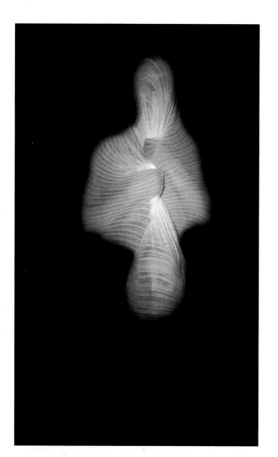

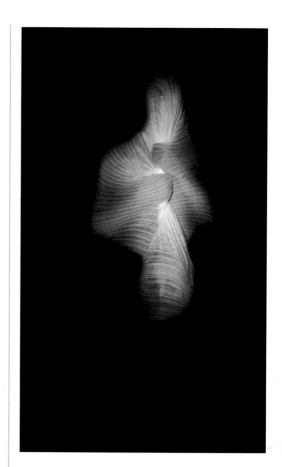

6 To create the "head in a bag" look, use the technique outlined in steps 4 and 5, painting out the area under the lower head, but still leaving either side sharp.

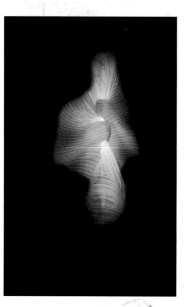

7 The image is almost finished and just needs tweaking a little. Select the *Burn* tool. Keeping the opacity at approximately 40% and still using quite a large brush size, work around the lit areas in the middle, concentrating on the faces and arms.

8 Go to *Levels* (*Image > Adjustments > Levels*) and drag the right-hand arrow to the right until you're happy with the result. It doesn't need to slide far, or it will spoil the effect. All it needs is a touch to help bring out the light in the center of the image.

9 Finally, go to *Filter > Sharpen > Unsharp Mask* and enter the following settings: *Amount*: 100%; *Radius*: 1.0; *Threshold*: 0. You may feel your image doesn't need this final stage, in which case, omit this step.

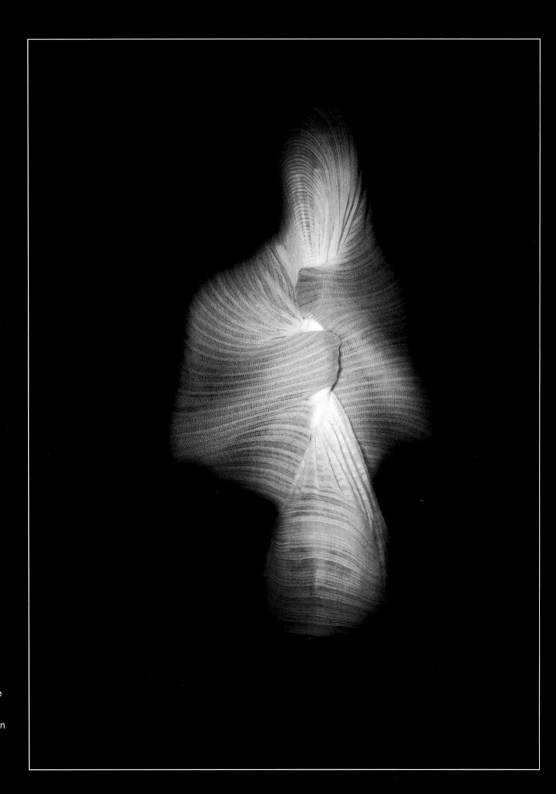

Final Image
This haunting image is
incredibly easy to create
using only one source
image and a combination
of blending modes and
brushes in Photoshop.
© Georgia Denby

SECRETS

by Simon Rudd

I don't know about you, but I am terrible at keeping secrets. Whatever the secret, I just blurt it out at the wrong time to the wrong person. So I created this Photoshop image to remind me that sometimes I need to keep my mouth under lock and key. The main tools used to create the image are the *Liquify* filter, the *Clone Stamp*, and the *Burn* tool.

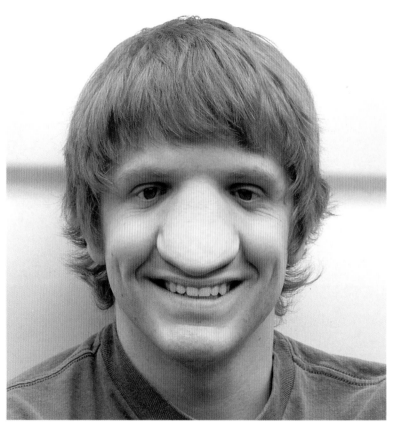

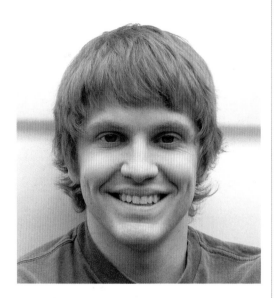

1 First of all, open the photograph in Photoshop and make a backup copy (Ctrl/Cmd+J). Then use the *Crop* tool to focus the picture on the model's face—click on the top-left corner of the part of the picture you want to keep, then drag your mouse right and down until you have a square or rectangle around your selection. The unselected part of the picture will turn gray to show what you will have left. When you're happy with the selection, click the checkmark in the *Tool Options* bar to finish.

2 The next step is to the change the shape of the face slightly using the *Liquify* filter. To load the filter, go to *Filter > Liquify* or press Shift+Ctrl/Cmd+X. When the new window has loaded, choose the *Bloat* tool—this is the one that looks like a large pillow (it's normally the fifth tool from the top). Change the settings to *Brush Size*: 300; *Brush Density*: 50; *Brush Pressure*: 50; *Brush Rate*: 40. Focus the brush over the model's nose and hold the left mouse button down until the nose has swollen up as shown. Click *OK* to accept the changes.

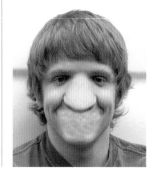

3 Now we are going to remove the mouth. This is a fairly straightforward procedure using the *Clone Stamp* and the *Patch* tool. Load the *Clone Stamp* and Alt/Opt+click on a section of skin to set the source of the clone. I used the model's chin. Set the brush size to 50 pixels and opacity to 70% and gradually remove the mouth. When you've finished, you may notice that the mouth looks flat and without texture, so to combat this we will use the *Patch* tool.

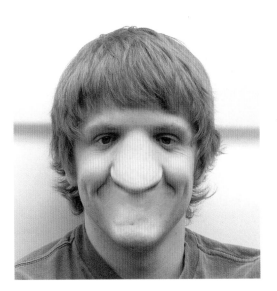

4 The *Patch* tool copies texture and is ideal for use on skin. Draw around a section of the mouth using your mouse and drag it onto the chin. When the mouse button is released, it will copy the texture of the selected skin to the mouth. When you are happy with the results, move onto the nose and smile lines.

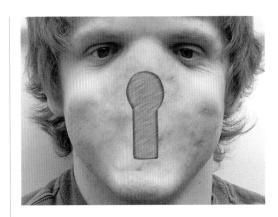

6 When you're happy with the keyhole shape, it's time to duplicate it and give it a metal texture. To duplicate the keyhole, click on the keyhole layer and go to *Layer > New > Layer Via Copy* or press Ctrl/Cmd+J. Rename this layer "Metal Keyhole." Create a selection around the new keyhole by pressing the Ctrl/Cmd key and clicking the graphic. Add noise to the layer using *Filter > Noise > Add Noise* at a setting of 400%. Follow this by going to *Blur > Motion Blur* and entering these settings: *Angle*: 21°; *Distance*: 30 pixels.

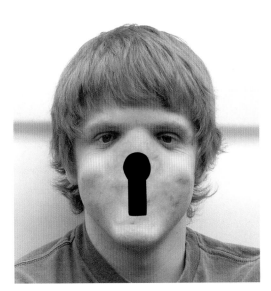

5 We are now going to flex our artistic muscles and make a basic keyhole shape—a round-edged rectangle and a circle is all that is required. Start by making a new layer (*Layer > New > Layer*) and calling it "Keyhole." Set the default colors by pressing D on the keyboard, then click on the *Rounded Rectangle* tool. In the tool options bar, set the *Radius* to 25 pixels and the shape options to *Fill Pixels*. Draw a long vertical rectangle from near the model's eyes down to where the top of his lips would be. Next, choose the *Ellipse* tool and draw a circle from the top of the rectangle to a quarter of the way down.

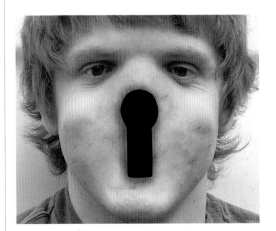

7 Now we need to add some depth to the keyhole to make it look more realistic. Select the *Burn* tool and set the options to *Brush Size*: 50 pixels with a soft edged brush; *Range*: Midtones; *Exposure*: 50%. Go to your manipulated layer and begin to trace around the edge of the keyhole image. This should make it look red and burned.

SECRETS

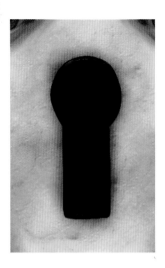

8 We'll use the *Burn* tool again to add some depth to the layer. Change the range from *Midtones* to *Highlights* and the brush size to 25 pixels, but keep the other settings the same. Trace around the keyhole as before, staying close to the keyhole shape and making sure some of the red midtones are retained.

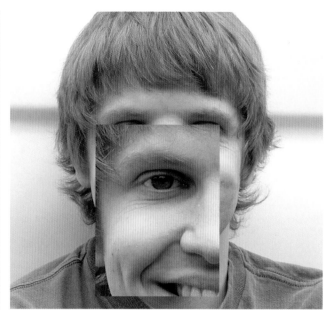

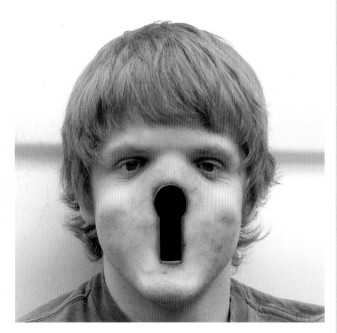

9 The keyhole is looking a little out of place now so we are going to adjust it. Select the Metal Keyhole layer and put a selection around the graphic by Ctrl/Cmd-clicking it. Go to *Select > Modify > Contract* and enter a value of 10 pixels. This will shrink the selection by 10 pixels. Press the Delete key to clear the area inside the selection. Deselect the keyhole by pressing Ctrl/Cmd+D. You should now have a metallic texture on the inside of the keyhole.

10 The final element of the image is an object inside the keyhole. You could use whatever you like, but I decided to use an eye staring out of the hole. Go to your first layer—this should be the original picture—and, using the *Rectangular Marquee* tool, draw a large selection around one of the eyes. Copy the selection by going to *Layer > New > Layer Via Copy* and name the new layer "Eyeball." Drag the Eyeball layer to the top of the layer stack.

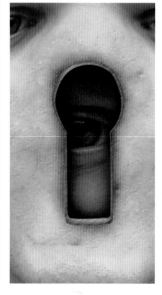

11 To change the size of the eyeball, go to *Edit > Transform > Free Transform*. While holding the Shift and Alt/Option keys, pull one of the corner anchors, making the picture roughly twice its normal size. Place the Eyeball layer over the keyhole shape. The final step is to mask the unwanted parts of the Eyeball layer. Add a layer mask to the Eyeball layer by going to *Layer > Layer Mask > Reveal All*, set the foreground color to black, and with a 30-pixel soft-edged brush, paint away the parts of the layer that are not needed.

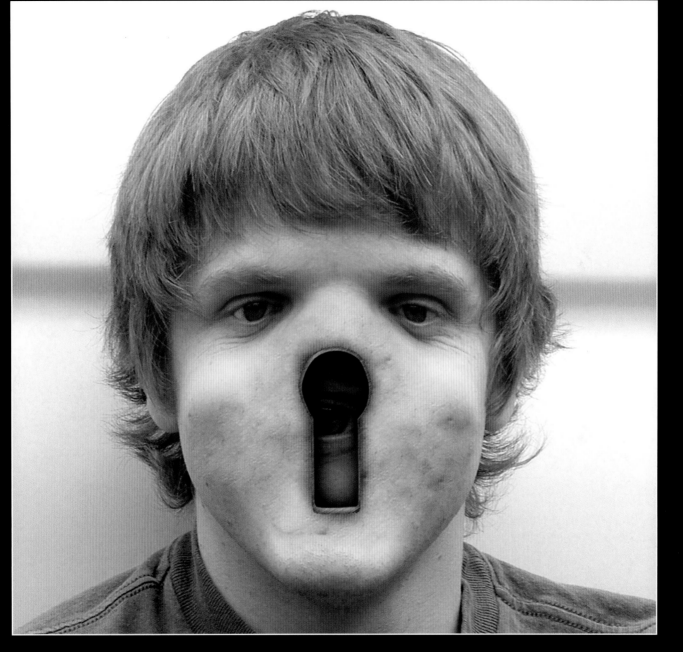

Final Image

This disturbing image focuses on the keyhole metaphor, but a multitude
of apertures can be created by using the *Custom Shape* tool to carve
new windows into people's souls!

© Simon Rudd

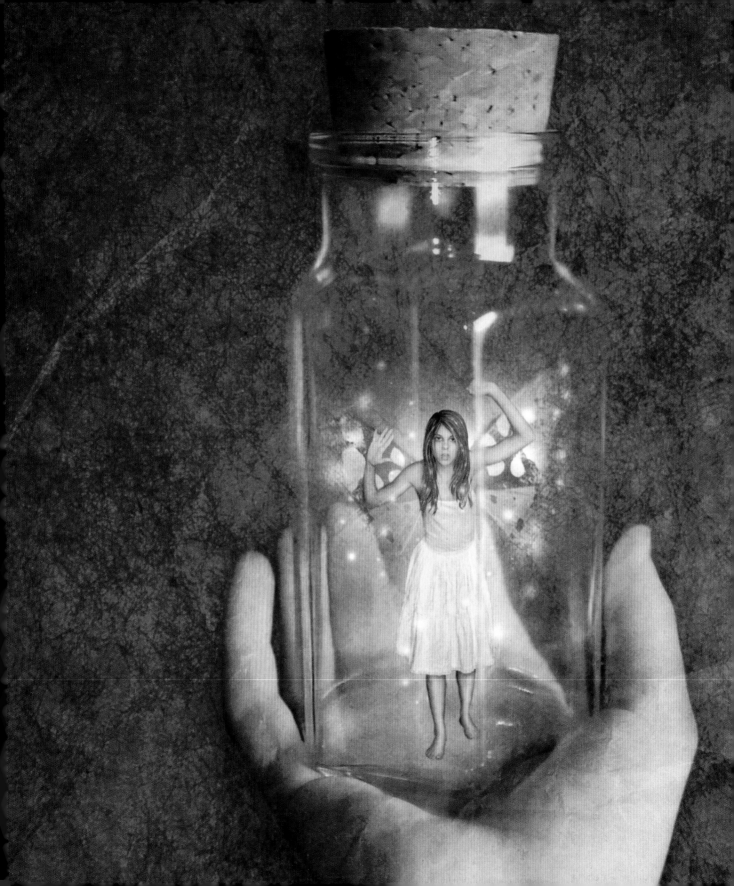

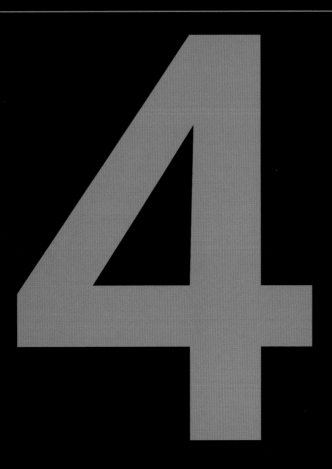

4

In this section of the book, we'll look at creating surreal creatures. Some of these will use human body parts, others will use children's toys and parking meters, but all of them will create creatures that you won't find in your local zoo. There is also a wide mix of themes—some of the creatures will be recognizably fantastical, while others will be surreal nightmares that you wouldn't want creeping up behind you on a dark night.

Boo!

creatures

Creatures

THING IN THE WOODS

by Hampus Samuelsson

You don't have to be Dr. Frankenstein to build creatures from body parts these days. With the help of your able assistant Igor von Photoshop you can chop and change limbs to create some truly wild lifeforms. If you go down to the woods today, you're sure of a big surprise!

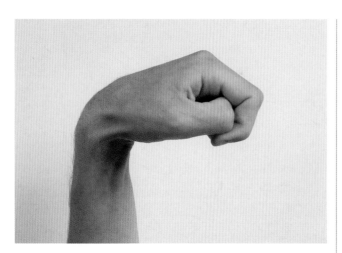

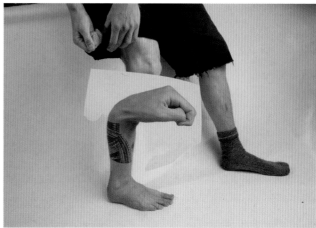

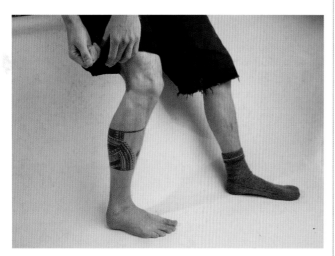

2 The tattoo is too high up the leg and it's too wide. I made a selection right below the tattoo and copied into a new layer, made it a smart object, and then warped it to fit the wrist. The quickest way to get into *Warp* mode is to press Ctrl/Cmd+T to make the layer transformable, then Right/Ctrl+click on the object onscreen and choose *Warp*. You will now be able to make a perfect fit. When the proportions are good, blend all of the separate areas together using layer masks.

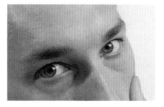 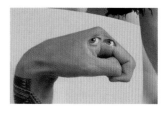

1 Open up your carefully chosen foot and hand image. First, we want to combine the hand with the foot and calf. Lower the opacity of the Hand layer so that you can see the calf through it and match them up. The wrist is currently much thinner than the calf, so we'll need to enlarge it to create a seamless join. We can't just scale the image because we don't want the hand itself to be much bigger than it already is. The answer is to warp it. First, make the layer into a smart object (*Layer > Smart Objects > Group Into New Smart Object*) so that you can go back and edit it again if necessary.

3 Now it's time to make our creature see. Import the eyes from the face image, and paste them into your PSD as two layers, one for each eye. Just merging them as normal eyes looks a bit boring, so switch them around putting the left eye on the right side, and vice versa. This will give him an odd look and the nose bone will fit nicely with the thumb. Merge the eyes into the hand using layer masks, make any necessary *Levels* adjustments to blend them seamlessly. I also changed the *Hue* and *Saturation* on the left eye to make it look better. Try to save some of the eyebrows if you can.

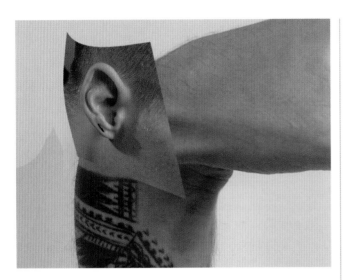

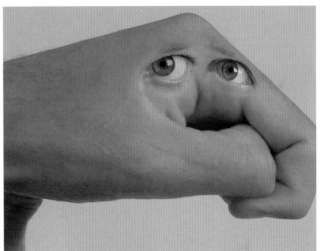

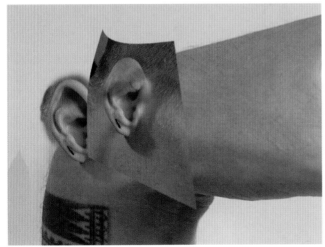

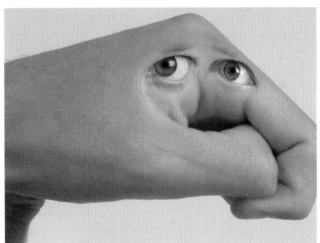

4 Now that the creature can see, it's time to let him hear, too. Open an image of an ear and follow a similar process as you did for the hand and the tattoo—warp the ear until you're happy with the shape, and then use a layer mask to merge it with the hand. The left ear is a bit trickier. Copy the first ear and use the *Clone Stamp* tool to build up the back of the creature's left ear. You only need to do the top section of the ear, and then use a layer mask to hide the rest of it behind the hand. Don't worry about the hair around it, we'll use another layer mask to deal with that later. Use the *Burn* tool or the *Airbrush* to make a shadow at the bottom of the ear.

5 To change the eye color, make a *Hue/Saturation* adjustment layer and check the *Colorize* box. Use the *Hue* slider to pick a color, then press *OK*. You will now have a new layer with a layer mask. Press Ctrl/Cmd+I to invert the layer mask, then use the *Brush* tool to paint out the eyes on the mask.

THING IN THE WOODS

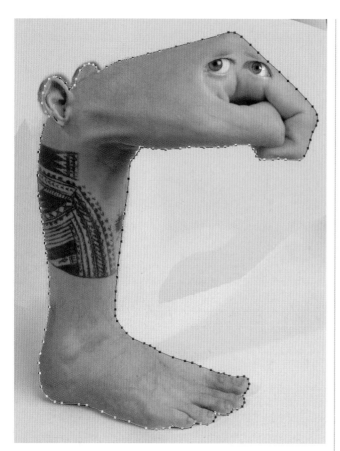

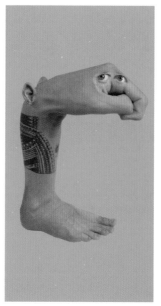

7 To mask the hair on the leg, select the channel with the highest contrast from the *Channels* palette–in this case it's the blue one. Duplicate this channel, and use *Levels* to make the contrast even higher. Invert the new channel and make it a selection by Ctrl/Cmd+clicking on its thumbnail. Click on the channel that you saved from the path you made earlier, and use a soft brush to paint in the missing hair. Select the whole of this channel and paste it as a new layer into your creature group. You may want to add a solid-filled background layer to give some definition to the piece.

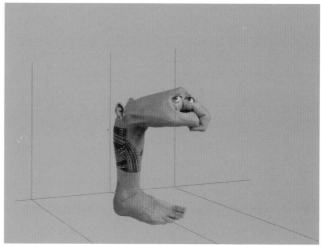

6 We now need to cut our figure out of the background. The method that I prefer is the path and alpha method. First, make sure that your figure is in the same group–make a group by clicking the *Create a New Group* icon at the bottom of the *Layers* palette, then drag all of the creature layers into it. Open the *Paths* palette and make a new path around your creature using the *Pen* tool. This takes some practice but don't give up! Once you get the hang of it, it's far quicker and more accurate than other methods. Once you've completed the path, Right/Ctrl+click on the path's thumbnail and choose *Make Selection* to transform your path into a selection. Switch to the *Channels* palette and click the *Save Selection As Channel* icon at the bottom.

8 I'm creating a background from scratch for my creature, so the first thing I'll do is draw some perspective lines on a new layer to use as guides. Next, choose an image to use as your environment. A nice barn wall will do for a floor–paste it in, and distort it to fit the guide lines. Now we need some paint. I have a great image of some rusty old machinery that will be perfect. Distort the paint on top of the floor, and change the layer's blending mode to *Hard Light*. Go back to the wooden floor and use the *Clone Stamp* tool to remove any obvious cracks under the paint.

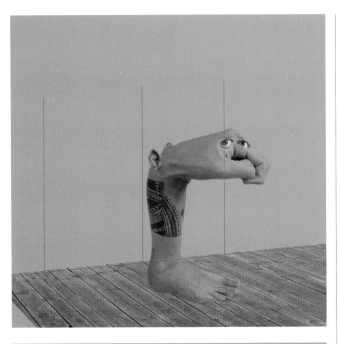

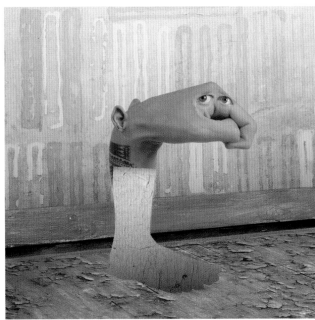

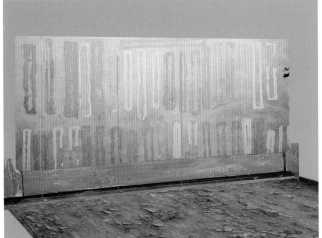

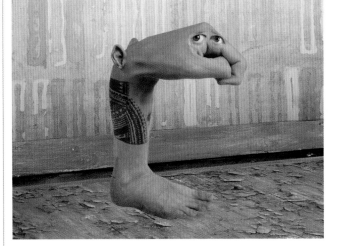

9 Add a wall in the same way as you added the floor. Make sure that you get the perspective right by sticking to your guides. Make any fine adjustments to the *Levels*, *Curves*, and *Hue/Saturation* that are necessary to make it blend. I've also added a strip of wood from a barn door as a skirting board—again, skewed to fit the perspective, and the colors adjusted slightly to blend in.

10 Almost done now, we just need to add some final details. If our creature's been hopping around without any shoes then his foot should have more scars. I've used another image of cracked paint with its blending mode set to *Soft Light* to create this effect. Next, create a new layer behind the creature and paint some shadows on with a soft brush. Change the blending mode of the shadow layer to *Soft Light*.

THING IN THE WOODS

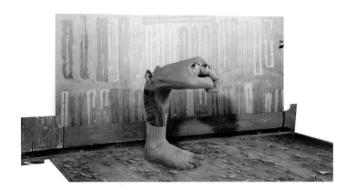

11 I made a few small color adjustments to the image using a *Hue/Saturation* adjustment layer set to *Colorize* and with the *Hue* changed to green. I set the blending mode of this color layer to *Soft Light*, with its opacity at 30%. With that done, crop the image to focus on the creature and a bit of the background.

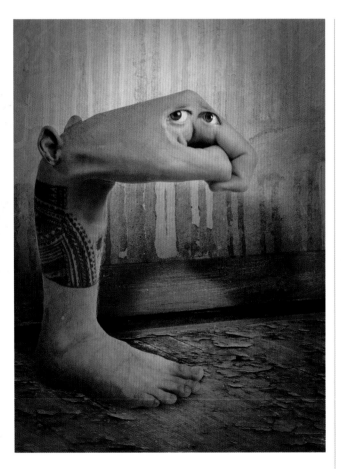

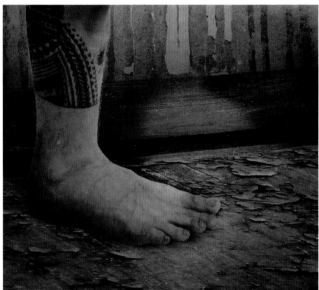

13 The final thing is to try and age the image a little using an overlaid texture. I imported an image of the cover of an old bible and put it on top with its blending mode set to *Soft Light*, and its opacity at 50%. Only one thing left, the paint on the floor isn't great, so make a *Hue/Saturation* adjustment layer above it and change the *Hue* to green and lower the *Saturation*. Select its layer mask, invert it, and paint out where you want the green color to appear, giving the floor a really dirty and moldy look.

12 To add a bit more atmosphere to the piece, we'll add a darkened vignette around the edge of the image. This will also help to draw the eye to the creature. Make a round selection using the *Elliptical Marquee* tool with *Feather* set to 150 pixels. Invert the selection, and make a *Levels* adjustment, lowering the white *Output* level to about 170.

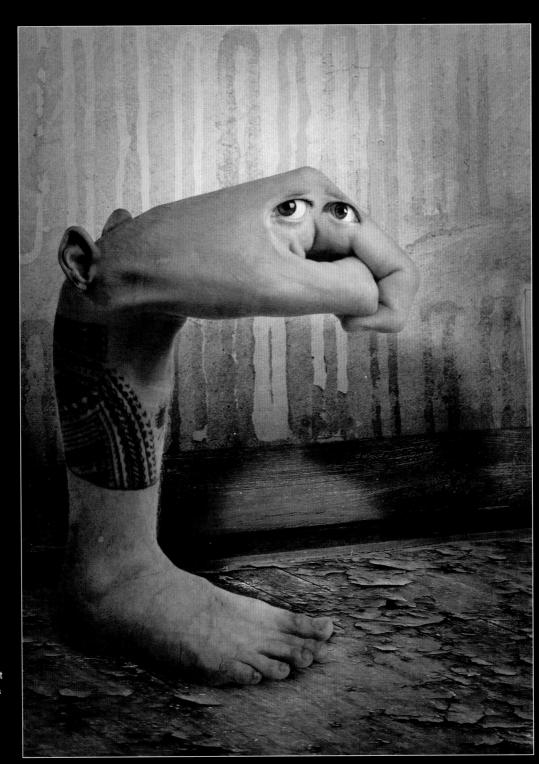

Final Image

This image goes to show that although you can make a striking creature, it won't be complete unless you spend time putting it in the appropriate surroundings.

© Hampus Samuelsson

Creatures

BEAR

by Anthony VenGraitis

Sometimes it's fun to experiment when creating an image from multiple photos, just to see what sort of results the combination of elements will produce. By using layer blending modes and adjustment layers to alter the color and brightness of a montage you can give it a more natural look, and a simple object can take on a life of its own.

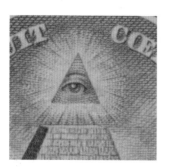

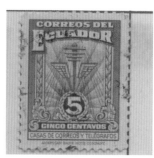

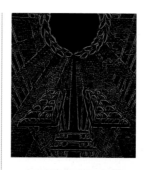

2 We now want to use Photoshop's *Glowing Edges* filter to give a more lively feel to the background. Use a higher setting in the *Brightness* and *Smoothness* fields and a lower setting in the *Edge Width* field. After we get the desired effect, we will need to make a *Hue/Saturation* adjustment to change the hue of the background to a cooler, greenish tone.

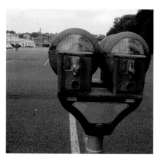

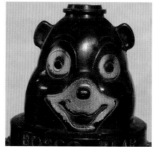

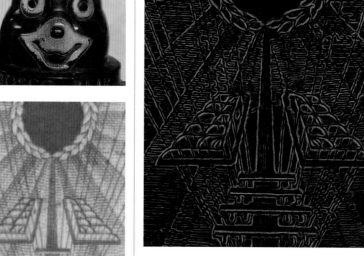

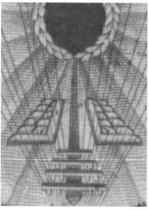

1 An old postage stamp will serve as the starting point, and will be the abstract background for the entire image. In order to capture enough detail, we'll need to create a high-resolution scan of the whole stamp. Rotate the entire scan 180 degrees, and then crop into the abstract design in the center of the stamp. We'll also need to use the *Clone Stamp* tool to eliminate the number 5 from the circular field at the top of the scan. Select a dark portion of the circular field (make sure that the *Clone Stamp* tool is not set to *Aligned*) and carefully clone out the number to create a blank, dark area in the circular field.

3 Now we can add the first element to the image. The all-seeing eye from a U.S. dollar bill will fit nicely in the circular field. After getting a high-resolution scan of the back of the dollar, select the triangular portion that contains the eye. Once the area has been selected, switch to the *Quick Mask* mode and use the *Blur* filter to soften the edges of the selected area. Switch back to *Standard Edit* mode, and copy and paste the eye above the stamp background. Use the *Linear Light* blending mode on the eye layer, and set the opacity of the layer to 25%. This will help the eye blend more naturally with the dark circular area.

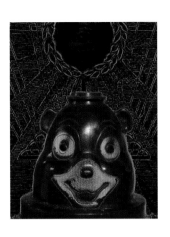

4 We'll need to select the bear from the photograph and cut away the background. It's helpful to plan ahead and take a picture of the object on a solid-colored background. This will allow us to use *Select > Color Range*, reducing the need to hand-select the edges of the bear. After we get the best selection from *Color Range*, we can fine-tune the selection by switching to *Quick Mask* mode and erasing any unnecessary selected areas. After we get a clean selection, we can switch back to *Standard Edit* mode and copy and paste the bear photo on top of the background. Make any necessary scale and rotation adjustments to make sure the bear is set correctly in the frame.

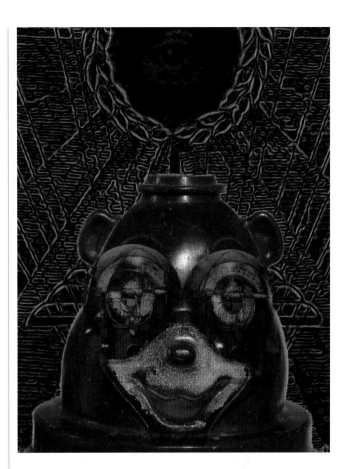

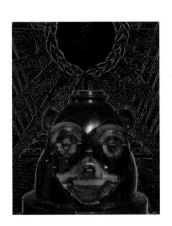

5 This time we'll need to select and copy the parking meter image for the bear's face. We won't be able to use the *Color Range* selection tool here, so it will require some patient use of the *Quick Mask* to select the object. Use the *Brush* tool to carefully mark the selected area on the mask. Once selected, use a light blur on the mask to soften the edge of the selection. Then, copy and paste and change the blending mode of the layer to *Difference*. In this mode, the bear's face will show through the parking meter. This will allow us to adjust the scale and rotation so that the meter aligns properly on the bear's face.

6 Create a layer mask for the parking meter layer. Use the mask to clean up the stray bits of the parking meter around the bear's mouth and eyes and beneath its chin. It's important to watch the effect of the mask on the image when we mark the areas. If necessary, reset the *Hardness* of the brush or reduce its opacity.

Creatures

BEAR

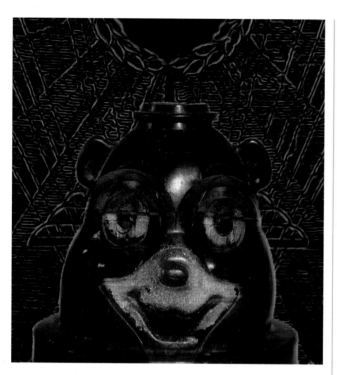

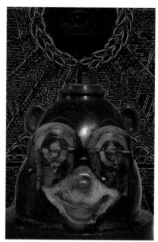

9 We'll need to make two more adjustments to the separate layers to get more "pop" from the image. To help accentuate the meter portion of the image, we can add a separate *Hue/Saturation* effect to the meter layer. Click on the meter layer thumbnail, and add a *Hue/Saturation* adjustment layer. Make sure to check *Use Previous Layer to Create Clipping Mask*, then click *OK*. Set the *Hue* to +160, the *Saturation* to +50, and the *Lightness* to +20.

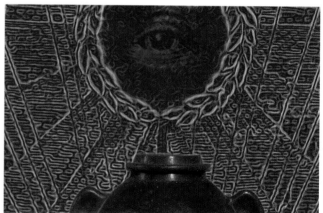

7 Ctrl/Cmd+click on the meter layer's thumbnail in the *Layers* palette. This will automatically load a selection area to match the meter. Click on the bear layer to select it, and make a *Brightness/Contrast* adjustment layer. Set the *Brightness* to about 30% and click *OK*. The layer will automatically be set to only affect the area included in the selection.

10 The last adjustment will be to add a *Brightness/Contrast* adjustment layer to the background portion of the image. Click on the stamp background and add the adjustment layer. Set the *Brightness* to +40, and the *Contrast* to +15. This will give a more consistent look to the brightness of the overall image. Some of these adjustments can be changed according to your own preference for brightness and color, but any effort to change the appearance of one layers will likely require some additional amendment to all the other layers. Your eye will be the best judge of how to do this.

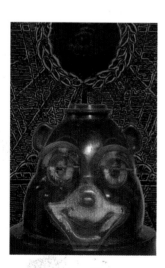

8 The image has already achieved an interesting look, but the blending of the layers is creating some areas of sharp blue color around the bear's eyes. This next step will help create a more uniform look to all of the separate layers. Apply a *Hue/Saturation* effect to the entire image. In this case, we set the *Hue* to +150, the *Saturation* to -75, and the *Lightness* to +15. By using a more consistent color treatment, the combination of odd elements will appear more natural.

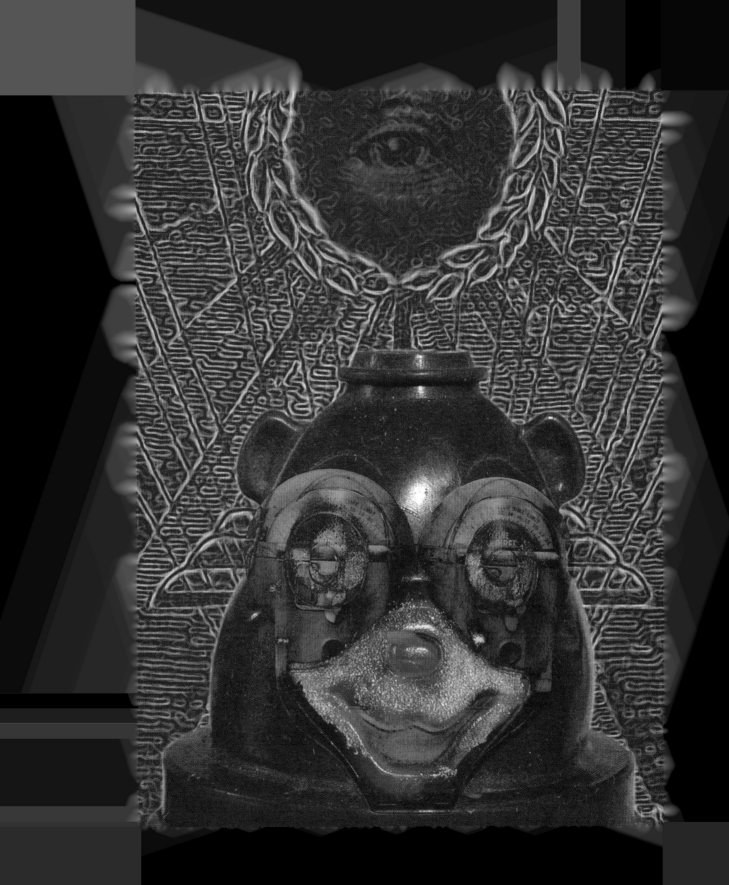

Creatures

YOU CAN'T OWN ME

by Nela Dunato
If you ever grieved because fairies don't exist in real life
and you weren't born as one, now you can learn how to make
yourself appear as a part of an old fairytale.

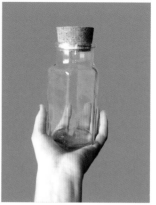

2 Invert the selection (Ctrl/
Cmd+Shift+I) and click the
Quick Mask icon, then double-
click it and change the mask
color to green (R: 0, G: 255,
B: 0) at 100%. Now use a black
brush to mask any parts of the
background where it's still not
clear green, and a white brush
to bring back parts of the hand
and bottle that are hidden.

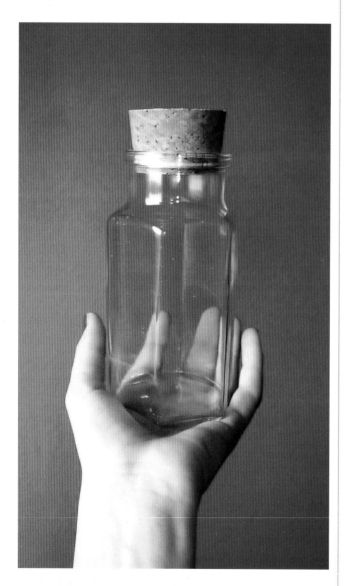

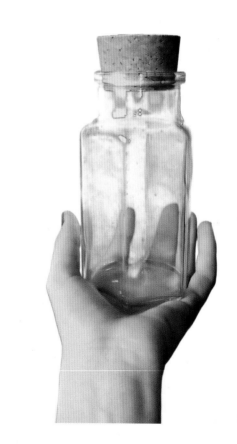

1 Open the image containing the glass bottle (bottle_01.jpg). Set the
foreground color to a bright red (R: 201, G: 24, B: 40–the color in the
background of the image) and go to *Select > Color Range*. Make sure
that the hand and bottle edges are black, while the background and glass
are white. Increase the *Fuzziness* slider until you achieve the right effect.

3 Press Q to switch back to *Standard Edit* mode, and apply a layer
mask. Go over the glass with the *Sponge* tool to remove any red
tint from the reflections. Go to *Image > Adjustments > Color Balance*
and change the settings to: *Shadows*: 1, 0, -6; *Midtones*: 11, -11, 37;
Highlights: -1, -8, -9.

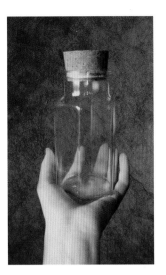

4 Make a new layer set called "background." Create a new layer and fill it with medium brown, then add some texture images to create a satisfactory background. Either download those provided (texture_02.jpg, texture_03.jpg, texture_04.jpg), or use your own to create a different effect. Set the blending modes of each texture layer to *Overlay*, *Hard Light*, or *Soft Light*, and vary their opacity between 30% and 50%. Experiment with these settings until you're satisfied with the result.

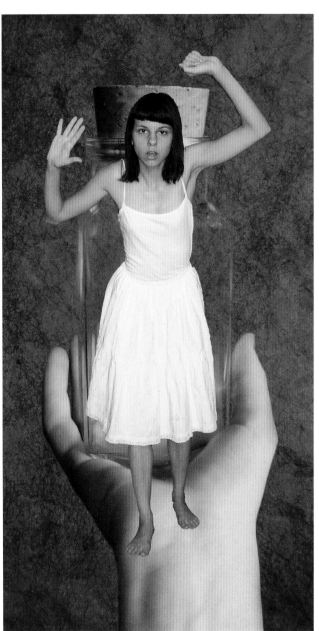

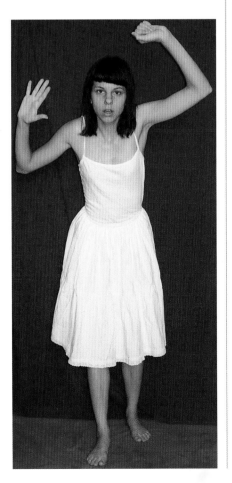

5 Open the girl image (girl_06.jpg) and select the area around the girl loosely with the *Polygonal Lasso* tool. Press Q and paint over the remaining background with a black brush (the mask will appear red). If you make a mistake, use the white brush to bring the deleted part back. Press Q and copy the selected girl to your working document. Flip the bottle image horizontally so that the shadows on both images match.

Creatures

YOU CAN'T OWN ME

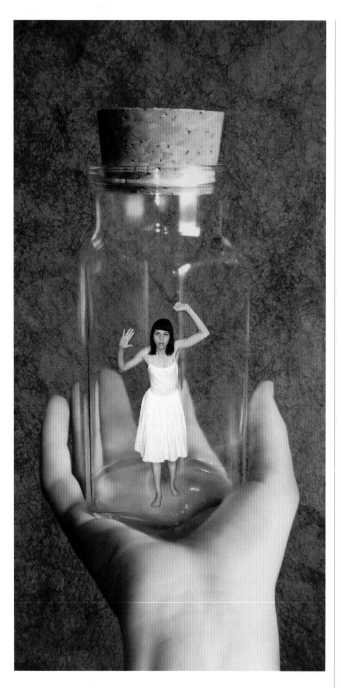

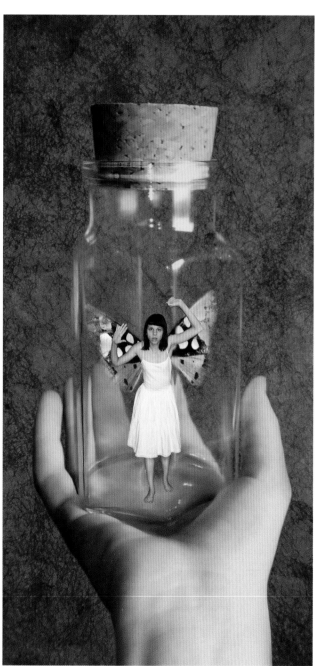

6 Select the *Dodge* tool and use it to lighten any areas where the light should fall. Burn the left edge of the palm a little to make it look more believable.

7 Copy both butterfly wings under the girl layer, and transform them so that they fit the pose. Adjust the *Hue/Saturation* and *Brightness/Contrast* of the layer to your liking. Next, apply a layer mask and paint around the wing edges to make them fade softly.

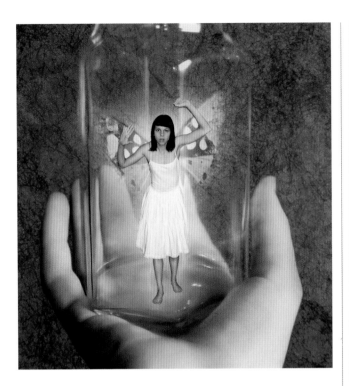

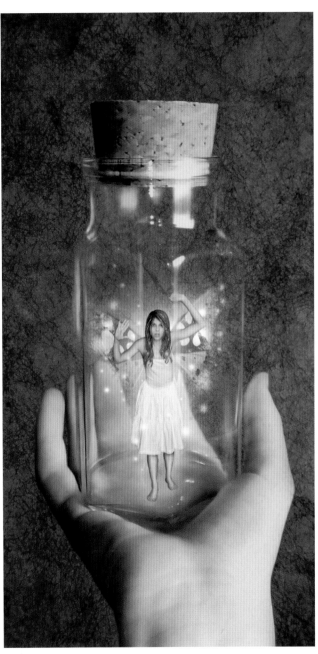

8 Lower the opacity of the wings layer to 70% and add an *Outer Glow* layer style with the following settings: *Color*: white, *Blend Mode*: *Overlay*, *Opacity*: 100%, *Size*: 115px. Lower the girl layer's *Opacity* to 95% and add another *Outer Glow* layer style with these settings: *Color*: light yellow, *Blend Mode*: *Hard Light*, *Opacity*: 70%, *Size*: 120px.

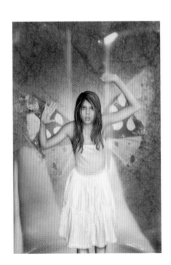

9 This step is optional, and depends on the girl model you are using—because I don't like the hair on the original photograph, I painted new hair on a layer above. Even if you can't paint, you can do the same by using custom hair brushes that are available for free on numerous websites.

10 Creating fairy dust is very easy. Make a new layer with the blending mode set to *Overlay*, at about 75% *Opacity*. Take a soft white brush and click around randomly on a separate layer, varying the brush size as you do so. Repeat this on a layer between the body and wings; this will add to the feeling of space.

Creatures

YOU CAN'T OWN ME

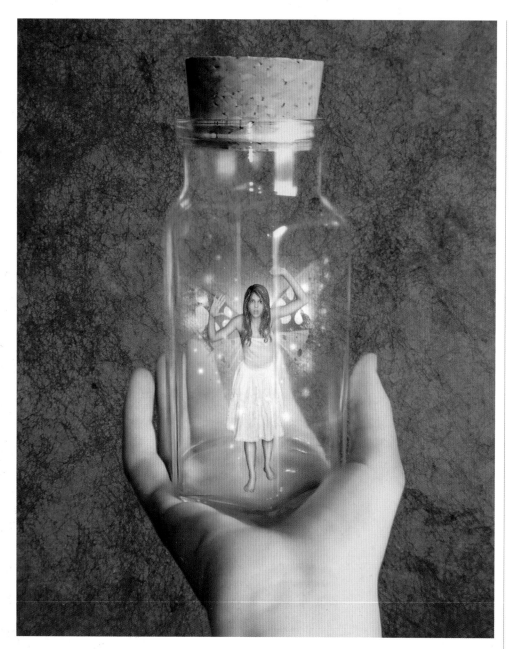

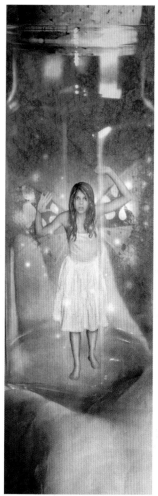

12 The last thing to work on is the atmosphere of the image. Add two textures (texture_05.jpg, texture_07.jpg) on top of the document. Set the blending modes of these textures to *Soft Light* and lower their opacity until you achievable a suitable effect. Mask the parts where the texture looks too intensive, especially the face and hands. Shade the background beneath the hand to get a more three-dimensional look.

11 Next, we need to add the glass bottle in front of the model. Make a new layer at the top of the *Layers* palette and draw a vertical line with a soft white brush (about 30% *Opacity*), then a thin black one next to it. Use the *Blur* tool and blur the body and wings directly beneath this line. Then blur some more on the parts that are further from the glass, while leaving the face and right palm completely crisp.

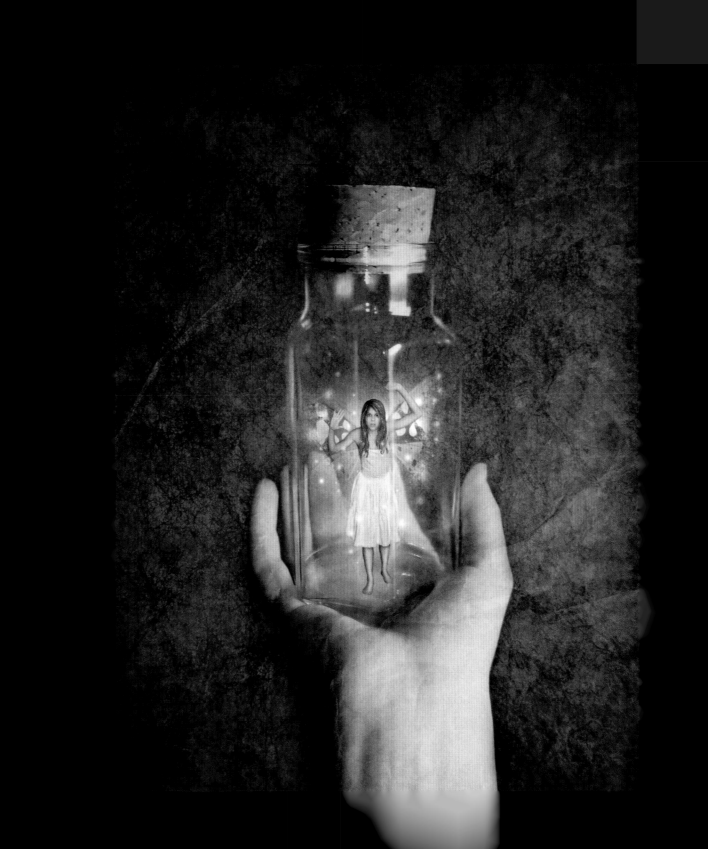

Creatures

HEARTBROKEN

by Patrik Blomqvist
This image is inspired by Salvador Dali's *Sleep* and, like the painting, we'll build it from scratch. Just like an artist you will start out with an empty white canvas and piece this surreal composition together from a number of sources. The broken heart pieces are made from two similar photos taken from slightly different angles then blended together to get the distorted effect. The environment is a simple texture with some lighting effects. The outdoor source photos are taken with a Canon 400D and we'll change the hue and light to make the heads fit their new indoor environment.

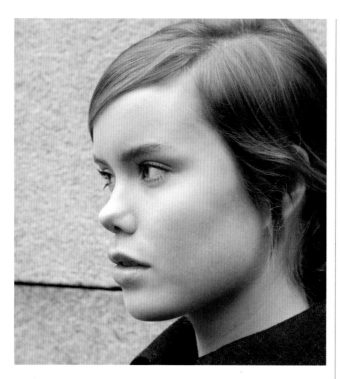

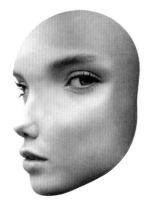

2 Now to create the shape of the new skull. The back of the head will actually be built from the chin. Make an oval selection over the chin and copy merged. Enlarge and place it at the top of the head. Add a layer mask set to *Reveal All* and erase the desired parts. Repeat and complete the head. Merge your layers, then make a selection around the head. Invert the selection and delete the background. You should now have the basis of the head shape.

1 First, we'll build the rough distortion of the face. Open "Face1.tif" and "Face2.tif." Copy "Face2.tif" and paste it over "Face1.tif." Add a layer mask to hide all of "Face2.tif," then reveal the desired parts of the image with a broad, 250-pixel soft-edged brush. Use the *Healing Brush* tool [J] to restore the texture between the eye and the nose. Pick a texture from the chin by holding down the Alt/Option key to set a sample point.

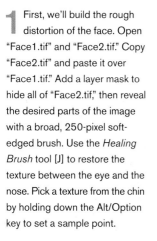

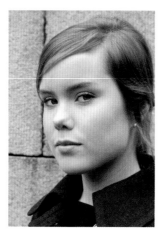

3 Adjust the hue and saturation to balance the colors in the image. Add a *Levels* adjustment layer and tighten the levels. Bring out the warmth with a *Color Balance* adjustment layer. Erase the red hues in the eyes in the adjustment layer mask. Optionally you can brighten the white parts of the eyes and teeth and increase the saturation of the lips with a *Hue/Saturation* adjustment layer or using the *Sponge* tool (O on the keyboard) set to *Saturate*.

TIP

I recommend the *Pen* tool for selections. It's hard to learn but very precise and the curves can be saved and reused in the *Paths* palette.

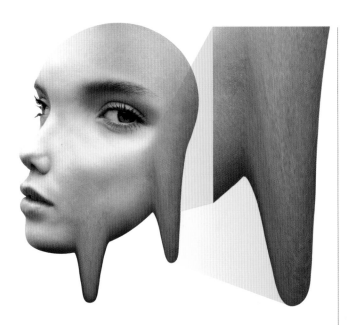

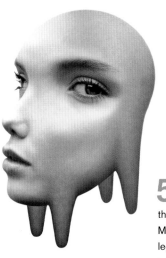

5 Once you have created the fore legs, you can just copy them to create the hind legs. Make a selection over the front legs and copy and paste them into a new layer and place them behind the head. Add a *Levels* adjustment layer to make the extra set of legs a bit darker.

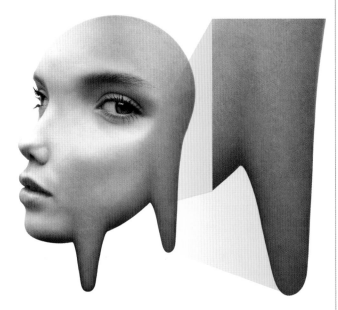

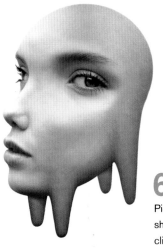

6 Now it's time to add some modeling to the creature. Pick a dark brown color and paint shadows in a new layer set as a clipping mask with a broad, soft-edged brush. Set the opacity of this layer to about 35%, and set its blending mode to *Multiply*. Paint the highlights in yet another layer set as a clipping mask with a broad, soft-edged white brush. Set this highlights layer's blending mode to *Soft Light*.

4 The next step is to create the "legs." The *Liquify* filter is often used for the creation of smoke and other things, but it's also just what we need to create additional legs for our face. Go to the *Liquify* filter and drag out the legs with a big brush about 250-300px with high *Density* settings. The *Liquify* filter is very destructive to the texture, and it will have to be restored with the *Healing Brush* tool. Pick a texture from the chin holding down the Alt/Option key, and paint it on the newly created legs.

Creatures

HEARTBROKEN

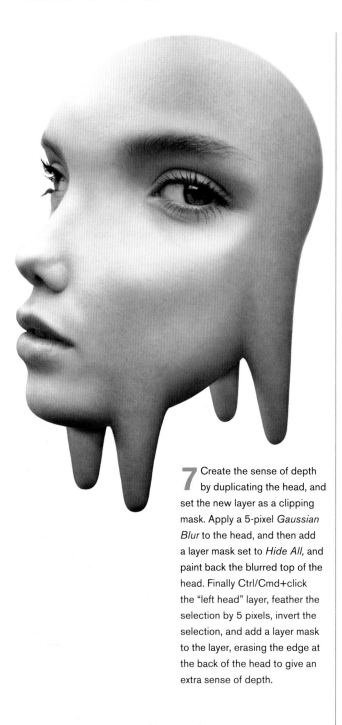

7 Create the sense of depth by duplicating the head, and set the new layer as a clipping mask. Apply a 5-pixel *Gaussian Blur* to the head, and then add a layer mask set to *Hide All,* and paint back the blurred top of the head. Finally Ctrl/Cmd+click the "left head" layer, feather the selection by 5 pixels, invert the selection, and add a layer mask to the layer, erasing the edge at the back of the head to give an extra sense of depth.

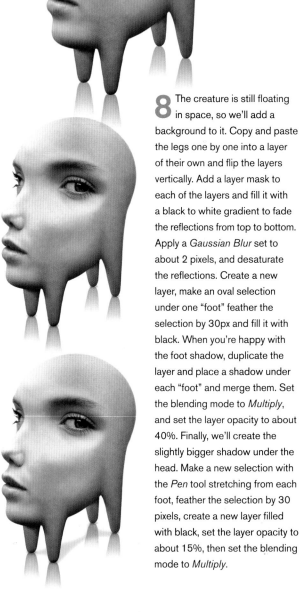

8 The creature is still floating in space, so we'll add a background to it. Copy and paste the legs one by one into a layer of their own and flip the layers vertically. Add a layer mask to each of the layers and fill it with a black to white gradient to fade the reflections from top to bottom. Apply a *Gaussian Blur* set to about 2 pixels, and desaturate the reflections. Create a new layer, make an oval selection under one "foot" feather the selection by 30px and fill it with black. When you're happy with the foot shadow, duplicate the layer and place a shadow under each "foot" and merge them. Set the blending mode to *Multiply,* and set the layer opacity to about 40%. Finally, we'll create the slightly bigger shadow under the head. Make a new selection with the *Pen* tool stretching from each foot, feather the selection by 30 pixels, create a new layer filled with black, set the layer opacity to about 15%, then set the blending mode to *Multiply.*

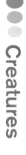

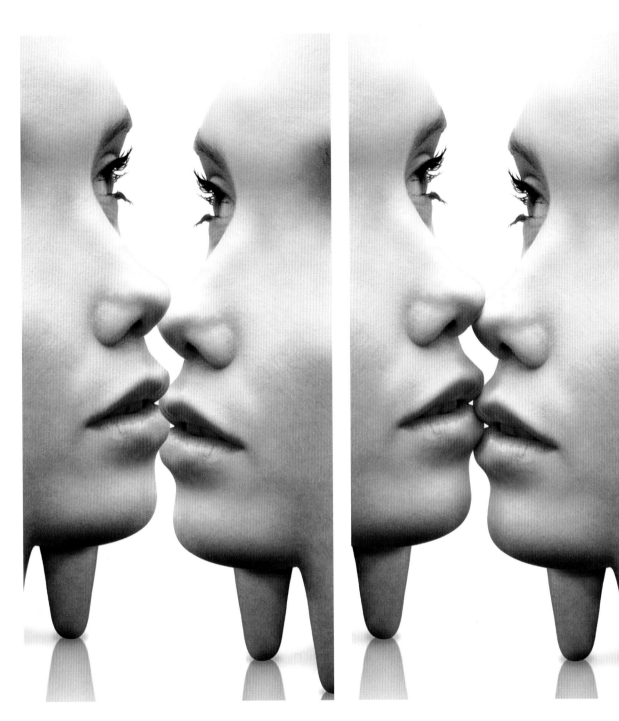

9 Duplicate all the layers and flip them horizontally in order to get the other part of the heart. Add layer masks to the right and left head, and erase parts of the lips in order to make them interact. It still looks kind of flat, so paint shadows on the right hand face in a new layer set as a clipping mask. Set this clipping layer's opacity to about 40%, and set its blending mode to *Multiply*. Repeat with the left face.

Creatures

HEARTBROKEN

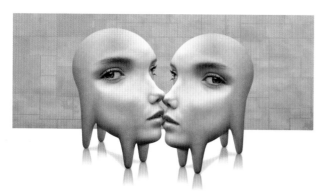

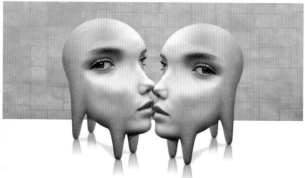

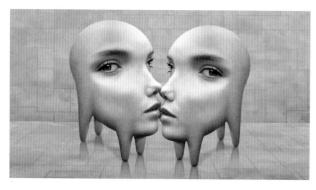

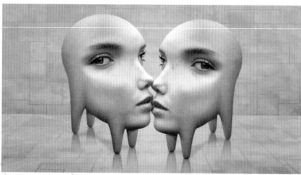

10 Open "texture.tif" and place it as the wall in the background. In order to make the texture a little more dynamic, and to replicate lens vignetting, you can create a new layer and draw a black-to-white radial gradient. Set the layer's opacity to 20% and the blending mode to *Multiply*. Duplicate the wall layer and apply *Edit > Transform > Perspective* to make the floor tilt, and again add a gradient, in the same way as above, on the floor. Set a soft source of light behind the heads by creating a white-to-transparent radial gradient from the center of the image in a new layer set to *Soft Light*. Adjust the *Hue/Saturation* and *Levels* of the environment with adjustment layers to match the hue of the heads. Tighten the *Levels* even more by copying merged and applying *Auto Levels* faded to about 50% to keep the warmth.

Final Image
The shape and position of the two heads creates the subtle appearance of a broken heart.
© Patrik Blomqvist

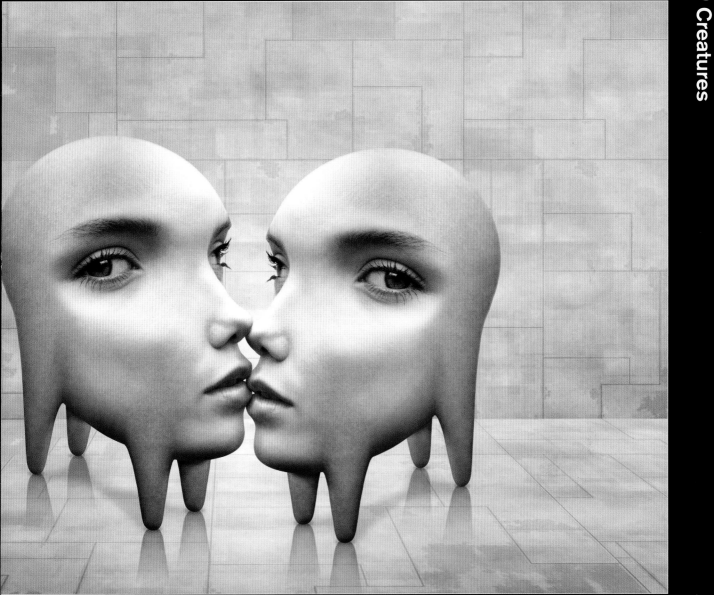

ELECTRIC MEDUSA

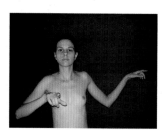

by Nela Dunato

The idea of combining organic and mechanical elements is very popular among surreal photomanipulators. Take a look at how an ordinary female model was transformed to a futuristic bionic woman inspired by Greek mythology.

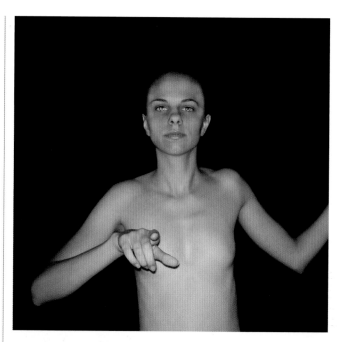

1 Extract the model from the background by applying a layer mask and painting over portions containing the background with a black brush. Rename the layer "body".

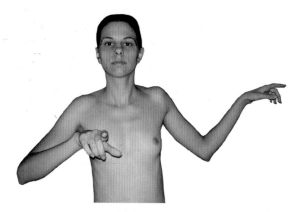

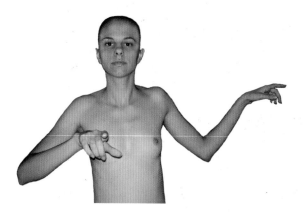

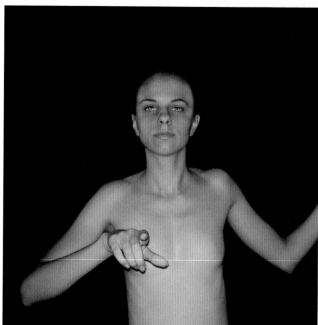

2 To remove hair, piercings, and tan imperfections, first cover them with a piece of clear skin copied from another part of the face, then use the *Healing Brush* tool to blend edges. Correct the shading using the *Burn* and *Dodge* tools.

3 Go around the body layer using the *Smudge* tool (*Strength*: 10-12%) to make the skin smooth, without any texture. Use the *Dodge* tool to whiten the iris of the eyes. Adjust the *Brightness/Contrast* and *Color Balance* to get a less natural skin color.

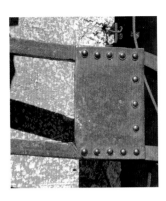

4 Paste a part-metal texture onto a new layer, remove the white blotches using the *Healing Brush* tool, then duplicate the layer a few times and move the copies around until they cover the whole body (except the head). Flatten down all texture layers to one and set the blending mode to *Overlay*, 50% *Opacity*.

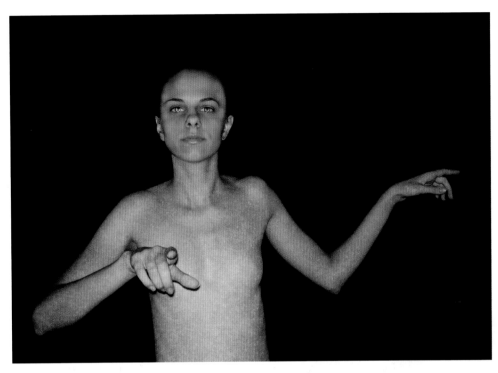

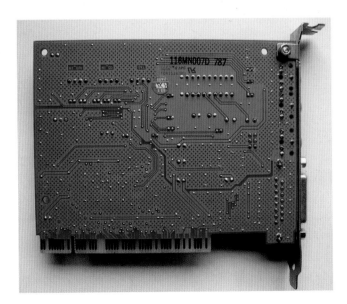

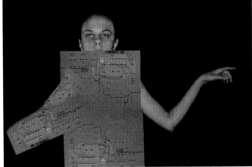

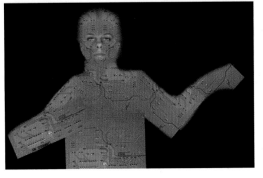

5 Copy a chip pattern on a new layer and name it "chip", desaturate and set the blending mode to *Soft Light*, 100% *Opacity*. Rotate parts of the pattern so the electronic elements flow more naturally across the body. Put the face texture on another layer and name it "chip face."

ELECTRIC MEDUSA

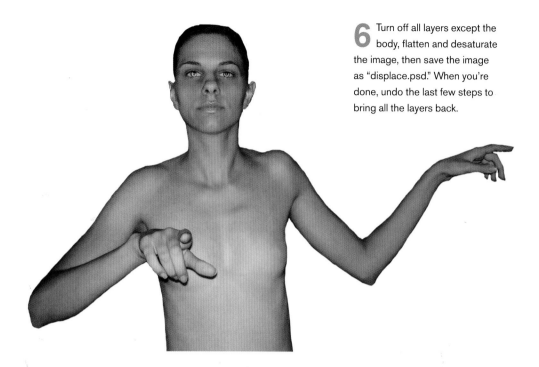

6 Turn off all layers except the body, flatten and desaturate the image, then save the image as "displace.psd." When you're done, undo the last few steps to bring all the layers back.

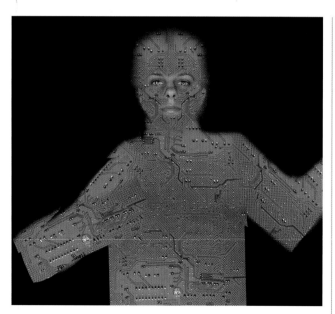

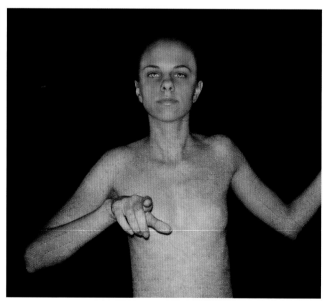

7 With the chip layer selected, go to *Filter* > *Distort* > *Displace* and set the following settings: *Horizontal Scale*: 10%, *Vertical Scale*: 10%, *Stretch to Fit*, *Wrap Around*. When asked for a file, select "displace.psd." Repeat for the chip face layer, but change the scale percentages to 5%.

8 To make sure that the textures are only applied to the body, Ctrl/Cmd+click on the body layer mask to create a selection. Apply a layer mask with this selection to all of the texture layers.

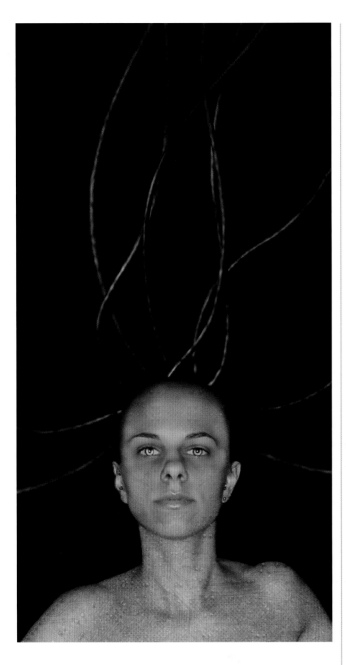

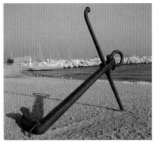

10 Cut round metal shapes from a photo and paste them into your document—these will be used as "plugs" that connect cables to the scalp. Transform the size, angle and position of each plug then shade it using *Burn* and *Dodge* tools.

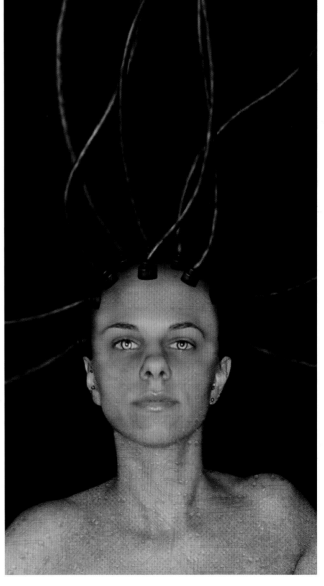

9 Using the *Pen* tool, draw cable shapes on a separate layer. In the *Paths* palette, Right/Ctrl+click the *Work* path and select *Fill Path*. Apply a *Bevel and Emboss* style to the layer, then flatten it. Make a few separate layers of hair. Go around the cable edges with the *Burn* tool to give them a more realistic, worn look, then shade the scalp to create shadows according to an imaginary light source.

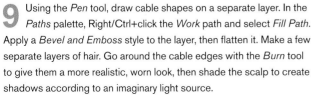

ELECTRIC MEDUSA

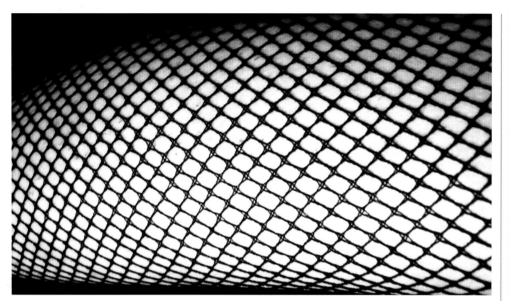

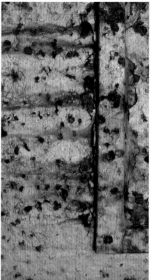

11 Open a picture of some fishnet, desaturate it, and increase the contrast. Then go to *Edit > Define Brush* and name it "fishnet." Use this brush to stamp a white pattern on a layer above the hair. Set the blending mode of this layer to *Soft Light*, 50% *Opacity*.

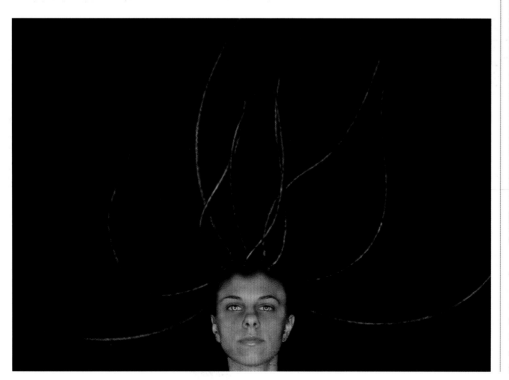

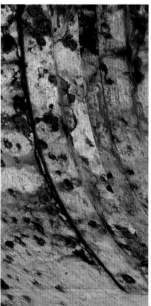

12 Open an image of rusted metal and apply *Filter > Distort > Shear* to make a curved shape. Cut a narrow curve from this and paste it into your working document, it will be used for the ribs.

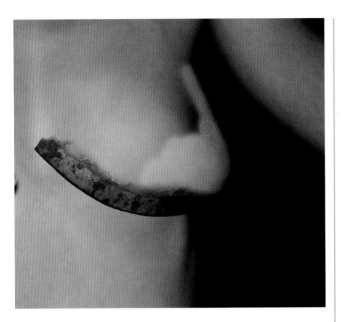

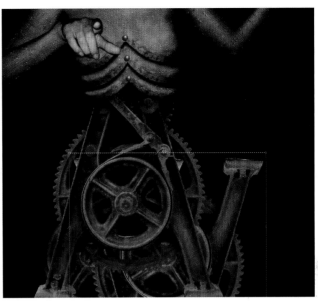

13 Blend the metal part with the torso and, if necessary, repaint a part of body using the *Clone Stamp* tool to fill the gap. Duplicate the rib layer and repeat this step for all 3 pairs of ribs.

15 Cut the mechanism from its background and paste it under the body layer. Resize it, adjust the *Color Balance*, and shade it using the *Burn* tool. Duplicate the layer a few times and move it around to get more complex machinery. Delete unwanted parts using a layer mask.

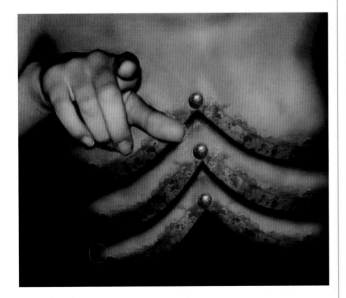

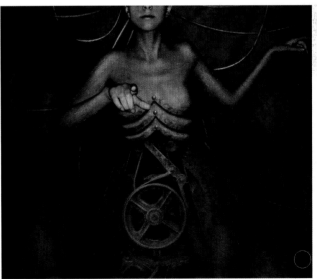

14 Copy a nail image and position it between each pair of ribs. Burn the skin under the ribs to create a drop shadow effect.

16 Make a "background" layer and fill it with light brown, then paint over it with a large dark brush, or use the *Clouds* filter to generate a random surface. Paste a wall texture on a layer above it, set its blending mode to *Overlay*, and adjust its *Contrast* and *Saturation*.

Creatures

ELECTRIC MEDUSA

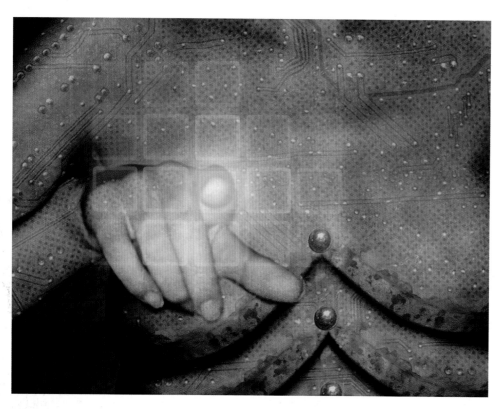

17 Draw a white rectangle, set the blending mode to *Multiply*, and apply the following layer style: *Stroke* (9px, light yellow), *Inner Glow* (white) and *Outer Glow* (light yellow). Duplicate the layer a few times and form a keyboard, lowering the opacity of each layer. Arrange all the key layers into a single layer set named "keyboard."

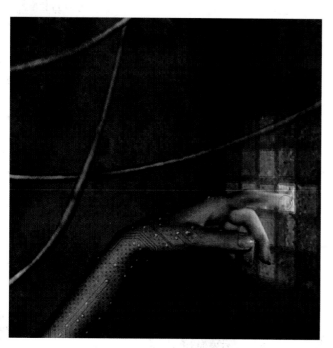

18 Duplicate the keyboard layer set, move the copy next to the left hand, and perspective transform it to fit. Paint over the fingertips using the *Dodge* tool so that they reflect the keyboard light. Add more glow to the keys and eyes by painting with a light yellow brush on a layer above them.

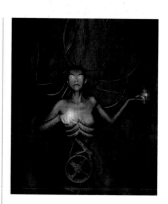

19 Make a new layer on top and fill it with olive color, set the blending mode to *Color*, 36% *Opacity*—this will unify the colors on the image. Do a final check to see if anything stands out too much and, if so, blend it using a layer mask.

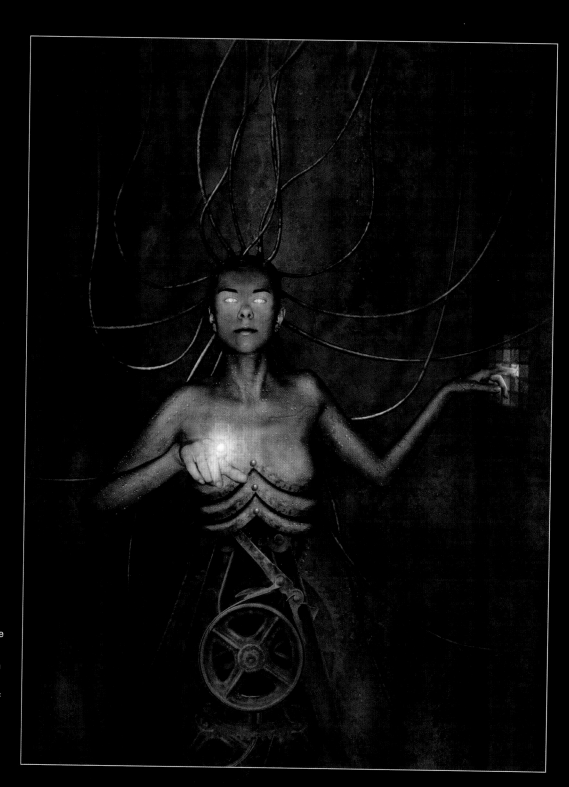

Final Image
This Medusa for the modern age has come a long way from its simple human form in the original picture. Again, the creation of a simple background really helps to tie the image together.
© Nela Dunato

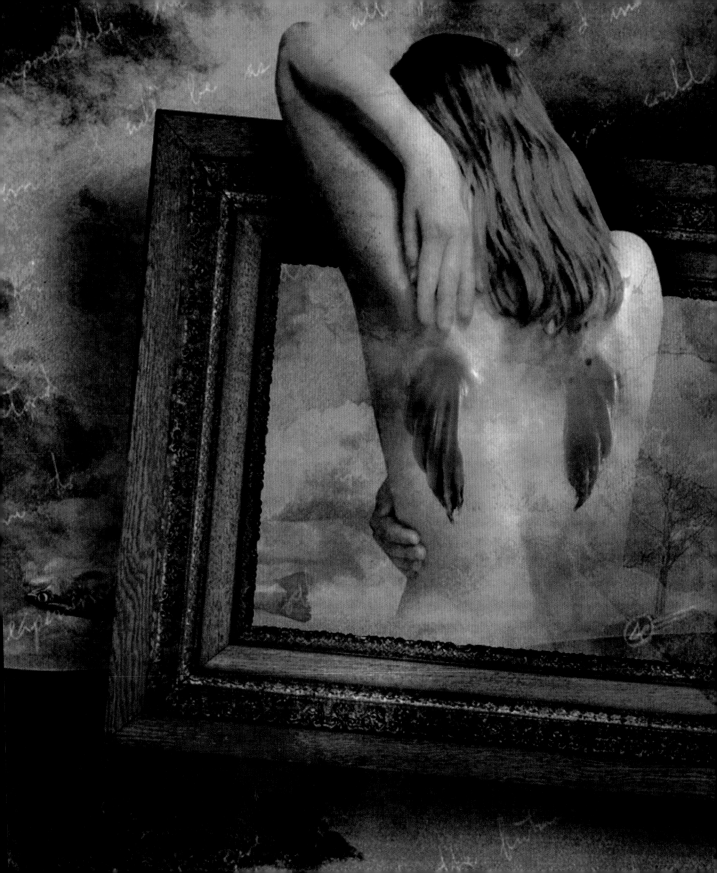

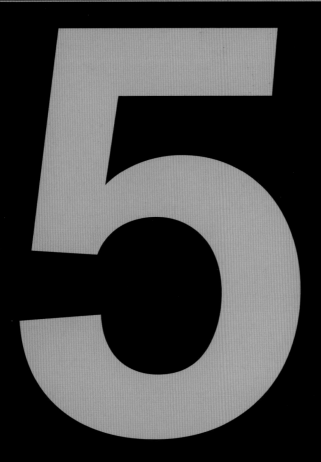

5

The obvious evolution from building single surreal portraits and creatures is to move on to constructing entire surreal scenes. These can be anything from subtly odd landscapes to complete artworks ready for hanging in a gallery. The most important consideration when building a scene is the composition of all of the elements, and careful planning is required from the outset in order to successfully bring the project together. The results, as you'll see, can be stunning.

scenes

Scenes

INVASION

by Tony VenGraitis

Taking an element out of one picture and adding it into another will almost always create entertaining results. But if you let yourself get carried away with Photoshop's tools, you can sometimes make the combination of elements more convincing than you had originally thought possible.

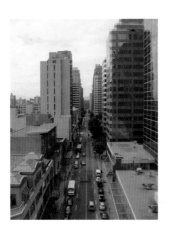 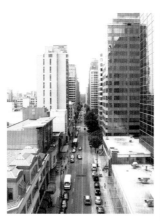

1 We'll begin with a simple photograph of a city street with lots of tall buildings. Since we are planning to add elements from different photographs to the cityscape (in this case, a couple of giant bugs), it will be helpful to change the color and feel of the photograph. We can do this by applying a *Brush Stroke* filter and by using some blending techniques and color adjustments. We'll start by duplicating the entire cityscape layer, and applying Photoshop's *Accented Edges* filter to the top layer. Go to *Filter > Brush Strokes > Accented Edges* and set the *Width* and *Smoothness* to 1, and the *Edge Brightness* to 18. Immediately after applying the filter, go to *Edit > Fade Accented Edges*. Leave the *Opacity* at 100% and set the *Mode* to *Linear Dodge*.

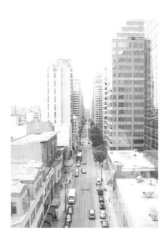

2 Change the blending mode of the top cityscape layer to *Hard Light*. Then add an *Invert* adjustment layer to the bottom cityscape layer. As a final change, add a *Hue/Saturation* layer above the top layer, reducing the entire cityscape's *Saturation* to -30, and increasing the *Lightness* to +15.

3 Now comes a more difficult part. We have two photographs of a praying mantis that we want to insert as our alien invaders. Removing the mantises will require the painstaking selection of each of the bugs. The best method is to use the *Quick Mask* tool (located toward the bottom of the toolbar). It's best to do this type of intricate selection with an input device, such as a graphics tablet, rather than a standard

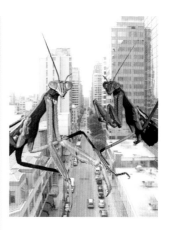

mouse, but either will get the job done with a little patience. Once the bugs have been selected, copy and paste them onto their own separate layers; the smaller Bug 1 on the top layer, and the larger Bug 2 below. Use *Edit > Transform > Scale* and *Edit > Transform > Rotate* to position the bugs in the gaps between the buildings, and to make them the correct size in proportion to each other.

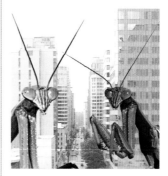 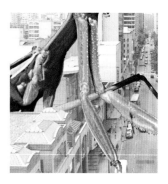

4 We need to touch up the bug layers to help them fit better into the cityscape. The first step is to add a layer to repair the broken antennae on both bugs. Copy a portion of the good antenna, and use the *Scale* and *Rotate* functions to align it to the end of the broken antenna. Next, to improve the appearance of the bugs coming out from between the buildings, add a layer mask to each of the bug layers, and mask out the portions of the buildings that should be in front of them.

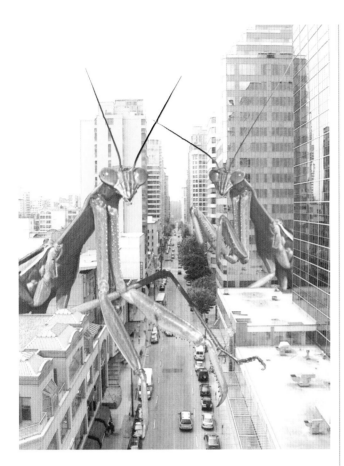

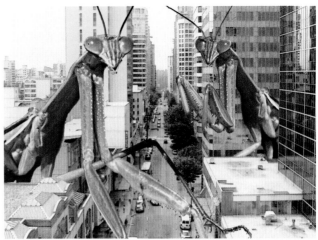

6 To eliminate the washed-out look, add a *Brightness/Contrast* adjustment layer to the entire image. Set the *Brightness* to -40 and the *Contrast* to + 20. This will help strengthen the details of the image, and give the bugs a more dramatic appearance.

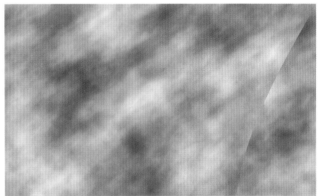

5 The color and shading of the two bugs makes them look entirely out of place (yes I know, giant bugs are not supposed to look like they belong on a city street, but you know what I mean), so our next task is to make adjustments to each bug so they look more natural against the cityscape. To our smaller Bug 1, we will add a *Hue/Saturation* adjustment layer. Make sure when you create the new layer that you check the box marked *Use Previous Layer to Create Clipping Mask*. Adjust the color sliders so the bug's color matches the surrounding buildings (*Hue*: +135, *Saturation*: -50, *Lightness*: +30). To add a little more pop to Bug 1, we can also add a *Brightness/Contrast* adjustment layer. Set the *Brightness* to +15, and the *Contrast* to +30. On Bug 2, we'll need to add a *Hue/Saturation* adjustment layer using the same settings as we used for Bug 1. The second bug does not need to have the brightness or contrast adjusted.

7 Now let's add some smoldering fire to the horizon. The best way to do this will be to use the *Clouds* filter. Start by presetting the color palette on the toolbar. Use white as the foreground color, and dark gray as the background color. These colors will be used to render the clouds. Create a new layer at the top of the image. Then go to *Filter > Render > Clouds*. The filter will fill in the entire layer with clouds. To make it look more like drifting smoke, go to *Filter > Distort > Shear*. A box will appear with a graph and a "shear line" that is used to distort the layer. Click on the center dot of the shear line and drag it half way to the left edge. The curved distortion of the clouds will give the appearance of drifting pillars of smoke.

Scenes

INVASION

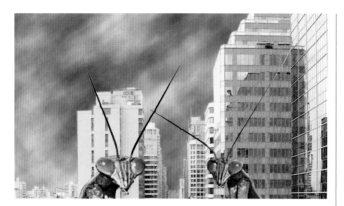

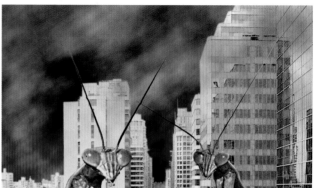

8 We'll need to create a mask on our smoke layer. Since the sky above the cityscape is a consistent shade of white, we can use the *Magic Wand* tool. First, hide the smoke layer by clicking off the layer visibility. Then set the *Magic Wand* at a *Tolerance* level of 5, and check the *Anti-Alias*, *Contiguous*, and *Use All Layers* boxes. Clicking the *Magic Wand* on the white sky should select most of the area where we want the smoke to appear. Click on the smoke layer to make it visible again, and then click the *Add Layer Mask* button. This will create a layer mask on the smoke layer using the selected sky area. Click on the new layer mask and use the *Brush* tool to adjust the selected area so the horizon is cleanly masked. Finally, set the blending mode of the smoke layer to *Multiply*.

10 Let's add an additional layer of smoke to the image. First, reset the color palette on the toolbar, making the foreground white and the background black. Create a new layer at the top of the image, and apply the *Clouds* filter. Set the blending mode of this layer to *Darken*. Next, add a layer mask to the new smoke layer. Select the mask, and use the *Gradient* tool to gradually fill in the mask area with black. Start the gradient with white at the top of the frame, and allow the black to fill in until it is at full strength at the midpoint of the image. The mask will allow the new smoke layer to darken the sky a bit more, and will add some smoke-like shadows to the upper sections of the buildings.

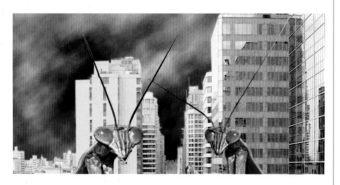

11 A final tweak of the color can be made by using a *Selective Color* adjustment layer over the entire image. As you become more comfortable making color adjustments, you can experiment with *Selective Color* layers to give a more striking look to your images. For this image I used the following settings:

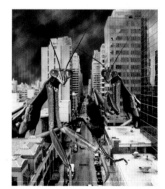

9 To add the appearance of fire glowing below the horizon and within the smoke, we will need to blend some color into the smoke layer. Insert a new layer above the smoke layer; make it a clipping mask for the smoke layer, and then use the *Gradient* tool to fill in the new layer with a red-brown linear band of color. Start the gradient with full transparency at the top of the layer, and allow the color to gradually fill in until the color is at full strength at the very bottom of the horizon (right above the building rooftops in the distance). Set the blending mode of this color layer to *Color Burn*.

Reds:
C: -20 / M: +5 / Y: +45 / K: 0
Yellows:
C: -100 / M: 0 / Y: +100 / K: 0
Greens:
C: 0 / M: 0 / Y: 0 / K: 0
Cyans:
C: 0 / M: 0 / Y: 0 / K: +100
Blues:
C: +100 / M: 0 / Y: 0 / K: +40

Magentas:
C: 0 / M: 0 / Y: 0 / K: 0
Whites:
C: -50 / M: -30 / Y: +40 / K: -15
Neutrals:
C: +5 / M: 0 / Y: 0 / K: +20
Blacks:
C: 0 / M: 0 / Y: +60 / K: +5

Scenes

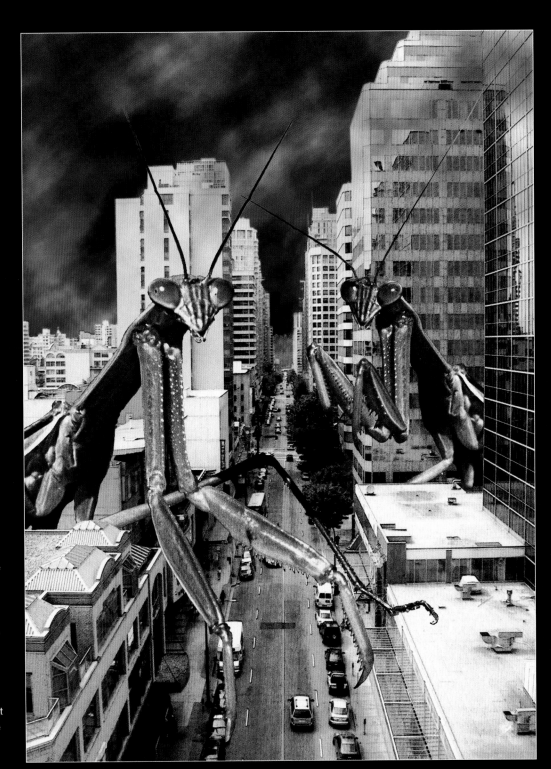

Final Image

The surreal colors in this scene are what make the image. Very little work was required to blend the bugs into the city street because the colors immediately inform us that something weird is happening here, so we aren't looking for the visual inconsistencies that we might be if the picture was colored naturally.

© Tony VenGraitis

THE GATE OF EDEN

by Ben Goossens
In my professional life as an advertising Art Director, surrealist painters were a source of inspiration for my visual concepts— and they still are now for my hobby. This image pays a particular debt to my fellow Belgian, René Magritte.

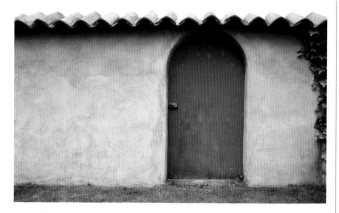

3 The photograph was taken at the Ommegang in Brussels, an annual reenactment of the pageant that took place in the city in 1549. The figure needs to be extracted from its background so that it can be combined with our new background. First, double-click on the background layer so that it becomes a standard layer. Select the *Eraser* tool with a 5-pt hard brush. Erase around the edge of the figure, Shift-clicking to create straight lines where necessary.

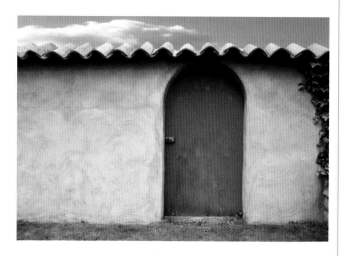

1 The starting point for this image was a photograph of a white wall with a red door, taken at an outdoor party. The door seemed to suggest some intriguing possibilities. The sky in the original image was a rather flat blue, so it was erased using the *Magic Eraser* tool in Photoshop.

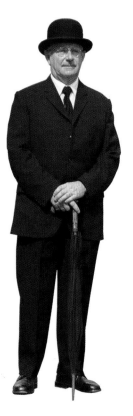

4 Once the man has been separated from the background, the rest of the background can be removed quickly, using either the *Magic Eraser* tool or the standard *Eraser* tool at a larger brush size. Then, I felt I should replace the face with an apple.

2 A replacement sky with clouds was added on a new layer and given a horizontal *Motion Blur (Filter > Blur > Motion Blur)*. The background layer containing the wall was dragged on top of the sky layer and the image flattened. The background inspired me to go on creating a surrealist image.

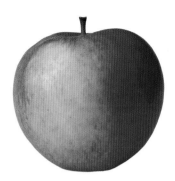

5 I took a simple photograph of an apple to use in place of the head. The apple was extracted using the same methods as in Step 3. There are many ways to extract images from backgrounds in Photoshop, including the simple *Eraser* tool, the more complex *Extract* filter, and the use of masks. For more difficult extractions I prefer to use the *Eraser* in conjunction with the professional plug-in MaskPro.

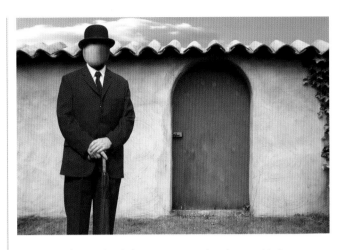

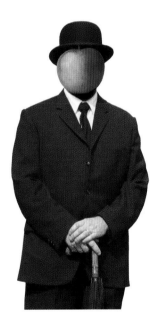

6 Once the apple has been extracted from the background, it is added as a new layer in the "man" image. The *Transform* tool (*Edit > Transform* or Ctrl/Cmd+T) can then be used to reduce the apple to the right size to fit the man's face.

8 When the man/apple image was complete, it was added as a new layer in the wall image. The man was reduced to the right proportions using the *Transform* tool (*Edit > Transform* or Ctrl/Cmd+T) and moved to the correct position using the *Move* tool.

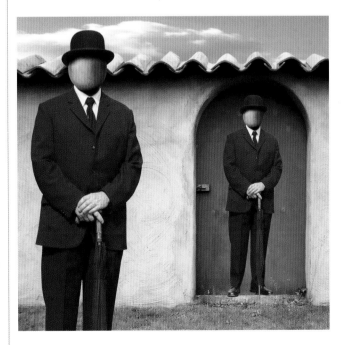

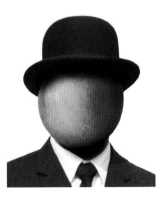

7 I erased the part of the apple that would appear under the hat, and used the *Burn* tool to darken some parts of the apple to make it look realistic. Shadows were added below the hat rim, and along the right side of the apple. While I was using the *Burn* tool, the apple layer was locked; otherwise it would also affect the layer of the man below.

9 A selection of the complete man/apple image was made using the *Magic Wand* tool with a *Tolerance* setting of 120. The selection was reduced to the right size using the *Edit > Transform* command (Ctrl/Cmd+T), and moved with the *Move* tool into the correct position on the door.

Scenes

THE GATE OF EDEN

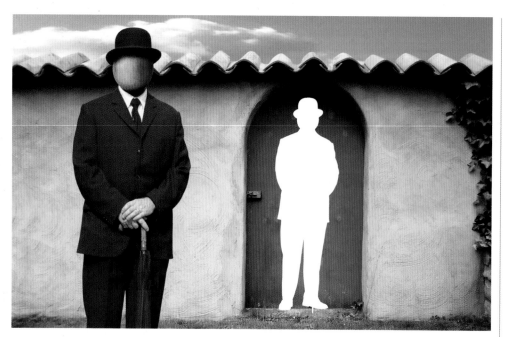

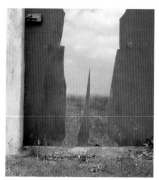

11 While the selection was still active, a square selection was used to create the grass at the feet of the cut-out man in the door. Using the *Clone Stamp* tool, the grass of the main background was cloned into the selection of the man's feet. Afterwards, the grass was blurred a little using the *Gaussian Blur* filter set to a radius of 7 pixels.

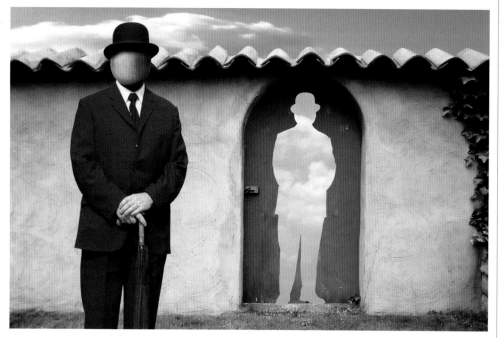

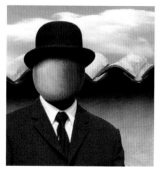

10 The selection was first saved (*Select > Save Selection*) so that it could be used again if necessary. While the selection was still active, the part of the door behind the man's selection was erased. A second image of a cloudy sky was then pasted into the selection.

12 Lastly, the *Blur* tool (not to be confused with the *Blur* filter) set to a size of 5 pixels was used to soften the borders of the man so he would not look like he was just pasted into the background. Draw around the figure using the *Blur* tool, Shift-clicking to cover straight areas quickly.

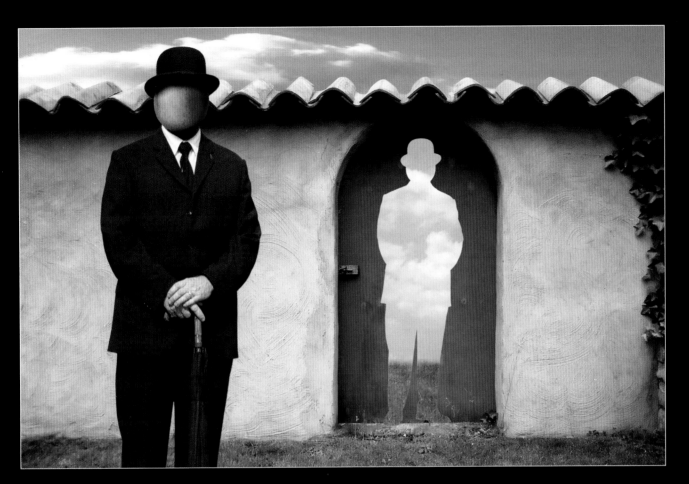

Final Image

This quintessentially surreal image was created from very simple elements. Its success lies in the strong composition and the initial concept.

© Ben Goossens

Scenes

SWEET HOME

by Ben Goossens

During a photoshoot in a very big, very grand house, I saw a giant sculpture of a marble hand in the garden and I knew it was the beginning of a new surrealistic image.

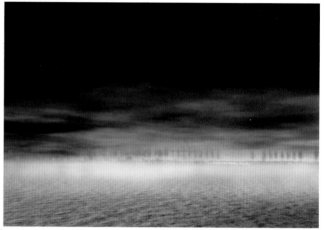

1 I started with a simple, broody landscape rendered in Bryce. Opening the image in Photoshop, I then altered the *Levels* (*Image > Adjustments > Levels*) and *Color Balance* (*Image > Adjustments > Color Balance*). I also added different colors to the sky using a big soft Paintbrush set to *Color* mode, with a low *Opacity* of 10%.

3 On a new layer, the mist is added to the background with a large, soft brush set to *Normal* mode at low opacity. This came easily to me, because I have years of experience of traditional airbrush painting. A *Motion Blur* (*Filter > Blur > Motion Blur*) set to an *Angle* of -18° and a *Distance* of 18 pixels was applied to the white mist.

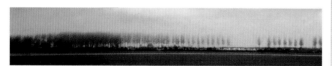

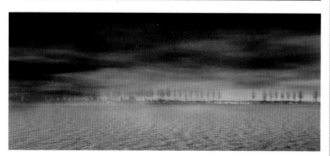

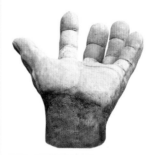

4 Once that was completed, I extracted the marble hand from the grass background, transformed it in height using *Edit > Transform > Scale*, placed it in the correct position with the *Move* tool, and darkened the bottom with the *Burn* tool. The hand layer was locked to prevent the *Burn* tool affecting other layers.

2 An image of a line of trees was added to the horizon, on a new layer set to *Overlay* with 100% *Opacity*. Parts of the sky and the ground in the tree image were gradually erased with a large, soft eraser at low opacity. This process was repeated many times over to achieve the desired effect.

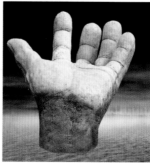

5 The next step was to add the door, which was extracted from a photograph I shot in the south of France. The door was placed on a new layer and dragged into the correct position at the base of the hand. I altered the *Color Balance* and *Levels* settings so that the door image matched the hand more closely. The areas of the hand adjoining the sides of the door were darkened using the *Burn* tool, and the section of the hand at the foot of the door was erased. I also darkened the palm of the hand as a shadow in readiness for the apple I'll add in the next step.

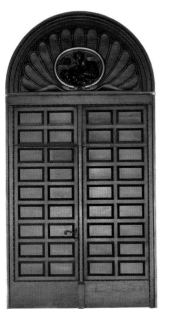

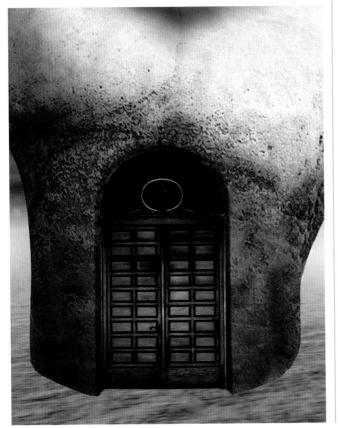

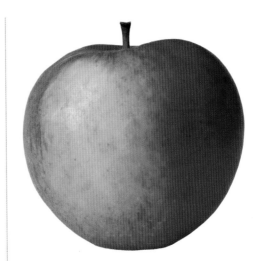

6 As promised, here's the apple. It's the same photo that I took for my project on pages 118-121, but we'll be changing it beyond recognition. Cut the apple from its background but keep it as a separate file—we need to turn it to stone before we add it to the main image!

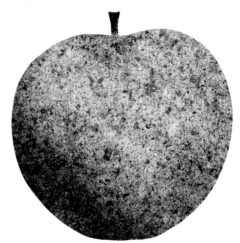

7 I took a photograph of some marble and used a selection to quickly cut out the exact apple shape. I then used the *Burn* tool at low pressure to darken the left side of the apple as it was on the original fruit, and switched to the *Dodge* tool to lighten the right side and the top of the apple.

SWEET HOME

Scenes

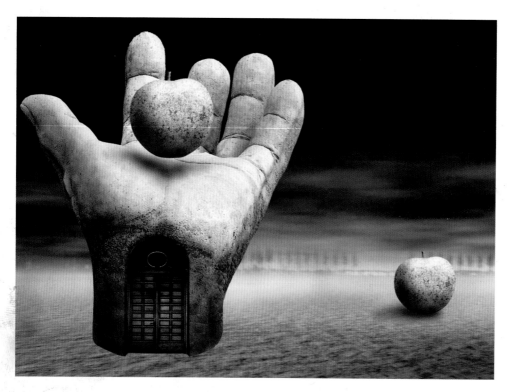

8 The marble apple was then pasted into the image above the hand and scaled to create an appealing dynamic. I then duplicated the apple and moved it to the right of the hand. I created a shadow under it in the same way using the *Burn* tool. I also brushed in some red color into the shadow as if reflected from a real apple.

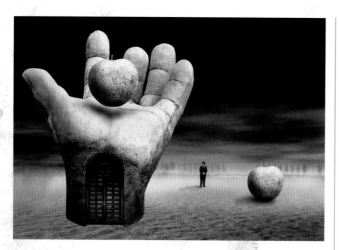

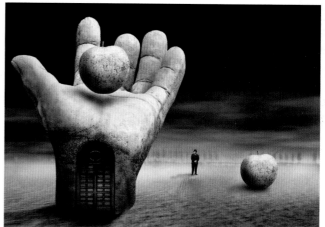

9 The man/apple image that I used in the previous project was added on its own layer and scaled to fit in the background. I created a shadow of the man by duplicating him, coloring him black, and then blurring him extensively using the *Gaussian Blur* filter. Finally, the *Transform* tool was used to skew the shadow into the correct position, and the opacity was lowered to blend it into the background.

10 Once everything was in place, I adjusted the background colors slightly, and darkened the right corner with a large brush at low pressure.

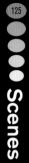

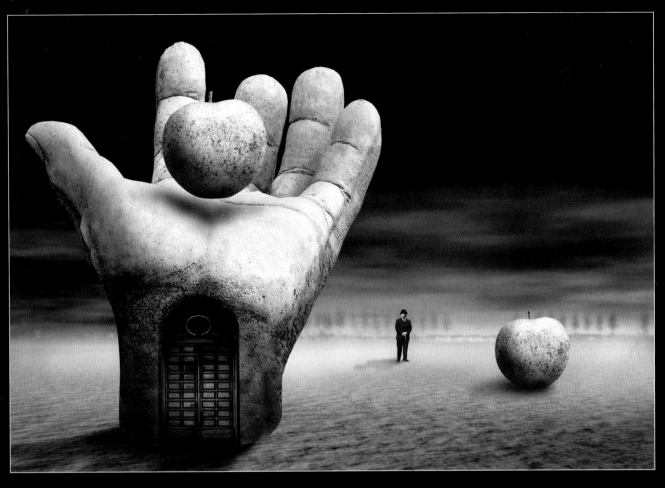

Final Image

Again, the strong composition
and color balance tie this image
together. A real sense of depth
and scale is achieved by adding
the figure and small stone apple
onto their own planes.

© Ben Goossens

Scenes

GUARDIAN ANGEL

by Domen Lombergar
Guardian Angel is an experimental piece in which I wanted to visually interpret several emotional
states. I wanted it to convey sensuality, surrounded by a grotesque, surreal environment. The angel
represents a higher force, yet the immaturity demonstrated by the not yet fully developed wings would suggest
that the angel was either just born or had just materialized. The anonymity of the model is another interesting
aspect of the image, since the identity of the guardian angel cannot easily be transferred onto a human. Her
face is hidden but she will be watching over you.

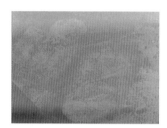 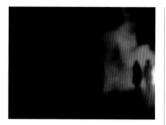 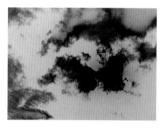 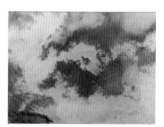

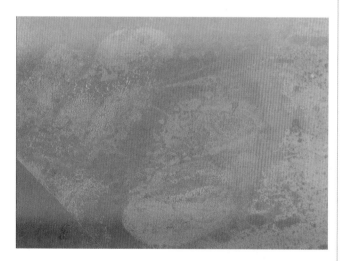

1 Open bg.psd and texture-bg.psd. Make sure both images are visible
in the Photoshop workspace, select the *Move* tool (shortcut V), click
on the image, and drag and drop it into the composition. Holding the Shift
key while doing this will horizontally and vertically center the new image.
Now set the blending mode to *Color* and the *Opacity* to 40%.

2 Open up overlay-texture.psd and drag it into the image. Set its
blending mode to *Overlay* and leave the *Opacity* at 100%.

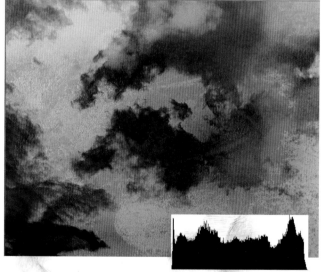

3 We're going to darken several areas of the current image. Go to
Layer > New Adjustment Layer > Levels, and enter a value of
78 in the first of the *Input Levels* boxes. Click *OK* and then click on the
layer mask, which is the white square next to the *Levels* icon in the new
layer we just created. With the *Brush* tool (shortcut B), start to paint on
the layer mask. Everything that is black will not be visible and everything
white is opaque. Create a layer mask that's mainly dark with several
white spots. These spots will darken the image below.

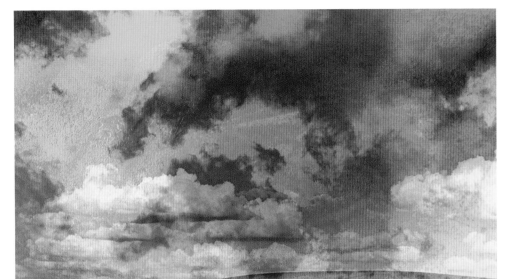

4 Time to bring some landscape into the composition. Open up the clouds.psd file and drag them onto the image. Set the blending mode to *Overlay* at 100% Opacity. The effect isn't quite strong enough, so drop another layer of the clouds onto the image, this time setting the blending mode to *Lighten* at 50% Opacity. You should see a dramatic increase in cloud visibility.

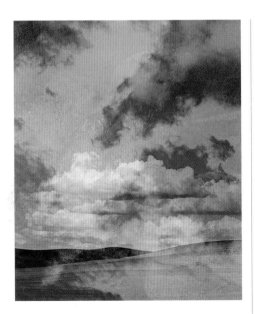

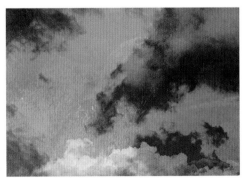

5 Let's drop down the saturation a little. Go to *Layer > New Adjustment Layer > Hue/Saturation* and set the *Saturation* tab to -50.

6 Go to *Layer > New Adjustment Layer > Color Balance* and set the following changes to the shadow colors in the image: -5 (more cyan), -4 (more magenta), and +39 (more blue). Click on *Midtones* on the bottom part of the dialog and set their color balance to: -68 (more cyan), +7 (more green), and -100 (more yellow). Now click on *Highlights* on the bottom part of the dialog and set the color balance of those to +5 (more red), -7 (more magenta), and +6 (more blue). Hit *OK* to close the dialog box. At this point you've probably already noticed that I prefer to do all the color adjustments via adjustment layers, which means that the pixels below will not be changed in any way and I can always come back and tweak each individual setting to my liking. It does make for a much bigger file size, but trust me, it's worth it.

GUARDIAN ANGEL

Scenes

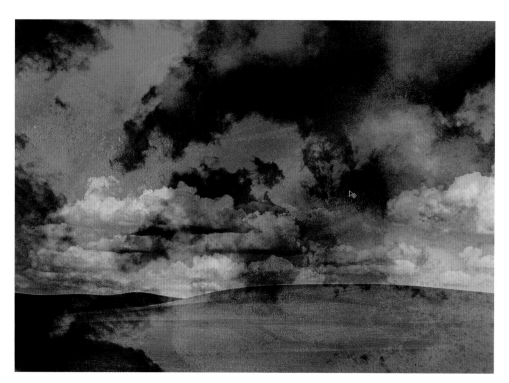

7 Open up the SL-texture.psd file and drop the texture right below both adjustment layers. Set the blending mode to *Soft Light* at 100% opacity.

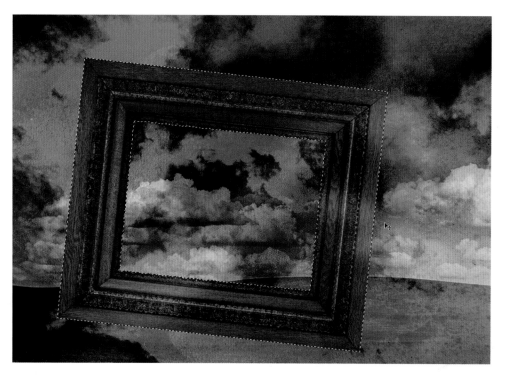

8 Open up main-frame.psd and bring it into the image. Place the frame as shown. Remember that we will be adding many more elements, so don't experiment with the placement too much if you want your image to look the same as mine.

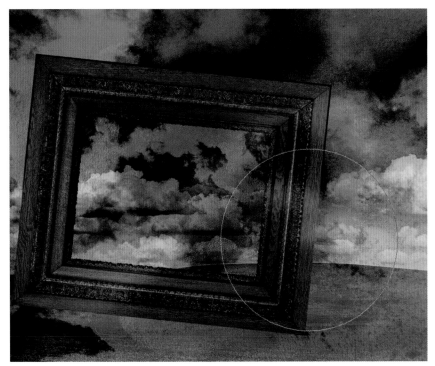

9 Let's add a stroke around the frame. Go to *Layer > Layer Style > Stroke* and choose a 4-pixel stroke with a black color (click on the default red color to choose another one) and change the *Position* from *Outside* to *Center*. Hit *OK* to close the dialog box. Now, right-click on the frame layer and choose *Create Layer* from the menu. This will create a new layer from the stroke layer style so we can further manipulate it. At this point, erase the stroke on the inside of the frame with the *Eraser* tool (shortcut E). We want to use the stroke to make the frame stand out against the sky, but then fade out as it crosses onto the landscape. Make a new layer mask by going to *Layer > Layer Mask > Reveal All*. Take a big soft brush, and with the black color selected as the foreground, start to paint on the lower part of the frame. The stroke will softly dissolve, leaving us with the effect we wanted.

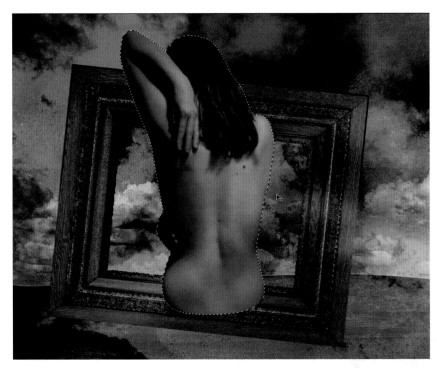

10 Open up girl.psd and drag it into the composition. Alternatively, you might like to try using one of your own photos, but make sure that the photo is in a similar pose to avoid confusion in the next steps. Put the girl in a group (*Layer > Group Layers*) so that we can experiment with the transparency later.

Scenes

GUARDIAN ANGEL

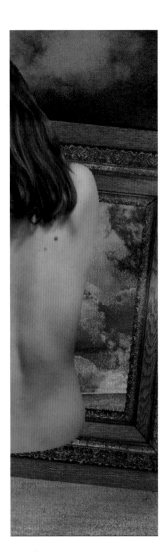
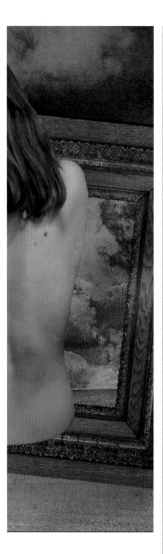
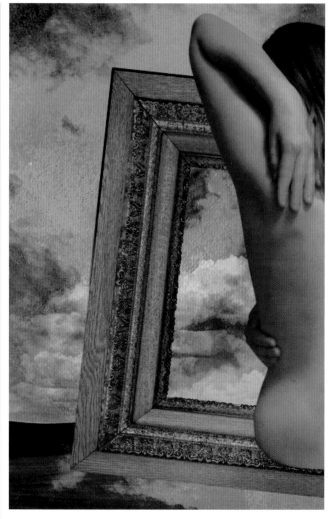

11 Create another *Hue/Saturation* adjustment layer above the SL Texture layer. This time we will be using the *Colorize* feature. Go to *Layer > New Adjustment Layer > Hue/Saturation*, click on the *Colorize* option and set the *Saturation* tab at 42 and *Hue* at 5. Click *OK* and then reduce the opacity of this layer to 30%. This will help to tie together all of the tones in the image. Now that's done, we can alter the overall color of the image. First, add one more texture. Open up sl-color-texture.psd and drop the texture right above both *Hue/Saturation* adjustment layers. Set the blending mode to *Soft Light* at 40% opacity. This will bring in some additional sporadic color and texture.

12 Now we're going to make some more dramatic changes. Create a *Selective Color* adjustment layer by going to *Layer > New Adjustment Layer > Selective Color* and make the following adjustments to *Reds*: *Cyan*: -13%; *Magenta*: -8%; *Yellow*: +34%; *Black*: +7%. Next, select *Yellows* from the *Colors* drop-down menu and make the following adjustments: *Cyan*: +19%; *Magenta*: -7%; *Yellow*: +34%; *Black*: -58%. Select *Greens* from the *Colors* menu and make these adjustments: *Cyan*: +100%; *Magenta*: 0%; *Yellow*: 0%; *Black*: +100%. Select *Neutrals* from the menu and make the following adjustments: *Cyan*: -4%; *Magenta*: +1%; *Yellow*: +44%; *Black*: 10%. Finally, select *Blacks* from the drop-down menu and make these adjustments: *Cyan*: 0%; *Magenta*: -3%; *Yellow*: +3%; *Black*: +6%.

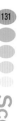

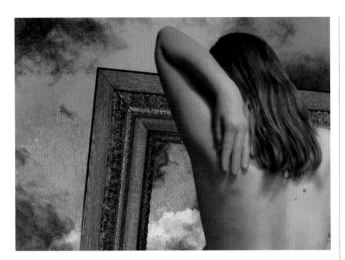

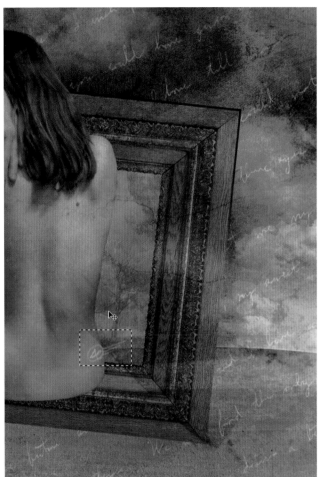

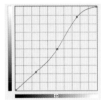

13 Now let's do some *Curves* adjustments. Go to *Layer > New Adjustment Layer > Curves* and make a curve like the one shown. This will boost up the contrast a little in the shadow areas and a lot in the highlights.

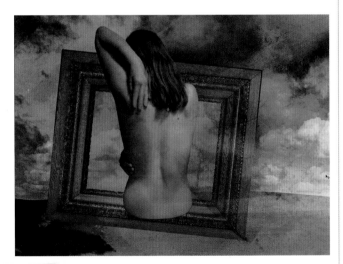

14 Let's add some more texture to the background. Open up handwriting.psd and drag it above the two cloud layers. Set the blending mode to *Screen* and the opacity to 62%. While we're adding some writing, let's also add a signature to the image. Open signature.psd in Photoshop and bring it into the composition. Set the blending mode to *Screen* and the opacity to 50%.

15 Open three more texture files in Photoshop: vl-texture.psd, cb-texture.psd, and texture.psd. Drag each into the image, and stack them below the SL Texture layer. Set VL Texture to a blending mode of *Vivid Light* at 10%, CB Texture to *Color Burn* at 50%, and Texture to *Soft Light* at 100%. We'll also add the image that resides in the main frame where the girl appears from. Open image-in-frame.psd, or use another image of your own choosing. We still need to manipulate the colors a bit, so make a new adjustment layer by going to *Layer > New Adjustment Layer > Hue/Saturation*. Check the *Colorize* box and set the *Hue* to 70 and the *Lightness* to -50. To make a nested layer as I'm using here, hold down the Alt/Option key while moving the mouse in the area between the two layers. When the cursor changes, click on that area. The top layer will now only affect the layer directly beneath it.

GUARDIAN ANGEL

Scenes

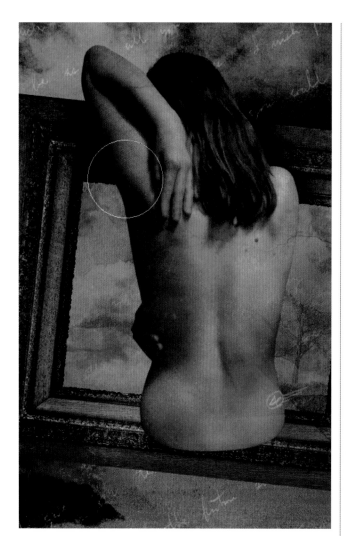

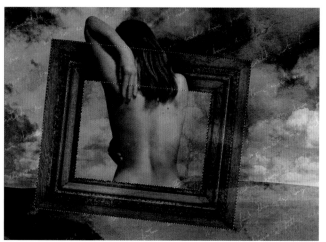

17 Now duplicate the frame and place it above the girl. Create a new layer mask for that frame by going to *Layer > Layer Mask > Reveal All*, and then with a big brush paint the top areas that overlap the girl with black. Leave the bottom parts alone.

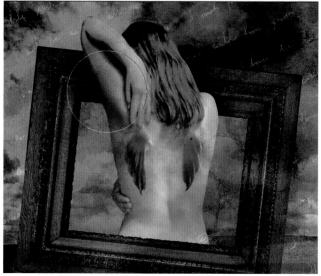

16 Create a new layer below the girl and with a large, soft brush, start painting in some shadows falling on the frame. The most important places are the top left and top right of the frame because we want to achieve the most obvious 3D effect in these areas. Take the time to make some more adjustments on the frame, such as darkening the corners.

18 Open wings.psd and nest it on the girl image with a blending mode of *Overlay*. Remember the layer nesting technique we used while we were changing the color of the image in the frame? Use it again here.

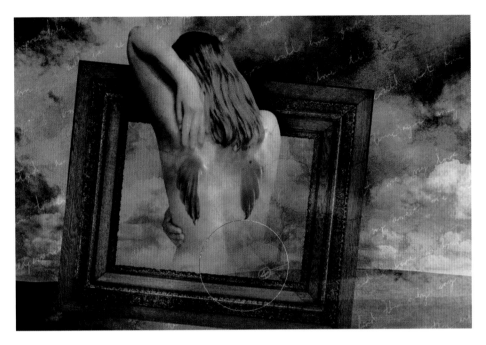

19 Make a new *Hue/Saturation* adjustment layer directly above the Wings layer. With *Colorize* checked, change the *Hue* setting to 54 and the *Lightness* to -38. Click *OK*. Turn the layer mask black and then play around with a white brush to make some parts of the girl green. Again, a soft brush will work much better than a brush with hard edges. Remember that we made a new layer group for girl.psd earlier? This is why. Make a new layer mask on the group (*Layer > Layer Mask > Reveal All*), and with a soft brush at a low opacity (around 20%) start painting with black on the bottom part of her body. This will slowly make her disappear.

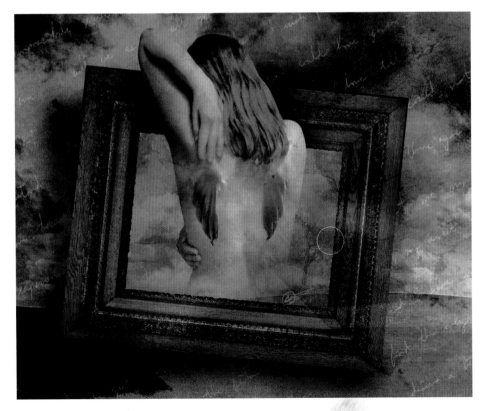

20 Open the next image, main-frame-shadow.psd, and drag it below all the frame layers. You can also create your own version by duplicating one of the frame layers, locking the transparency (the first of the four icons below the blending mode options), filling it with black, unlocking the transparency and blurring the result using the *Gaussian Blur* filter at a fairly high setting. Then make a new layer mask (*Layer > Layer Mask > Reveal All*), and hide the shadow that's inside the frame using a black brush.

Scenes

GUARDIAN ANGEL

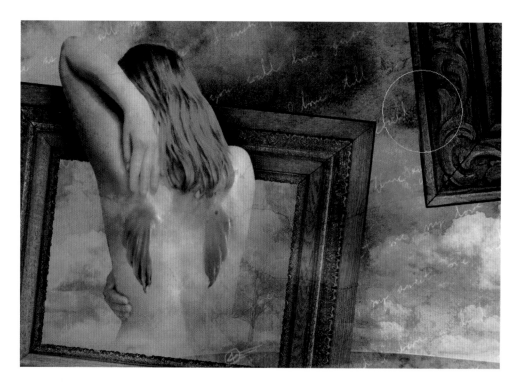

21 Open up top-frame. psd and drag it into the image. Repeat the same process of creating the faded black stroke on this frame that we used earlier, in step 9.

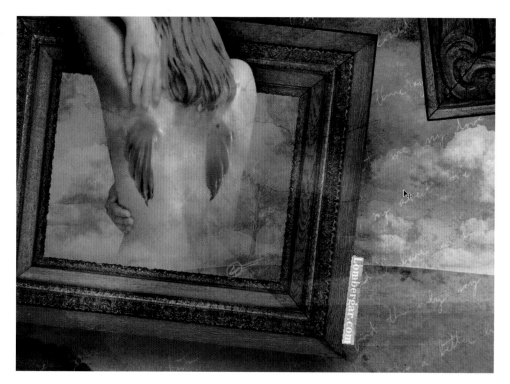

22 At this point, I'm adding my website URL because I know that I'll be displaying the piece on the Web, and I want it to be immediately obvious where the piece came from. You'll be amazed at how fast someone can "borrow" your image and show it as their own.

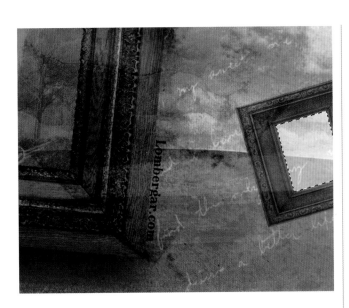

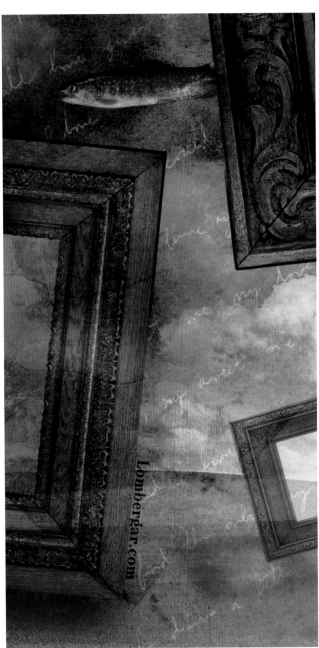

23 Now open small-frame.psd and move it into the composition. For the sake of keeping things tidy, make this into its own layer group as well. Fill the inside of the frame with a little color and set the blending mode to *Color Dodge* at 70%.

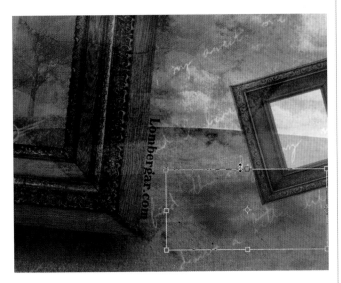

24 Duplicate the frame and blur it. Then select *Free Transform* and deform it so that it looks like a shadow.

25 Open up fish.psd and bring the first fish into the composition. Drag it below the top right frame, as if it were emerging from behind it. Then make a new layer and with a soft black brush paint some shadows, as if they were cast by the frame. Alt/Option+click between the shadow and the fish layer to nest the shadow to the fish.

GUARDIAN ANGEL

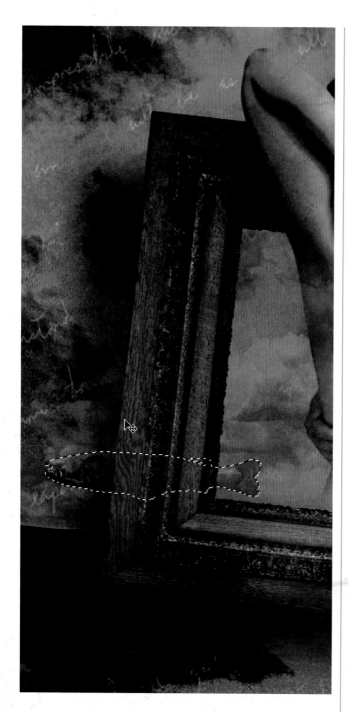

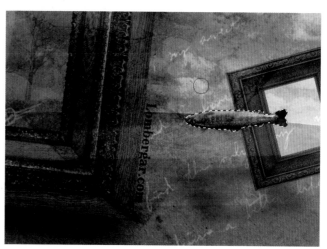

27 Duplicate the fish again and make it smaller with the *Free Transform* tool. Move it toward the small frame as if the fish was passing toward it.

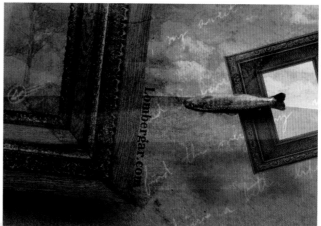

26 Duplicate the fish, and, using *Free Transform*, flip it around and move it below the main frame. There's no need to do the shadows here since we created them previously.

28 Now make a new layer behind the fish and with a soft black brush start painting the shadow of the fish. Alternatively, you can use the same technique as on the shadow of the main frame (filling the duplicate layer with black and blurring it). Play with the opacity until you achieve the look you like, then nest the shadow layers to the layer containing the small frame. And this brings us to the end. By now I hope you've grasped the use of layer masks, nesting layers, and using adjustment layers to modify color and luminosity. You've also hopefully gained some useful hints and tips on compositing and building complete images from disparate parts.

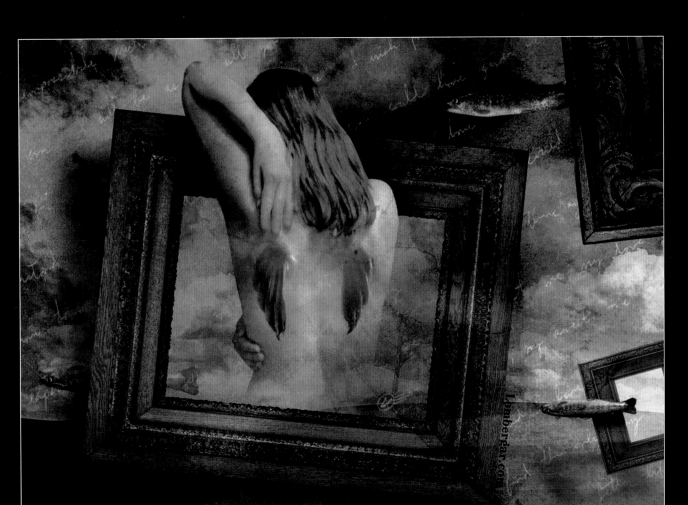

Final Image

This complex piece makes
full use of Photoshop's
layering abilities to create a
work of depth and subtlety.

© Domen Lombergar

Scenes

TIRED TIRE

by Patrik Blomqvist

Shape-shifting something familiar, such as a round tire, can give you a striking and unexpected effect. This tutorial can be applied to anything round—balloons, oranges, heads—and while you're at it, you can also go the other way and make something square round. This trick utilizes the *Warp* tool in Photoshop. There is a very easy way to turn something round into a square using *Warp*. Select the round object and apply *Transform > Warp > Inflate* (set *Bend* to 100). Though the method is too destructive for this project, we will still make use of the *Warp* tool and the *Smudge* tool to create the square tire.

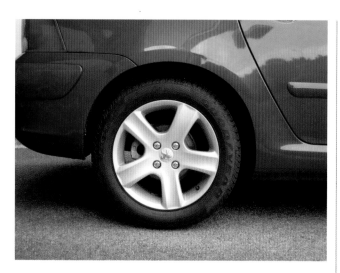

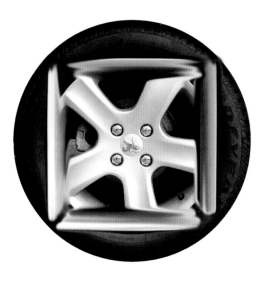

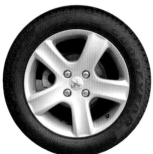

1 Make a rough selection of the tire and copy and paste it into a new layer. A good tip is to make a duplicate of any layer you will manipulate as a backup in case it doesn't turn out as planned.

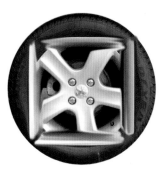

2 First we'll make the rim straight and later on we'll straighten out the rubber. Select the *Smudge* tool and set the brush size to about 30 pixels. Hold Shift for straight brush strokes. Pay extra attention to the corners—you might want to use a smaller brush for them.

3 The Smudge tool is very destructive to the texture, and we'll need to add some dynamics to the aluminum to restore the texture. Apply *Filter > Texture > Grain* and choose the *Enlarged* setting from the *Grain Type* menu. After you've applied the filter, fade it by going to *Edit > Fade Grain* and setting the *Opacity* to 50% and the *Mode* to *Soft Light*.

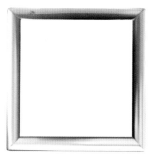

4 In order to make the rim look a little more three-dimensional, click on the *Add a Layer Style* icon at the bottom of the *Layers* palette. Select *Outer Glow*, and, in the resulting dialog box, set the blend mode to *Multiply*, the color to black, the *Opacity* to 75%, and the *Size* to 13 pixels.

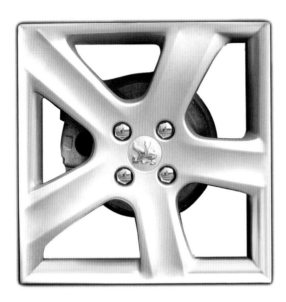

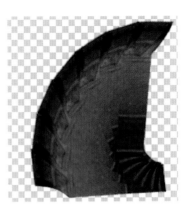

5 Copy the inner part of the rim from the original image. The *Pen* tool with its Bézier curves can be hard to handle, but with a little practice it will give you the most accurate selections. Merge the square frame with the inner part. Now you need to blend the two parts with the *Clone Stamp* tool and the *Healing Brush*. Finally, erase the outer glow from the inside of the rim.

7 Making the corners of the square tires is not as hard as it looks, but you need to be careful to make it look right. Make a small selection of the rubber and copy and paste it into another layer. Duplicate and rotate the small part and repeat until you have something that looks roughly like a curved corner. Now you need to clone and paint the inner part to make it look realistic. Duplicate, rotate, and place the corners where they belong. Now you have four sides and four corners in eight different layers. Merge them and make the tire seamless with the *Healing Brush*. Since the *Warp* tool is destructive, you need to bring back the sharpness with an *Unsharp Mask*. Go to *Filter > Sharpen > Unsharp Mask* and enter the following settings: *Amount*: 74%; *Radius*: 2.5 pixels; *Threshold*: 9 levels.

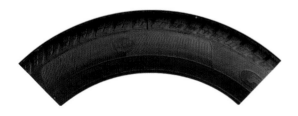

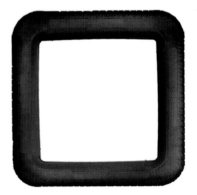

6 Now we are going to straighten out the rubber. Select a slice of the rubber as shown. Paste it into a new layer and go to *Edit > Transform > Warp*. Select *Arc* from the drop-down menu in the *Tool Options* bar and enter a value of -41.8% in the *Bend* box. You might want to compensate with the *Bulge* option and experiment with the *Bend* percentage to make it absolutely straight. When you're done, duplicate the straight part and place the duplicates on all four sides of the rim. Squeeze the bottom part slightly to imply the weight of the car pressing down on it.

8 Go to *Layer > New > Layer* and check the *Use Previous Layer to Create Clipping Mask* box. Set *Opacity* to 35% and *Mode* to *Soft Light* and click *OK*. Paint some highlights onto this layer with a broad, soft-edged white brush set to 35 pixels. Create another new layer in the same way, setting *Opacity* to 35% and *Mode* to *Multiply*. Paint in some shadows with a broad black brush. Optionally, you can clone parts of the tire to make it look less repetitive.

Scenes

TIRED TIRE

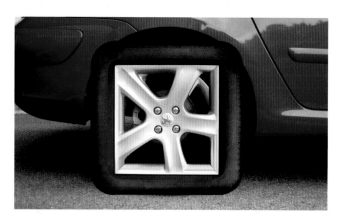

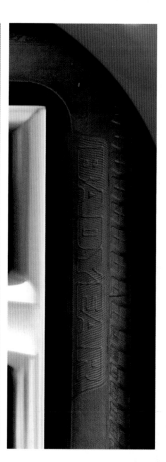

9 If you turn on the newly made rubber and rim layers, you'll still see the old tire behind them. Duplicate the original image of the car into a new layer, clone out the old tire, and add additional road surface from the back of the car. Add another layer and paint the black shadows behind the tire. Use the *Color Picker* to get the right black hue from behind the tire.

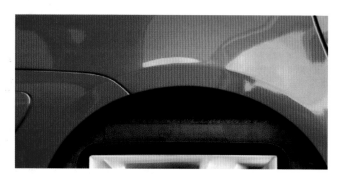

10 The new tire is still positioned outside the car, but that is easily fixed. Add a layer mask to it and erase the unwanted parts with a broad brush of 150 pixels.

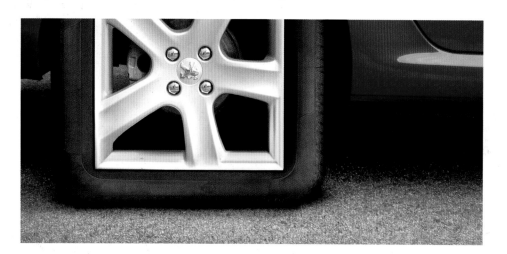

11 The new wheel is floating in the air and needs some shadow work in order to interact properly with the ground. Paint shadows with a broad 100-pixel soft-edged black brush in a new layer. Set the layer opacity to about 35% and the blending mode to *Multiply*. If a shadow is too hard, apply a *Gaussian Blur* to the layer. If you paint the shadows in different layers you can easily move and transform them to make sure they look exactly as you want them to.

12 As a final touch, we'll add a new logo to the tire and apply the layer style *Bevel and Emboss* with the following settings: *Style*: *Inner Bevel*; *Technique*: *Smooth*; *Depth*: 100%; *Direction*: *Up*; *Size*: 5 pixels; *Soften*: 0 pixels; *Angle*: 45°; *Use Global Light* checked; *Altitude*: 48°; *Gloss Contour*: *Default*, *Anti-aliased* unchecked; *Highlight Mode*: *Screen*, *Opacity* 17%; *Shadow Mode*: *Multiply*, *Opacity* 54%. Make sure the highlights and shadow settings match the tire. Copy the tire valve from the source image and place it on the aluminum rim.

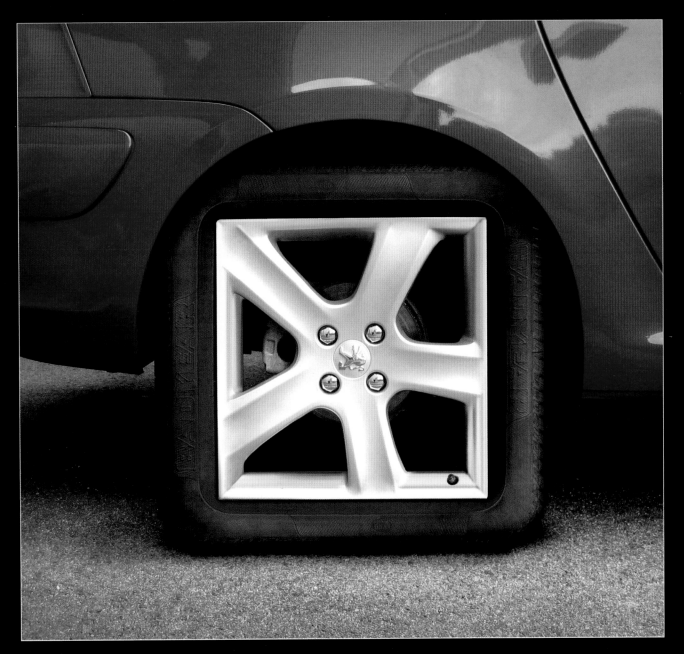

Final Image

The concept behind this piece was simple: create a square tire. The attention to detail is such that the final result is perfectly believable.

© Patrik Blomqvist

Scenes

YANKEE ROSE

by Thomas Speer

Texture mapping is a relatively simple process for changing the "material" of an object, but the problem becomes a bit more challenging when you try to map a complex pattern to the contours of an item. This process requires a good eye and a bit of patience but the results can be very rewarding.

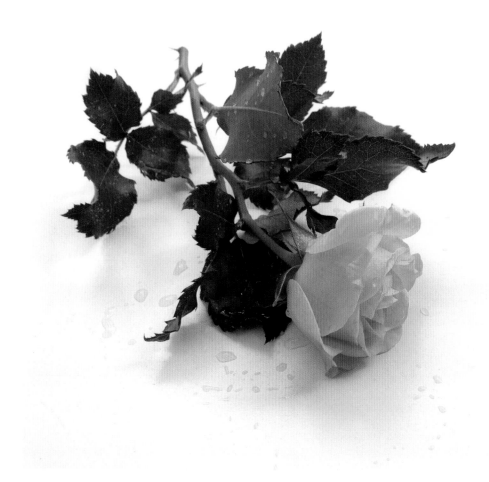

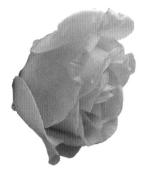

1 Start by selecting an appropriate flower. We are looking for a bright-colored flower with clean, unblemished petals and sufficient surface area to enable us to map out a recognizable flag pattern. This yellow rose is an excellent source for this project. Additionally, it is nicely isolated from the white background, which will provide better contrast for the final image.

2 Make a copy of the base image by duplicating the background image in the *Layers* palette. Click on the layer properties and rename this new layer "Yellow Rose." Now it's time to isolate the yellow flower from the rest of the image. Use the selection method that works best for you. Since the area to be cropped is relatively small, I prefer to magnify the image up to 200% and use the *Polygonal Lasso* tool to carefully outline the flower edges. Once you crop the yellow flower, make a copy and paste it into a new layer.

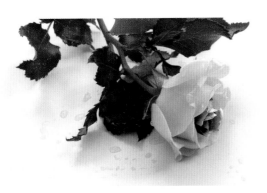

3 We are now going to use a grayscale gradient map to desaturate the yellow flower layer and give us a good white flower on which to "paint" our flag pattern. Go to *Image > Adjustments > Gradient Map* and select the *Grayscale* option from the drop-down menu.

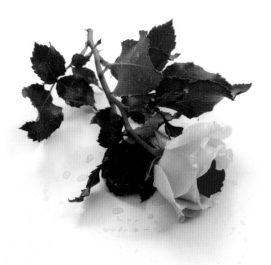

4 We now have a surface on which to paint our stars and stripes. Since the stars require a blue background, we will select a "core" section of the flower and create a blue mask. It doesn't matter how many of the inside petals you include, but leave the majority of the outside petals for the stripes. Again, we can magnify the image and use the *Lasso* tool to create a mask of the petals that we want to color blue. Once you have the mask outlined, create a new layer, rename it "Blue Mask," and fill the selected area with blue (Hexadecimal color value 000099). Don't worry about the solid appearance; we will blend the layers later.

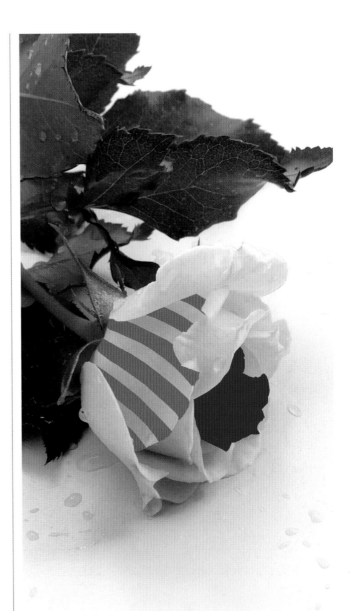

5 Next, create a new layer and rename it "Stripe Mask." It's now time to start laying out the red stripes on our petals. If you have a graphics tablet and pen, this is a little easier; otherwise, increase the magnification of your image, centering it on the white flower section, and use the *Polygonal Lasso* tool to lay out the first set of stripes.

Scenes

YANKEE ROSE

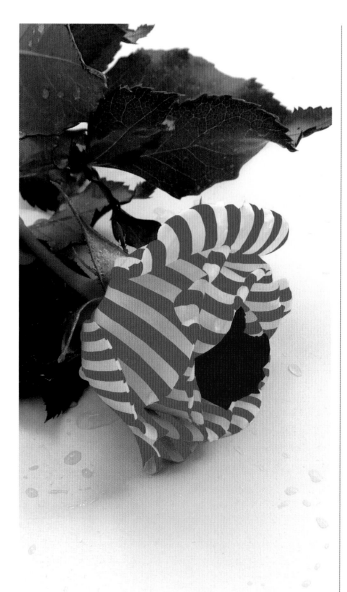

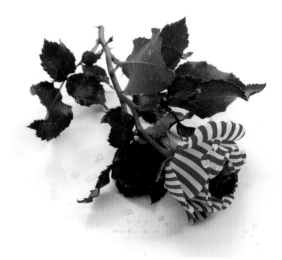

7 At this point, we want to bring a bit of contrast back to our flower. Select the Stripe Mask layer and change the blending mode to *Multiply*, with an *Opacity* setting of 80%. Next, select the Blue Mask layer and do the same.

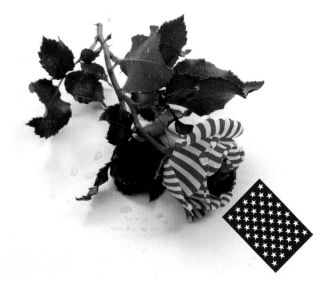

6 Few things in nature are perfectly symmetrical and our stripes should be no exception. We want them to be evenly spaced and to follow the contours of the flower petals as closely as possible, while still retaining some natural imperfections. As you mask each stripe, fill it with red (Hexadecimal color value CC0000). This may take a little patience but you will want to mask the stripes one petal at a time and take into consideration the curving surfaces of petals that bend back or overlap one another. If you haven't done so already, now is a good time to save your work!

8 Open the file Star Field–small.gif and drag the image layer over to your rose image. Rename this new layer "Star Field." Now rotate the star field image clockwise, so that the stars are roughly aligned with the surface of the blue flower section. In the next step, we will copy our star field over to our blue flower petals.

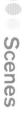

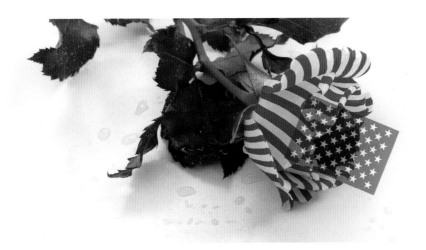

9 Select the Star Field layer and reduce the opacity to 50%. Using the *Move* tool, move the star field so that it completely covers the blue flower area. Try to position the stars so that quite a few overlap the blue edges of the flower section, as shown.

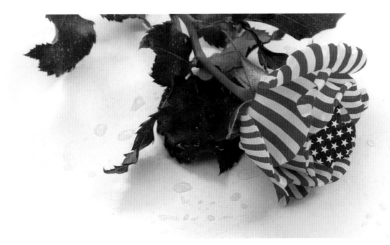

10 With the star field properly positioned, hold down the Ctrl/Cmd key and click on the Blue Mask layer to get a quick mask of the blue flower section. With the Star Field layer still selected, hit Ctrl/Cmd+Shift+I to invert the mask, then hit the Delete key. You should end up with a section of the star field that is equal in size to the blue flower area, with a number of the stars along the edge cut off.

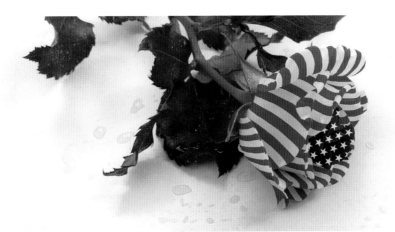

11 With the Star Field layer still selected, change the blending mode to *Luminosity*. The *Opacity* for this layer should remain at 50%.

Scenes

YANKEE ROSE

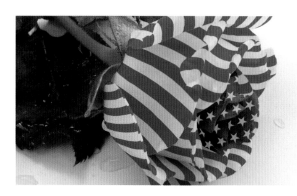

12 The star pattern looks pretty good but it is still a bit too uniform to look natural. We're going to make a few adjustments. Increase your image magnification to 200% with the image centered on the blue star pattern. With the *Opacity* still set at 50%, you can see where the edges of the petals run through the stars. We want to trim away some of that perfection to give the impression that some stars are on the front petals and some are on background petals. Make sure you have the same blue color selected (Hexadecimal color value 000099) that we used earlier. Using the *Brush* tool (size 9), carefully paint over areas where the tips of stars on one petal overlap another.

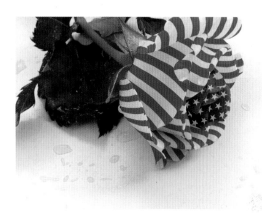

13 Now select the Copy layer that we made in Step 2. Change the image magnification to 100% and center the image on the lower-right section of the flower. You'll notice some yellow reflection remaining from the original flower. Hold down the Ctrl/Cmd key and click on the Flower Mask layer we created earlier, then hit Ctrl+Shift+I to invert the mask. Now select the *Sponge* tool with a diffused brush size of 100 (set the *Mode* to *Desaturate* and the *Flow* to 100%). Using the tool, carefully sponge out all the remaining yellow color (if this does not work, chances are that your mask is not inverted).

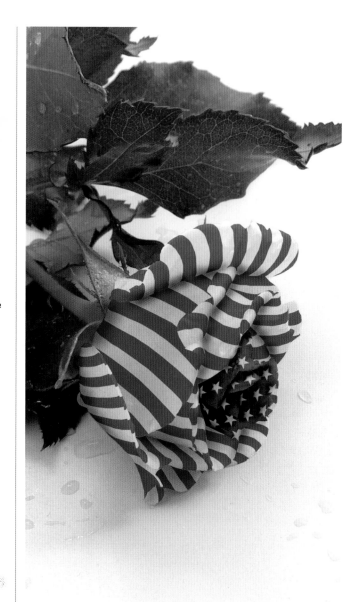

14 Everything is now in place, but the flower looks a bit flat. Select a diffused *Brush* tool (size 45) with the *Opacity* set to 10%. Change your palette color to black. Create a new layer above the Star Field layer and rename it "Shadows." Paint some pale shadows in along the creases of the petals to show some depth. Do the same thing where the stars fold down into the flower.

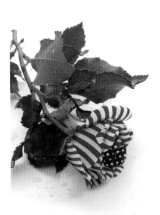

15 Change the opacity of your Star Field layer to 75%. Change the opacity of your stripe layer to 100%.

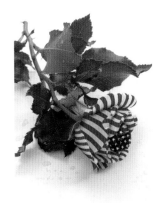

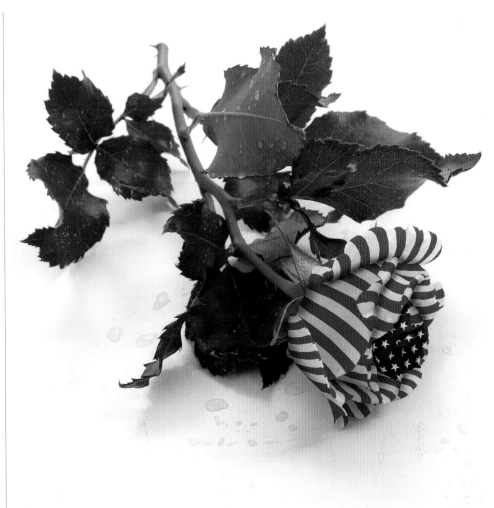

16 Change your image magnification to 25% so that you can see the whole flower with minimal distortion. Create a new layer just above the shadows layer and rename it Final Flower. With this new layer selected, hold down the Alt/Option key and select *Merge Visible* from the *Layers* menu. This will give you a composite picture of all the individual layers.

17 Using the composite picture layer that we just created, adjust the *Levels* in the image to enhance the shadows and darken the colors a little.

YANKEE ROSE

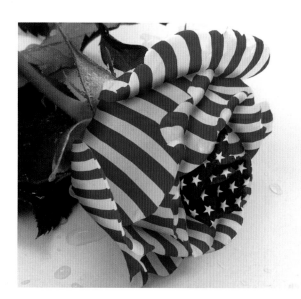

18 With the Final Flower layer still selected, hold the Ctrl/Cmd key and click on the Flower Mask layer we created earlier. This will isolate our adjustments to the flower section and not the stem and leaves. With your flower section selected, adjust the *Saturation* to -15. Our stars are looking better, but we still want to give them the right perspective. We will use the *Liquify* tool to selectively contract and expand parts of the stars so that they look as though they are at the same perspective as the surface of the flower petal. Make sure the Star Field layer is selected and the image magnification is still at 200%. Using the *Rectangular Marquee* tool, create a box around the blue star-filled section of the flower. Go to *Filter > Liquify*. Your image will open in a new window. The parts of the star that are closest to your point of view should be slightly expanded using the *Bloat* tool, and the parts of the star farthest away (deeper into the flower) should be slightly contracted using the *Pucker* tool. Set the *Brush Size* to 17 and the *Brush Pressure* to 75, and carefully distort the stars as needed.

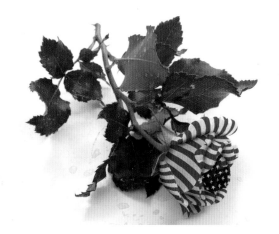

19 We'll make a slight adjustment to the brightness and contrast to give a much sharper and more lifelike appearance to the colors. Go to *Image > Adjustments > Brightness/Contrast* and in the resulting dialog box reduce the *Brightness* to -10 and increase the *Contrast* to 10.

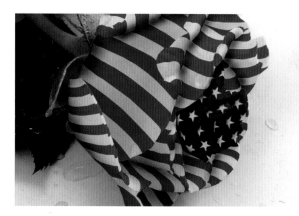

20 You may have noticed the water droplets on the flower petals. We want to enhance those slightly now that we've changed the colors of the flower. Set magnification to 100% and center your view on the flower section. Using the *Rectangular Marquee* tool, hold the Shift key and draw a box around each of the water droplets. Go to *Filter > Liquify* and use the *Bloat* tool (with a *Brush Size* of 40) to slightly expand each droplet. The visible lines of the stripes should be slightly curved as they pass through the water droplet.

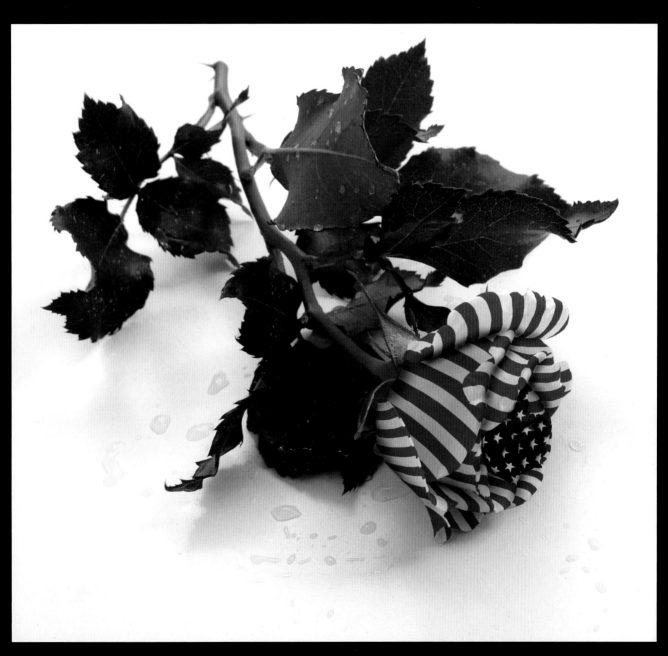

Final Image

The quality of the original image is a huge factor in
the success of the final result. The water droplets
in particular give the Yankee rose the look of
having been freshly picked from the garden.

© Thomas Speer

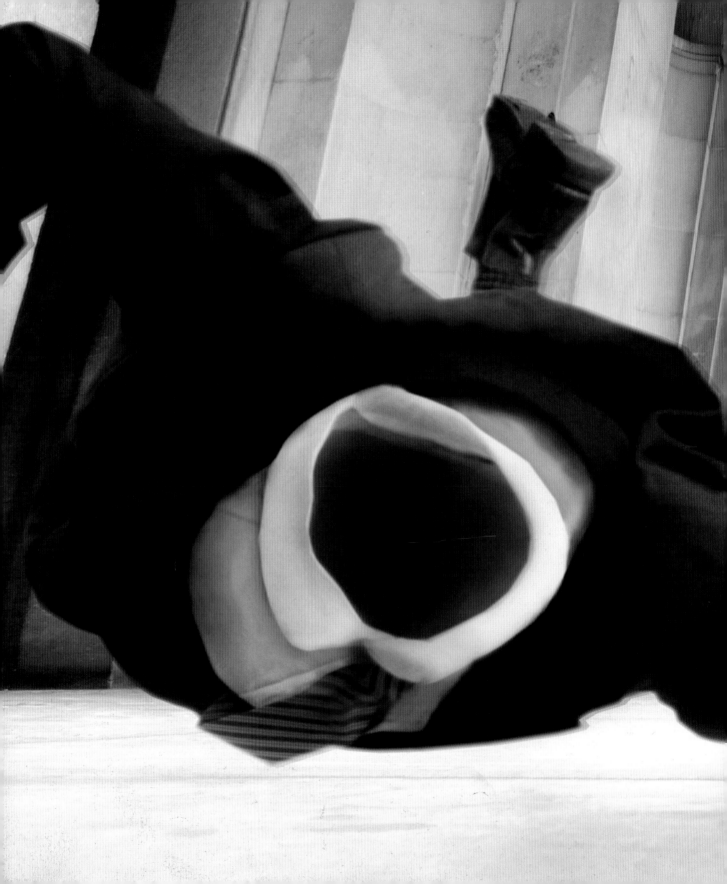

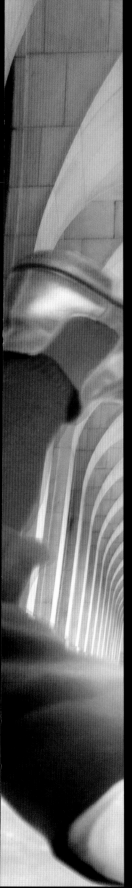

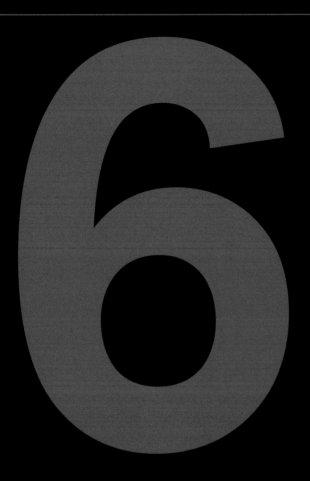

6

While it's true that you can create virtually any surreal image that springs to mind if you know
Photoshop well enough, there are still many instances when it's a darn sight easier to set up a
photoshoot in a studio to get the best possible images before you move from camera to computer.
Take the image at left as an example: without the initial studio work to get the correct pose from the
model, the image would have been impossible to construct.

studio photography

Studio Photography

FALLING MAN

by Andrew Brooks

With this shot, I was attempting to create a surreal image that was entirely photorealistic. The image is constructed from three main elements—the background, the man, and the briefcase—that were selected from about 20 different photographs.

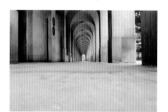

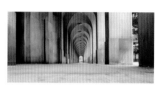

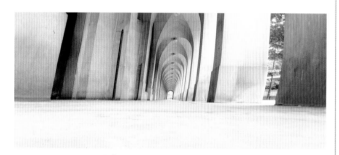

1 The first thing that we need to do is create a strong graphic background. Use the *Clone* and *Patch* tools to remove any unwanted details that could distract from the final image, such as signs on the wall. I want to create a widescreen cinematic feel, so I'm cropping the image to 5000 by 1970 pixels. Use the *Move* tool to position the background image within the new crop. Select the top half of the image using the *Rectangular Marquee* tool, then go to *Edit > Transform*. The image can now be warped and stretched to get the desired composition.

TIP

When moving the transform handles around to create the background, keep the top line of the marquee parallel. This will allow the bottom of the selection to join up exactly with the unselected area, leaving more scope to reshape and warp the image. This technique will enhance the surreal feel and can also be used to fill the left and right areas of the extended crop. Any gaps remaining at the edge, after the image has been transformed, can now be filled using the *Patch* and *Clone* tools.

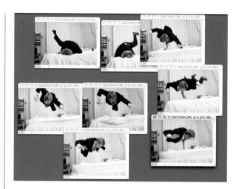

2 For the next element of the image we need to create the invisible man. The aim is to select the best bits of a number of shots, then make a composite of them to create the most graphic and dynamic version. These shots were lit with a mix of ambient light and flash to give the image a slight motion blur. The pictures have a soft light from the right side to match the light that would be flooding through the arches in the background image.

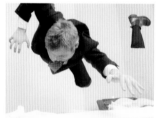

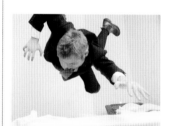

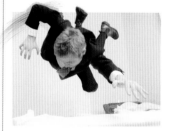

3 Use the *Lasso* tool to make a rough selection of the foot from RightFoot.tif. Copy and paste this onto the BestBody.tif image. Transform and position the rough selection of RightFoot.tif to where it works best with the body image. This should be done at 50% opacity so you can clearly see the join between the images. Return this layer to 100% opacity when you're done, and create a layer mask on the foot layer. On this layer mask, use a black brush to eliminate the parts of the image that are not required, and a white brush to paint through the parts that are required. For critical places, such as where the foot joins the body, use a feathered lasso (with a *Feather Radius* of 0.8 pixels) to get a soft edge. Repeat this on the other foot, the elbow, and around the portion of the image where the shoulder of the suit is covered by the head.

Studio Photography

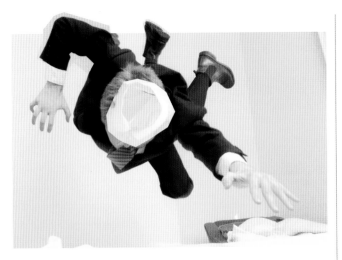

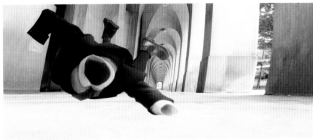

5 The invisible man element of the image can now be carefully cut out from the background using the *Lasso* tool. This can be copied and pasted as a separate layer onto the original background image. Lower the opacity of this layer to 50% and use the *Move* tool to rotate and position the body into the required position.

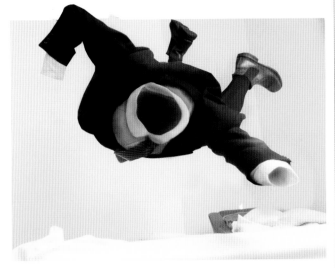

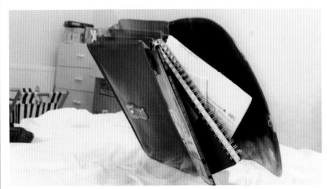

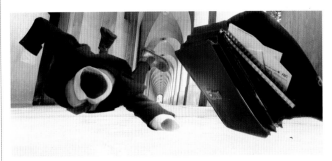

4 The next step in creating the invisible man element of the image is to create the inside of the suit. Firstly, copy and paste the new collar from shirt.tif and position it in the composition. Next, select the inside of the shirt using the *Lasso* tool (*Feather Radius* 1.0 pixels). Select a large brush (about 100 pixels), and paint in the shadow inside the shirt. Set the brush to 40% opacity, and create a graduated shadow area that is brighter at the edges. To achieve this effect, use the *Eyedropper* tool to select browns and blacks from the suit. Utilize the same technique for the shirt cuff. Using the *Patch* tool, sample areas of the suit and the shirt to add texture to the inside of the collar and the cuff. The image can now be flattened and any gaps or overlaps in the suit tidied using the *Clone* and *Patch* tools.

6 The third element that makes up the image is the briefcase, which is made up of the case and the objects within it. Drop the contents from CaseContent.tif onto Case.tif in the same way that the feet and elbow were added to the body element, as described earlier. Flatten this image, and carefully create a selection around it using the *Lasso* tool. Copy and paste it onto the original background image and position it using the same techniques that we used for the suit.

Studio Photography

FALLING MAN

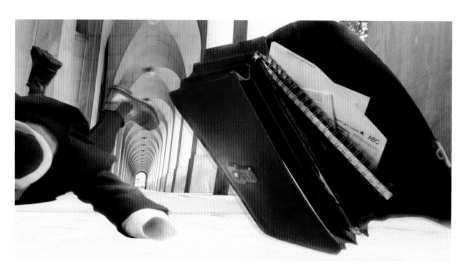

7 Now that all the images are in place, you can start adding motion blur, shadows, and lens flare effects to increase the realism of the shot. To add motion blur to the briefcase, you must duplicate the briefcase layer and place it underneath the original briefcase layer. Offset the duplicate layer so that it sits above and to the left of the original position. Lower the opacity on the new layer to about 30% to give a slight ghost image. This will add a feeling of motion. The same process can be applied to the body layer.

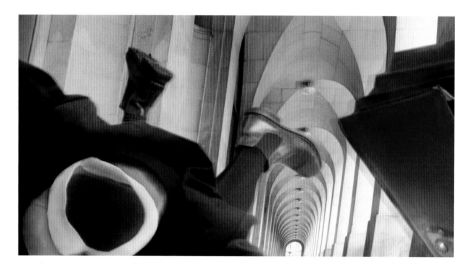

8 The edges of the case and the falling body may appear overly sharp in places. To soften these edges, create a layer mask and Ctrl/Cmd+click on the image thumbnail in the *Layers* palette. The option to *Select Layer Transparency* will appear. This will now give you a selection of all the information on that layer. Invert the selection and feather it with a *Radius* of 5 pixels. Use a black brush at 30% opacity to fade the edges. Soften your selection until it looks natural.

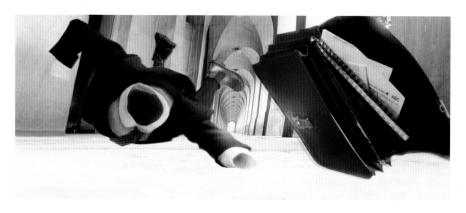

9 To add more realism to the shot and to tie all the elements together, you can create a little flare at the brightest area of the image. To do this, create a new top layer and use a soft brush (about 300 pixels) to paint some pure white into the end of the corridor and to the right where you can see the sky. Lower the opacity of this layer until it is flaring slightly. This will overlap both the dropped-in elements and the background and will add to the feeling that they are part of the same image.

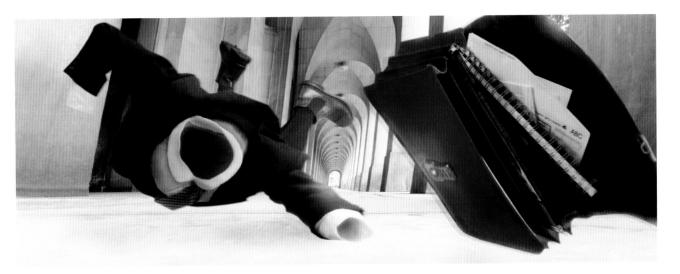

10 Create a shadow to add to the ground in front of the case and the invisible man. Copy and paste a selection of the floor from BackgroundHalfStopDark.tif. Move the layer containing this selection beneath the case and the suit layers, and transform it into a big enough area for the shadow. Create a layer mask and, using a black brush, (about 400 pixels) paint in a natural-looking shadow.

To create a more defined shadow at the point where the sleeve touches the ground, merge down the new shadow layer with the original background layer. Select a smaller area around the cuff and then feather it with a *Radius* of 40 pixels. Darken the shadow using *Curves*. Now that all of the elements are in place, the image can be saved and then flattened.

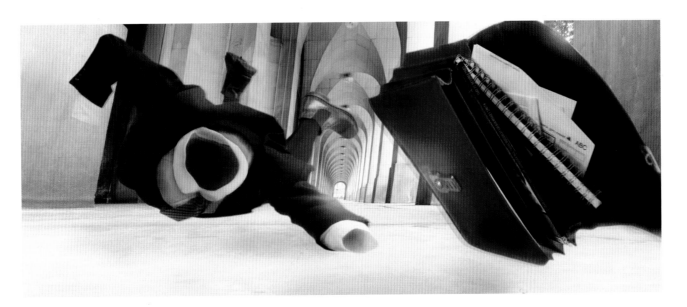

11 On the flattened image, you can now make more feathered selections to create highlights and shadows, adding to the realism. For example, make a selection on the case and lighten it so that it looks like the end of the corridor is reflected in the case. Control these highlight and shadow areas using adjustment layers to make the image look more natural.

FALLING MAN

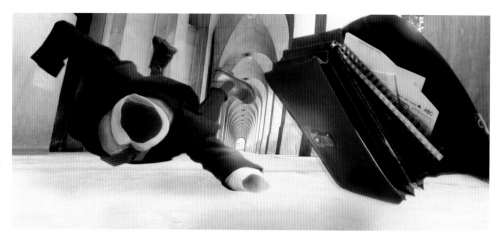

12 Once the image looks realistic and works as a whole, you can add a bit of atmosphere and feeling to the shot. To add a slight sepia tint to the shot, select *Hue/Saturation* then click on *Colorize*. Set the *Hue* to 40, and the *Saturation* to 29 to add a brown tint to the image. Immediately go to *Edit > Fade Hue/Saturation* and enter a value of 40% to create an image color that has a strong brown tone to it, but still retains the original colors.

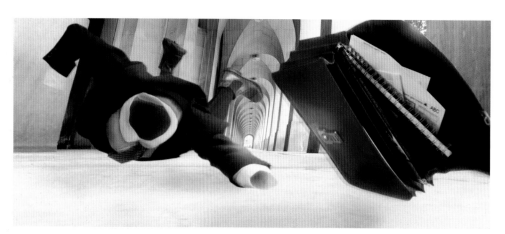

13 To give the entire image a more skewed feel, *Select All* and transform the image by pulling the corners with the Ctrl/Cmd key held.

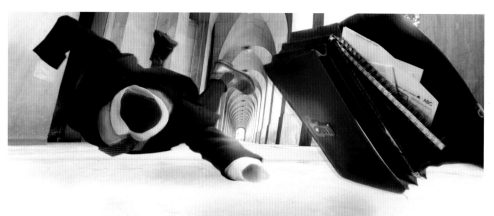

14 Finally, use *Curves* to add a little more contrast to the image, making the dark areas darker and the lighter areas slightly lighter, giving the picture a more graphic feel.

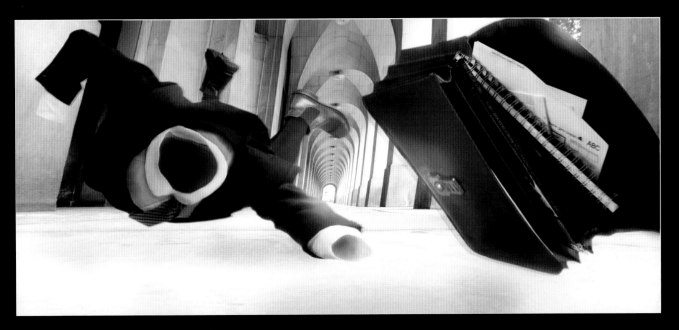

Final Image

The most important aspect of any studio shot (and most surreal artworks, for that matter) is careful planning. Consider the final effect you are looking for and photograph your models accordingly. If all goes to plan, you'll be surprised at how much of the compositing work that is usually required in Photoshop has been done for you.

© Andrew Brooks

Studio Photography

CHEERIO WORM

by Margot Quan Knight
I created this image as part of a series called *A Girl's Best Friend*. Almost any animal can become an ideal pet if you have Photoshop and the right camera lens.

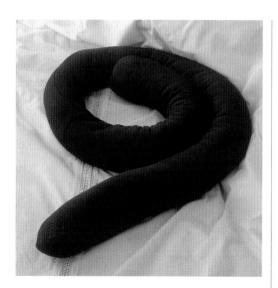

1 The first step is to make a very large worm. I used a sewing machine and made mine from stretchy brown fabric, quilting batting, wire, and Styrofoam peanuts for stuffing. Internal wires running the length of his body will help to hold him in position.

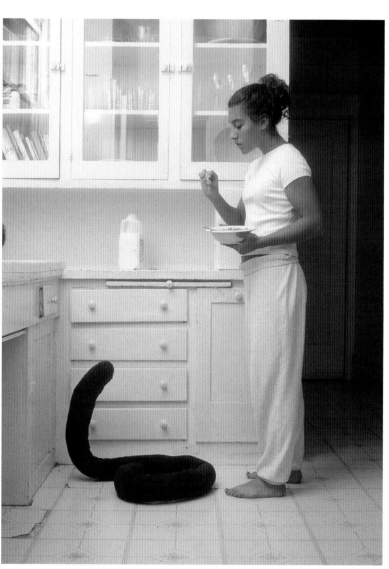

2 I used the worm prop at the photoshoot to help me compose the image. It also gave the model something to interact with.

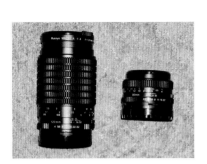

3 The key to making a Photoshop composite image look realistic is to photograph all of the elements of the image under the same lighting conditions. After I had photographed the model and worm prop, I photographed some real earthworms under the same lights. I used a macro lens to capture close-ups of the worms.

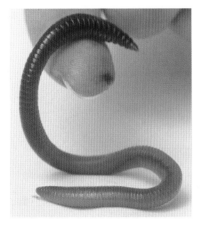

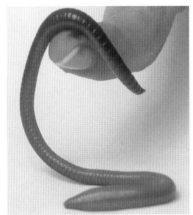

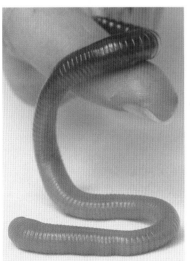

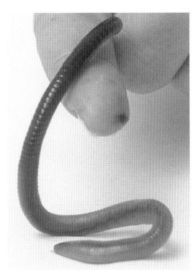

4 A macro lens has a very narrow depth of field, so it was hard to get the worm's head and tail in focus at the same time. I took many photos of the worms, but most of them were out of focus. If you dip your hands in ice water before handling the earthworms they will squirm less!

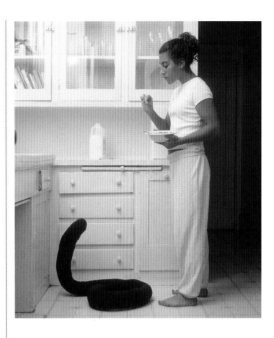

5 Before adding the worm to the background image, you should clean up any small details in the main picture. For example, I removed some lint on the woman's clothing, spots on the counter, stray hairs, and so on. Create a new "cover" layer, and use the *Clone* tool (with *Use All Layers* checked) so your cover-ups are separate from the background. If you make a mistake, your background file is still intact.

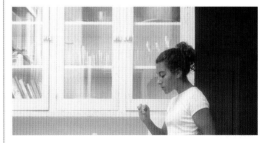

6 I also copied and pasted part of the cabinet glass to cover up the flare from my studio lights. Use the *Polygonal Lasso* tool to select around the area with the flare. Move the selection area up to the next shelf in the cabinet where there is no flare, then copy it. Move the copied fragment back down to cover the flare, and erase the edges with a large soft *Eraser* so that it blends in.

Studio Photography

CHEERIO WORM

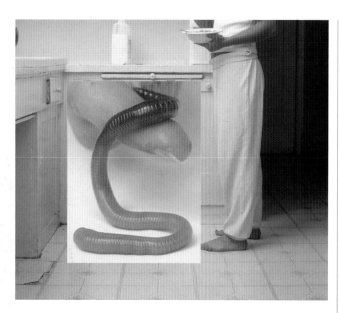

7 Drag the earthworm into your background file. Make a selection around the worm to remove it from the background. I do this by zooming in on the image and, using the *Polygonal Lasso* tool, work my way around the shape. I then save the selection and feather it slightly.

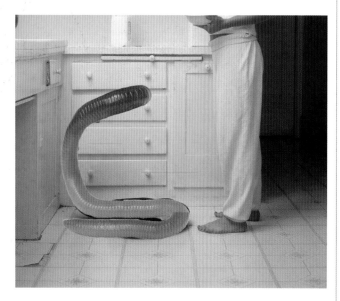

8 Hide the background around the worm with a layer mask. You can do this easily by clicking on the *Add Layer Mask* button in the *Layers* palette while the worm is selected.

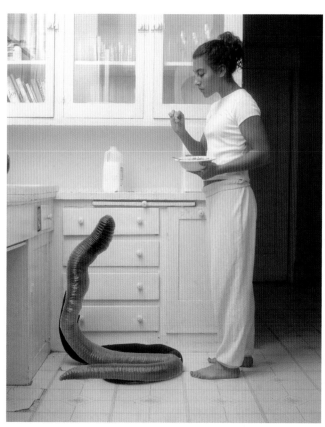

9 Now we can see that the prop worm sticks out from behind the earthworm in some places. For large cover-ups, select, copy, and paste background areas to hide the fabric prop worm. Erase the edges of the pasted fragments so that they blend in.

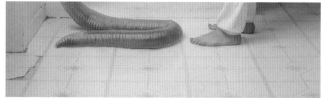

10 The shadow where the worm meets the floor is the hardest part. This will take some creative cutting and pasting to generate a smooth, realistic shadow. Because the floor is on a grid pattern, pieces of the flooring can be cut from elsewhere. I always use cut and pasted pieces of real shadow where possible rather than simply painting one, because it looks much more realistic.

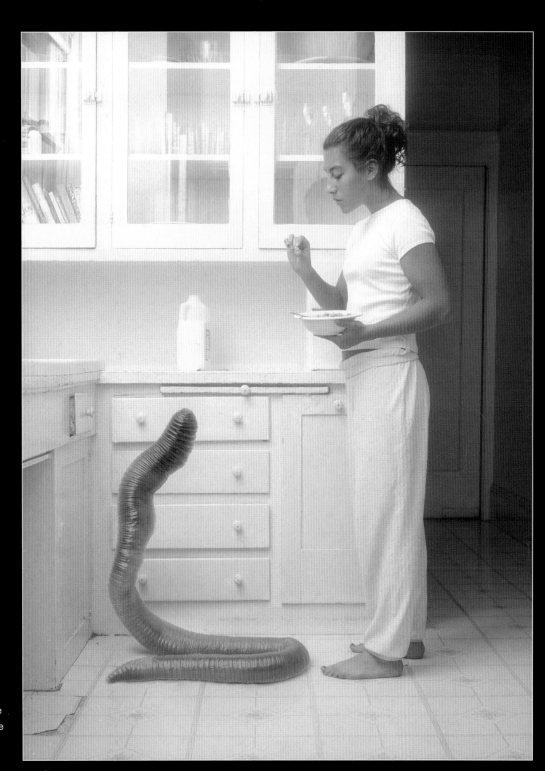

Final Image
The fabric model of the worm at the photoshoot has helped enormously in both showing where shadows should be correctly placed, and giving a convincing sense of interaction between the model and her pet worm.

© Margot Quan Knight

Studio Photography

SPILT MILK

by Margot Quan Knight

This image is part of my current series in which I am exploring timelessness. We have all been lost in thought or absorbed in a task when time seemed to stop or stretch. By using props, high-speed photography, and digital manipulation, you can create an image that conveys the feeling of stretched time.

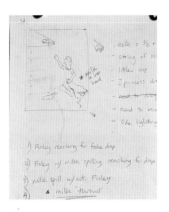

1 The first and most important step is to come up with an idea. What are you curious about? I brainstorm to come up with a number of different ideas, no matter how crazy and impossible. Afterward, I go back and pick the best one and think about how to make it happen.

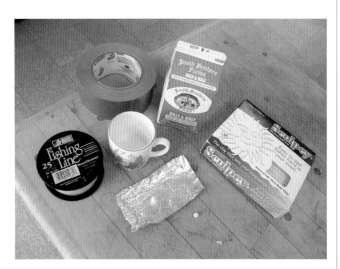

2 With an idea in my head to try and create a scene of a child plucking static drops of spilt milk from the air, I now need to sort out the required props for the shoot. I used Sculpey modeling clay to create three fake milk droplet beads, and used a pin to put a hole in each round bead before baking them in the oven. String the beads on fishing line, tying knots to keep the beads separate, then secure the string of beads to the kitchen counter using sticky tape. For the real fluid, I used Half & Half, which gives more substantial droplets than milk.

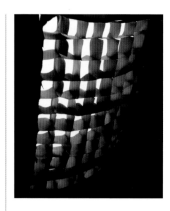
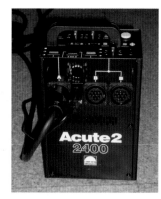

3 A strobe is necessary in order to "freeze" the milk droplets in mid-fall. I use a Profoto Acute 2 2400 kit on the lowest power setting. The lower the power setting, the faster the flash. A "soft-box" with nylon grid will focus soft light on the girl while allowing the background cabinets to recede into darkness.

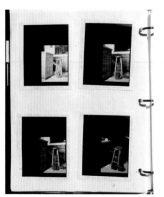
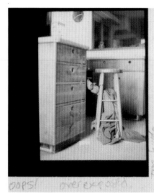

4 When working with models, especially children, I make sure to figure out my lighting ahead of time using a mannequin. If you don't have a mannequin to hand, you can create one using a stool and some cloth.

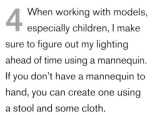
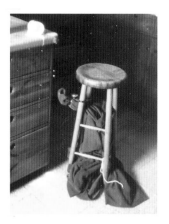

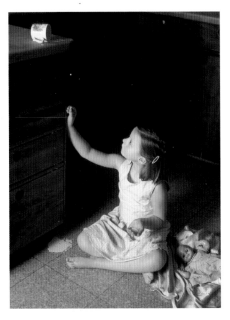

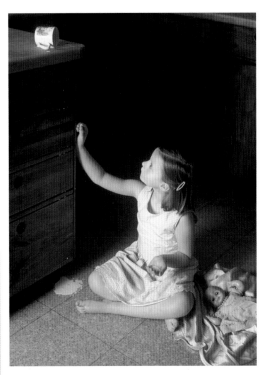

6 Clean up the background first. I cover any distracting details, such as the heating vent, by copying and pasting black from another area of the photo. I never use the *Brush* tool for this because I want to keep the subtle texture in the blacks. Use the *Clone* tool to cover up the fishing line and the extra white beads.

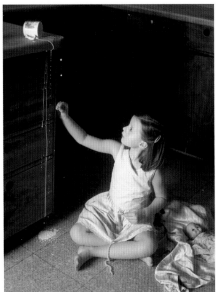

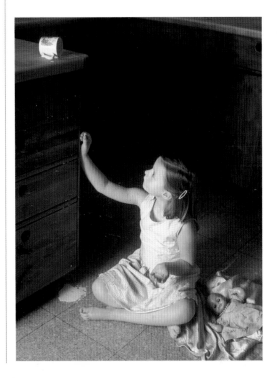

7 I didn't like the cropping on my best image, so I extended the canvas size and dragged in a piece of the counter from a different photo. To line up the new piece of counter, decrease its opacity to 50% and move the layer around until the drawers line up. I used the *Polygonal Lasso* tool to trace a natural break in the counter (below the drawers) and cut off the counter there. Any slight difference in color between the old and new cabinets will seem natural.

5 At the photoshoot, be open to the unexpected. I couldn't decide whether the girl should be holding milk or a string of pearls, so I shot both. I had planned to use Photoshop to arrange the milk droplets into a drip pattern, but I got lucky and caught the effect on film. I prefer the gesture of the girl holding the milk, so now I'll montage these two images together in Photoshop.

SPILT MILK

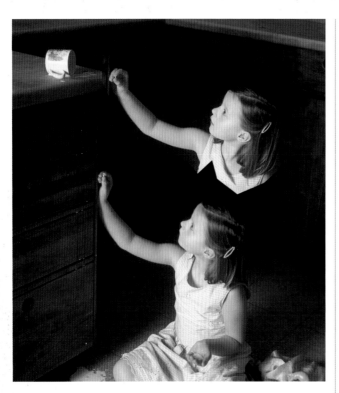

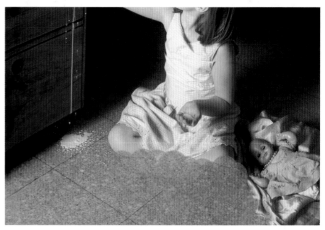

8 My favorite photo is of the girl holding milk, but the angle of her head and the gesture of her arm are not to my liking. This can be corrected by dragging in the head and arm from the other shot, aligning them at 50% opacity, and using the *Eraser* tool to blend them into the existing body.

10 Now I bring in the counter with the milk droplets. The girl's feet are in a slightly different position, so extend the flooring with the Clone tool so the new floor covers over the girl's legs. Turn off the new floor layer, then use the *Polygonal Lasso* tool to carefully select around her legs. I always save these selection areas as separate channels just in case I ever need to use them again.

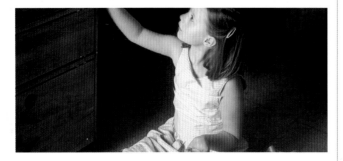

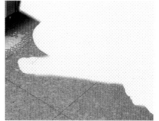

11 Turn the new floor layer back on. Use the *Eraser* (or a mask) to erase the new flooring. I erase the sharp edges first with the selection on, then deselect and use a large, soft *Eraser* to reveal the shadows of her feet on the floor.

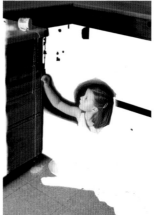

12 With the background layer switched off, you can see all of the composite elements that have been added to create the final image.

9 The new head and arm have squeezed the dress shoulder strap, so I cut a fragment of her shoulder strap from the original dress and pasted it on top of the new arm. The old arm is showing behind the new arm, so I cut and pasted black from the original image to cover the old arm. Here is the result so far.

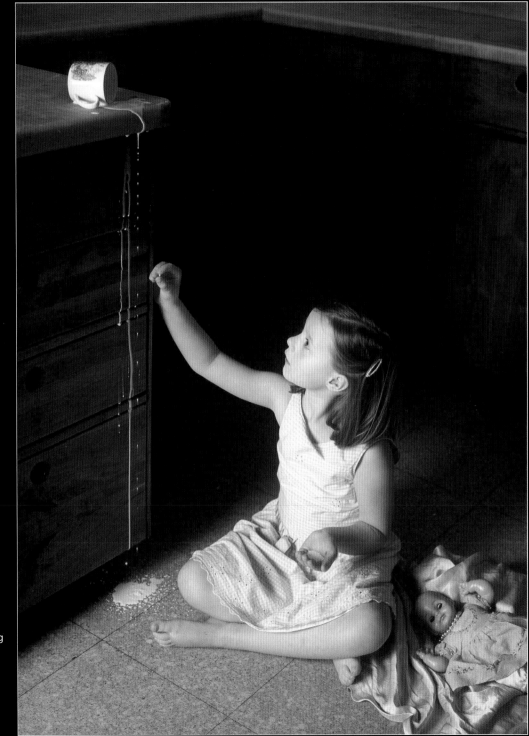

Final Image

The Photoshop compositing
work has been seamlessly
integrated into the final
picture, so that the result
looks convincingly like
a real photograph.

© Margot Quan Knight

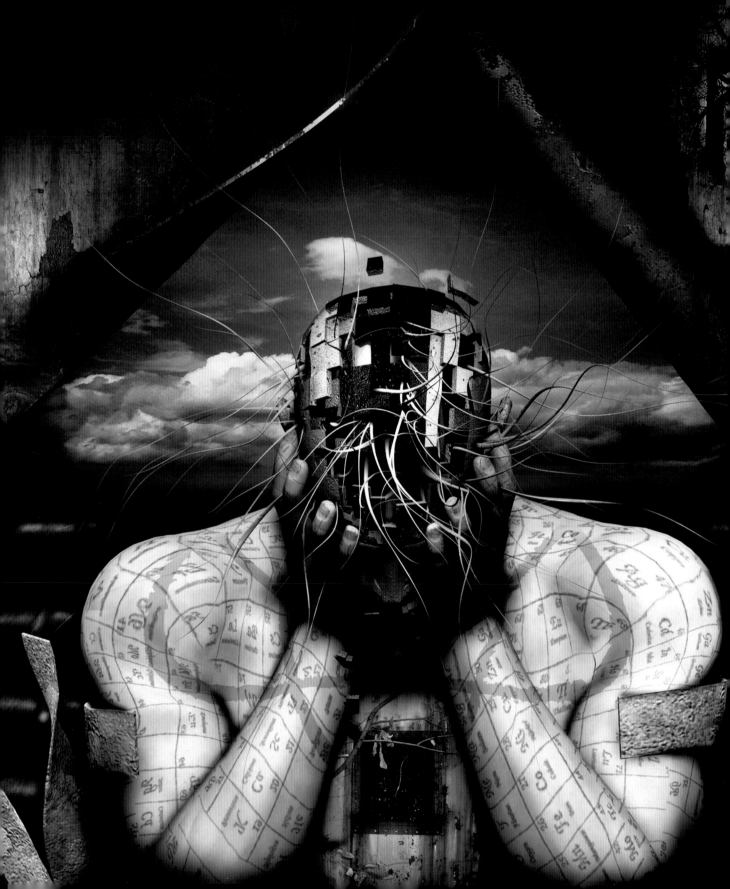

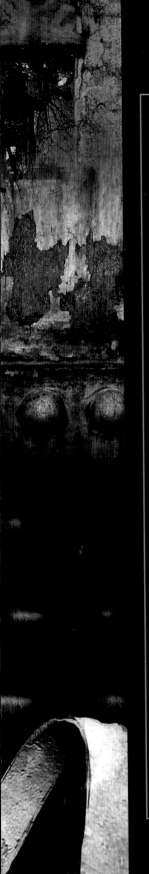

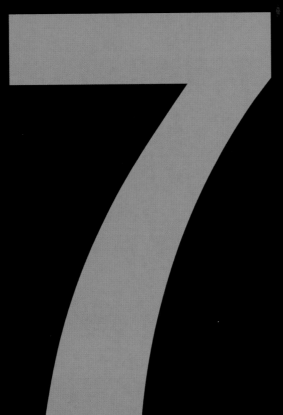

7

Photoshop is very good at combining photographic elements and adding textures and effects to existing images, but it's not always easy to create new objects from scratch in it. One solution is to use a 3D software package, such as Cinema 4D or Poser, to create new digital assets that can be imported into your Photoshop scene. It can take a while to master 3D packages, but once you've learned the basics, you'll be amazed at the possibilities that are opened up to you.

3D

3D

LOVER

by Liva Rutmane

This photomontage consists of one render made in Maxon Cinema 4D, with two photographs and four textures added on in Photoshop. Using 3D software to create elements gives them a solidity and depth that would be very difficult to create from scratch in Photoshop.

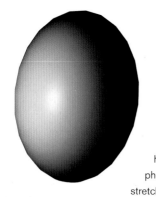

1 Primitives are the basic building blocks of 3D. They are the simple shapes, such as spheres, cubes, and cylinders from which all 3D graphics are made. In Cinema 4D, create a sphere primitive by going to *Objects > Primitive > Sphere*. We want this sphere to be roughly head-shaped for adding to our photograph later on, so we need to stretch it along one of its axes. Go to *Tools > Object Axis*, then *Tools > Scale* to set the correct mode. Click and hold on the Y-axis and stretch the sphere until you get a shape similar to that shown.

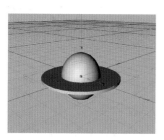

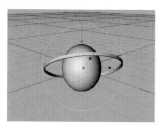

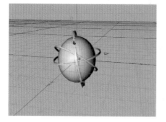

2 Create a primitive again, this time, a tube by going to *Objects > Primitive > Tube*. Use *Tools > Scale* to reduce the tube's height and increase its diameter. We only want the tube to be a thin ring, so change the tube's inner radius so that it's only a little less than its outer radius. Use *Tools > Rotate*, and click the *X, Y,* and *Z* axes to rotate the ring around the sphere until you have a pleasing composition. Make some copies of the ring, and distribute them around the sphere. Rotate the rings so that they cross over each other at different points. The shape only has to look good from one side, because it will be used as 2D image, so don't worry if the rings are a mess behind the sphere.

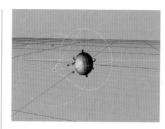

3 All of the photos used in the composition have one light source, so we'll match that light on our 3D model. Always pay attention to the light source because it needs to be similar to your real-life photo to achieve a realistic composition. Go to *Objects > Scene > Light* to add a light source to the image—I find *Spot (Round)* lights much easier to control. Go to the *Attributes > Details* panel for the light, and enlarge the *Spot Outer Angle* to around 80 degrees. You can alter the light placement and direction using the *Rotate* and *Scale* tools just as you would with a solid object. Make sure you also change the light's *Shadow* setting to *Soft* in the *Attributes > General* panel.

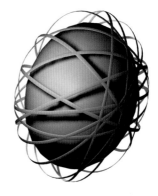

4 Once you've built up a good network of rings around your sphere, you're ready to render your image. In the *Output* panel of the *Render Settings* dialog box, you should change *Image Size* to at least 2000 pixels square, at 300 ppi. Save it as a PSD file, and check the *Alpha Channel* box in the *Save* panel. Then go to *Render > Render to Picture Viewer*.

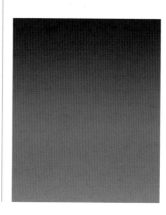

5 Create a new document in Photoshop at about 12 x 16.5 inches (30 x 42 cm) and at 300 dpi. Fill the background with a pale brown color—#655245. We'll use the *Gradient* tool over the top of this to add some texture to the background. Set the *Gradient* to run from black at the top to white at the bottom, with an overall gradient opacity of 40%. Save your working document and leave it for now.

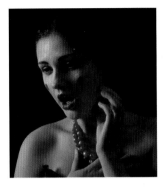

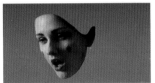

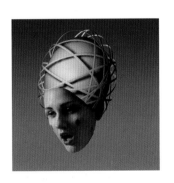

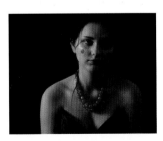

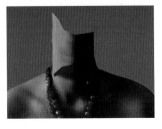

6 Open the main photo with the face. We're going to use the face from this photo with the body from another, and combine it all with our 3D head. Use the *Pen* tool set to make paths to roughly cut the face from the background. Go to the *Paths* palette, right/Ctrl+click on your paths layer and choose *Make Selection*. Don't forget to include an ear in your selection, as this will help blend our 3D head convincingly with the photo. After making the selection, drag it into the gradient background working image, and name its layer "Face."

7 Open your 3D render image. You won't have to cut the shape out, because there is an alpha channel already set. Go to the *Channels* palette and Ctrl/Cmd+click on the alpha channel to generate a selection. Now drag the 3D shape into the working document underneath the Face layer, and name it "Render."

8 Open the final photo of the girl. We'll use this image for the body, so you'll need to cut out just the neck and shoulders, including the beads. Drag this into the working file, and place its layer under everything else. As you can see, the objects are currently quite detached from each other, so the first thing to do is create a neck. To do that, select some parts from the existing neck and copy them several times—this won't be final, it's just to create a base on which you will paint later.

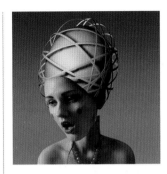

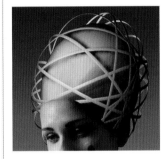

9 Next, start to blend the render with the face. First, select all of the parts of the rings that don't cross over the face, then copy it into another layer. Make a selection of this layer, and go to *Select > Save Selection* to save the selection as a new channel. This means that you will be able to go back to it whenever you need to. Leave this new layer underneath the Face layer. Now create a new layer for shading the 3D head. I find the easiest thing is to do all of my shading by hand using the *Brush* tool and a graphics tablet. Use the existing shading on the sphere and the photograph to guide you, and pick colors to blend with the face.

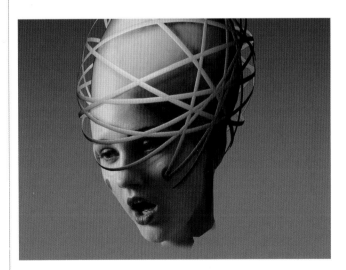

10 Now select the remainder of the rings—those that cross the face—and save this selection as a new channel. Copy the selection into a new layer, called "Lines," and place it above the Face layer. This part will need shading too. In a new layer between the Face and Lines layers. Pay particular care when drawing shadows over the nose and cheeks, as shadows act differently on these rounded surfaces. You should also paint in the rest of the neck at this stage, to make sure it blends in with the face.

3D

LOVER

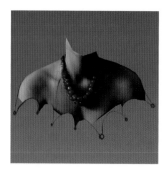
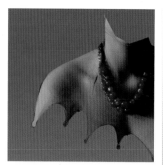

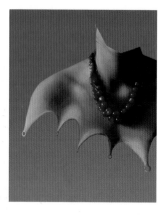
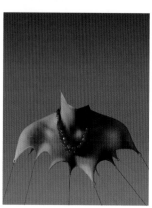

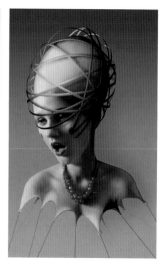

12 Next, we need to finish coloring the render. The sphere is mostly done, but we haven't worked on the lines yet. Load the selection of rings that you made earlier, create a new layer at the top of the palette, and fill the selection with #b46064, which is a dull pink. Set the layer to *Overlay*, and change its opacity to about 50%. Add any more shading that is necessary on the rings using a soft brush. To help blend everything together, create a new *Brightness/Contrast* adjustment layer and set *Brightness* to -30 and *Contrast* to +5. Make any final necessary touch-ups to the image, such as adding more shading in places to make it look more realistic. You should also paint some shadows above the background layer to help lift the head from the background.

11 I wanted to create an effect at the bottom of the image where the skin was being stretched out and tethered, almost like a giant balloon that was tied down to stop it from flying away. This effect is painted directly onto the photograph, and I find that a graphics tablet is absolutely essential for this kind of work. Start by sketching out the shape—this doesn't have to be too precise, just draw approximately how the whole shape should look. Create a new layer over the sketch layer, choose some appropriate colors from the photo, and paint in the main tones using the *Brush* tool. Vary the brush opacity from 30–50% to blend the colors better. Keep painting and blending—altering brush size, opacity, and color as you go—until you're happy with the tones of the shapes you've created. Once this is done, remove the sketch layer and merge the bottom section layers together. Copy and paste some of these "projections" and move them to a lower layer. Move these around so that they look like they are extending from the woman's back. Reduce the *Brightness* and *Contrast* of these to make them look more distant. When you're happy with the composition, the final thing is to add strings tying the figure down. Just use a hard, round brush for this and draw straight lines running straight off the image.

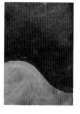

13 The final touch is to add some textures to the image. Textures not only enhance the mood and feeling of the piece, but they also help to tie the disparate elements together. I added three textures to the background and two overall textures that covered the entire image. These were applied as follows:

Background textures—
First texture: *Soft Light* blending mode at 7% opacity.
Second texture: *Hard Light* blending mode at 25% opacity.
Third texture: *Darken* blending mode at 25% opacity.

Overall textures—
First texture: *Overlay* blending mode at 21% opacity.
Second texture: *Overlay* blending mode at 5% opacity.

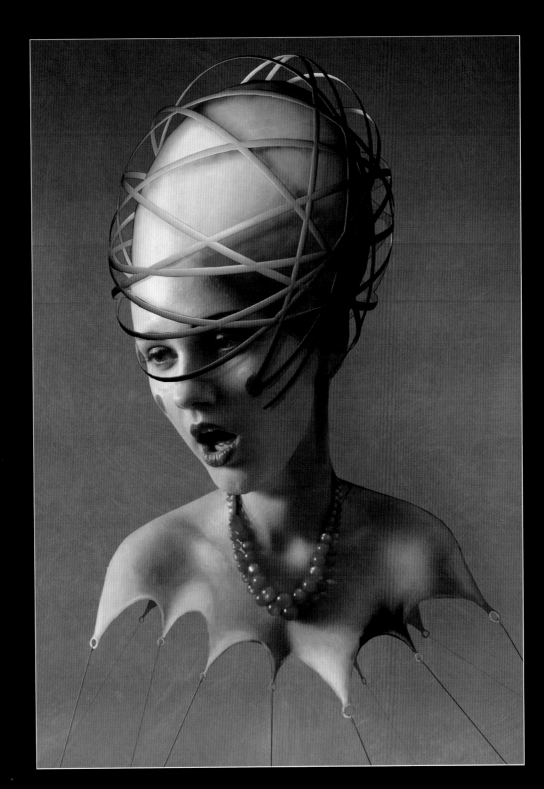

Final Image

3D packages make it
much simpler to create
complex shapes such as
this lady's headgear.

© Liva Rutmane

BLIND

by Liva Rutmane
In this project, we will create a series of objects in Cinema 4D and combine them with a set of photographs to make a hauntingly surreal final image.

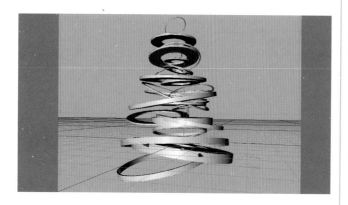

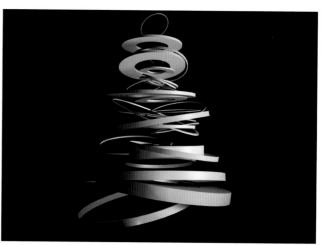

1 In Cinema 4D, go to *Objects > Primitive > Tube* to create a new tube object. Set the object's *Attributes* so that the *Inner Radius* is only a little less than the *Outer Radius*. Use the *Scale* tool to make the tube thinner, and rotate it to a pleasing angle. Place some more tubes on the screen, and position them using the same tools. Vary their *Outer* and *Inner Radius* values, and move, scale, and rotate them differently. The aim is to produce something shaped vaguely like a pyramid. Don't worry about viewing the other sides of the 3D object, because we will only be using it as part of a 2D image, so only seeing it from one angle.

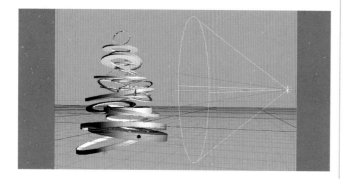

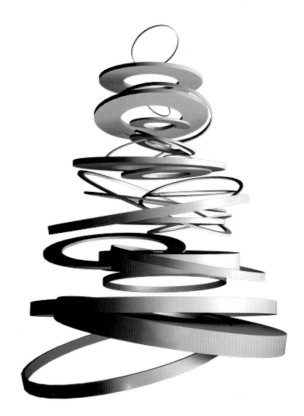

2 Add two light sources to the scene by going to *Objects > Scene > Light*. Use the *Attributes* panel to set the first light to *Omni*, with a *Brightness* of 70% and the *Shadow* set to *Soft*. This light will remain in the center of the pyramid and light it from within. The second should be set to *Spot (Round)*, *Brightness*: 90%, *Shadow*: *Soft*. Move this light farther away from the pyramid, and set the *Spot Outer Angle* value to 70 degrees.

3 You're now ready to render your image. Change the *Output* panel so that the *Image Size* is at least 2000 pixels square at 300 dpi. Save it as a PSD file and check the *Alpha Channel* box, then go to *Render > Render to Picture Viewer* and save your image.

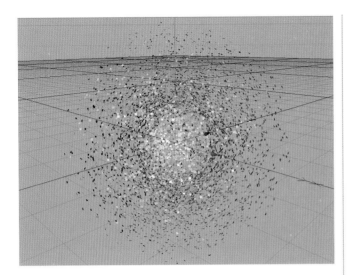

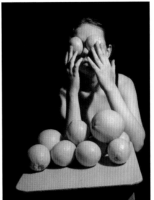

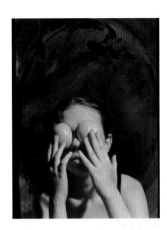

4 Now we'll create an explosion effect that will be used as a texture in the photomontage. Open a new Cinema 4D document and create a sphere primitive in the center of the scene. Go to the *Attributes* panel and increase the *Sphere Segments* value to over 100. This will make the explosion much more detailed. Next create the explosion by going to *Objects* > *Deformation* > *Explosion*. You will notice that an *Explosion* icon has now appeared linked to the sphere in your *Object* panel. Change the *Attributes* for the *Explosion* to *Straight*: 15%, *Speed* 140m. Render the explosion out as a picture with an alpha channel at the same dimensions you used earlier, and save it.

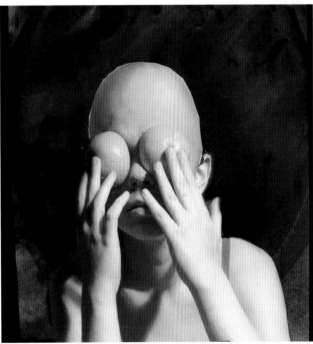

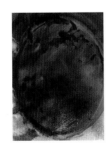
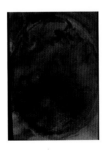

5 Create a new document in Photoshop. Fill the background layer with #4b4944, which is a murky brown color. Switch to the *Gradient* tool set to a low opacity and drag a *Foreground to Transparent* gradient using a lighter brown (#756b5c) to brighten the top of the image slightly. Next, add some texture to the background. I've imported two new images for my texture and changed the blending mode of the first image to *Multiply*, and the second to *Overlay*.

6 Open the main photo of the girl with the oranges. Use the *Pen* tool set to create paths to roughly cut it out from the background. When you're done, convert the path to a selection, and drag the girl across into background working folder. Name the layer "Face." We'll create a new orange head for the girl simply by painting it on with the *Brush* tool. I find that a graphics tablet is a huge help when painting freehand on the computer. The oranges in the image currently look a bit too yellow, but this can be remedied with an adjustment layer. Select the yellow parts of the face and go to *Image* > *Adjustments* > *Color Balance*, and set the color levels to *Red*: +33, *Magenta*: -28.

3D

BLIND

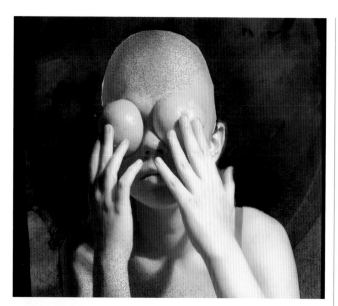

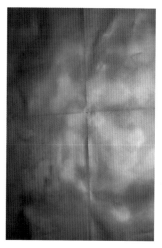

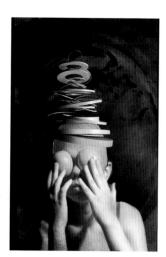

8   We'll make the girl grayscale, so select all of her skin apart from her face. Create a new *Hue/Saturation* adjustment layer, and set the *Saturation* slider to about -79. There's one last texture to add to tie the image together. Import the texture at the top of the layer stack, and set its blending mode to *Overlay*.

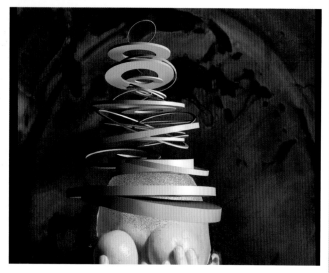

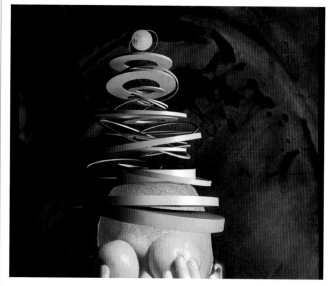

7   We'll now add our explosion render to create some more texture in the piece. You won't have to cut it out, because there is already an alpha channel set up. Go to *Window > Channel*, then Ctrl/Cmd+click on the Alpha layer to generate a selection. Drag the selected image over onto the working file above the Face layer, and name it "Explosion." Duplicate this layer twice, and arrange the explosions around the image to create a pleasing effect. This will also help to blend the face into the background a bit more. Open the render of the rings, make a selection using its alpha channel, and drag it into the working image at the top of the layer stack.

9   There are two final touches required to complete the image. The first is to cut out one of the oranges from our original photographs and add it to the top of the pyramid. The second touch is to paint in some shadows from the rings. Use a soft brush to paint these on where necessary.

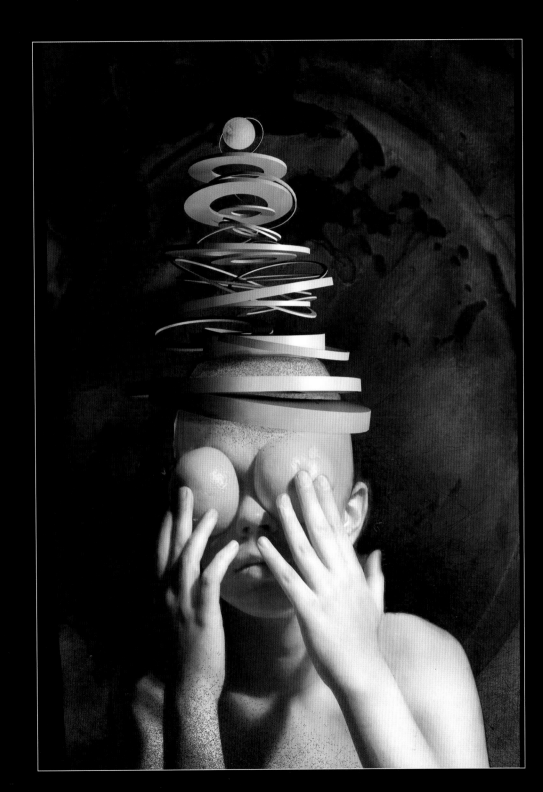

Final Image

This image looks
tremendously complex,
but it was simple to
create using Photoshop
and Cinema 4D, and
doesn't require any
advanced 3D skills.

© Liva Rutmane

3D

CONVENTUM ELEMENTUM

by Frank Picini

Conventum Elementum is a Latin phrase meaning the coming together of elements. In this illustration I wanted to compile imagery and textures from many sources and combine both natural and manmade elements. I was inspired by some great rustic photographs that I purchased for commercial use as textures in my 3D renders. This image uses a combination of software packages to create all of the separate elements and combine them all into the finished scene.

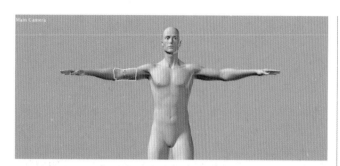

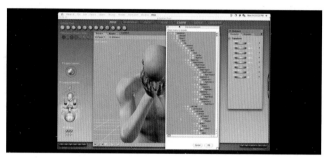

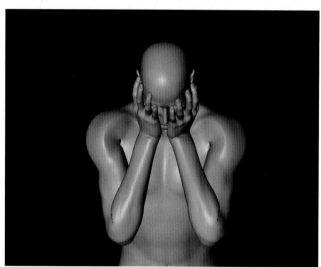

2 While exporting your .obj file there are many options to choose from, and you have the ability to choose which parts of the model you want to export. The only thing I did not export was the ground portion. You only really need the upper body with the arms and head since you're not rendering the lower half, but the rest of the polygons will not add much to the model size or to the export time so it doesn't really matter. Remember that if you want to import textures, etc., in Cinema 4D using a plug-in such as Interposer, then you must save your Poser scene with the same name as the .obj model you just exported.

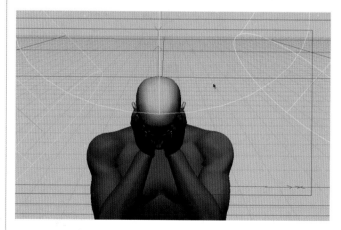

1 In this project, we'll make use of a number of applications to create the final image. We'll use Poser to create and pose a figure, Cinema 4D to edit the figure and add some extra elements, and then Photoshop to tie everything together and create a background. First, open Poser and create a new male figure. Pose the figure and any structural attributes, such as facial expressions and muscle tone. In this image, facial work was not as important as the body structure and muscles. You need not pay any attention to the lighting and texturing at this stage because these elements will be resolved later in Cinema 4D. Once the figure is posed, export the model as a single image .obj file.

3 Make a high-resolution Cinema 4D file at 3900 x 2083 pixels. We'll be adding all our own lights and textures to the model within Cinema 4D, so you just need to import the Poser model directly.

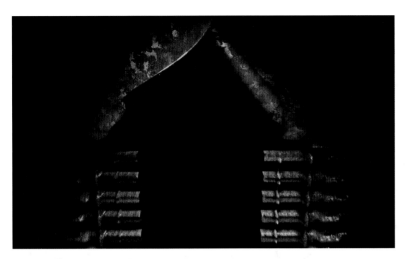

4 Set up the camera to the view of your choice. I first modeled the curled rusty walls from a simple thin elongated panel, making two panels, one for each side. I also imported some rusty bars that were made previously and brought them in as an object import. I applied a curl or bend deformer to the panel making each of them different.

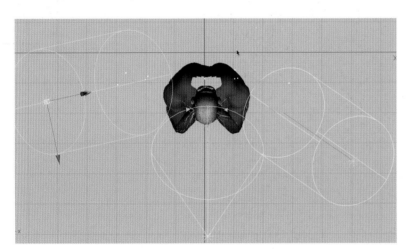

5 I prefer to use a 3-point lighting rig for my models. My main light was a spotlight placed slightly in front of the figure closer to the camera (foreground) and slightly above. The other two lights were above his shoulders. The right light was a *Parallel Spot* light set to *R*: 255, *G*: 219, *B*: 210 at an Intensity of 85% with *Diffuse*, *Specular*, *Show Illumination*, *Show Visible Light*, and *Show Clipping* checked. The left light was also a *Parallel Spot* light, this time set to *R*: 159, *G*: 195, *B*: 255 at an *Intensity* of 100% with the rest of the settings the same.

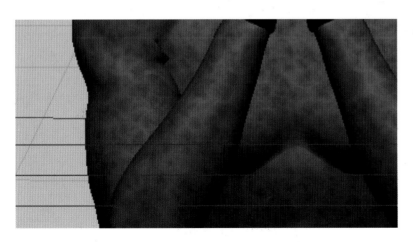

6 I added a rust texture to the models, then rendered out the image with an alpha mask as a high-resolution 32-bit image for compositing.

CONVENTUM ELEMENTUM

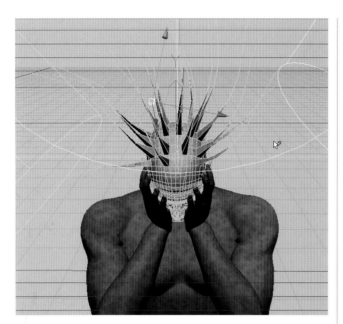

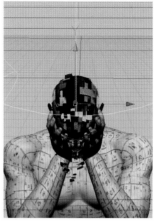

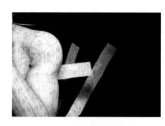

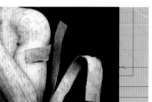

8 I created a new texture material and applied an image of the periodic table, then I UV-mapped this material to the body. I modeled some thin bars of metal, applied the rust material to them, and flanked them around the figure. Then I applied a twist and bend deformer to the shafts of rusted steel to wrap the figure. That's all for Cinema 4D, so render out your figure as you did in Step 6.

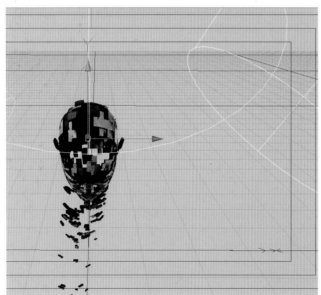

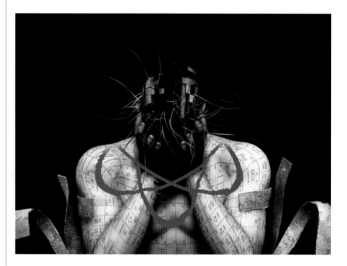

7 I made two copies of the head model. On the first copy, I selected a handful of polygons and applied a *Matrix Extrude* function to the polygons to create wispy tendrils. Play around with the *Matrix Extrude* function if you get the time, as it's worth becoming familiar with its parameters. I then applied a *HyperNURBS* object to smooth out the extruded polygons. On the second copy, I applied a deformer called *Explosion FX* to fragment the head.

9 Now we'll begin compositing the various pieces in Photoshop. Create a high-resolution file at 300 dpi at the same 3900 x 2083 pixel dimensions. I brought in both 32-bit images by just dragging them into the new file window. At this point, I decided to crop the panoramic canvas to a square canvas. Then I added a molecular symbol to the figure. This was achieved by applying a displacement filter and choosing the original file as the displacement source.

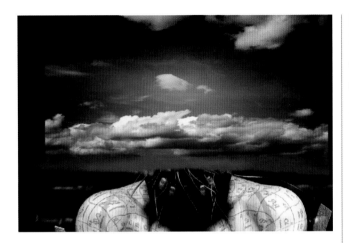

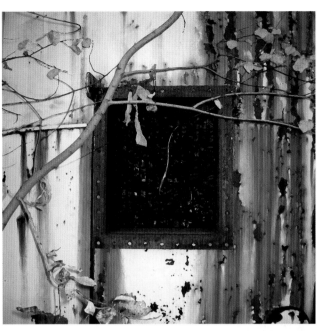

10 At this stage, I usually add a *Hue/Saturation* adjustment layer and desaturate the image to see the contrast in my object colors. That's when I decided to keep the final image black and white. I continued to toggle on and off the adjustment layer as I worked from color to black and white. Now I added the clouds photo. My source image wasn't quite big enough in the position that I wanted it, so I used the *Clone Stamp* tool to extend the bottom of the picture.

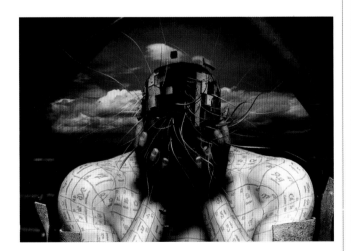

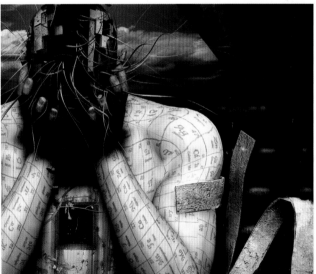

11 Now that the sky was composited, I needed to feather the bottom edge to graduate it to black. I decided to colorize the clouds image to complement the overall feel of the piece. I really liked the elongated cloud formation in this image with its floating single cloud above the head, and it worked fine as a strong contrast to the head of the figure while adhering to the design flow of the horizontal rusted bars.

12 I now realized that the curled edges of the rusted panels needed more highlight. On a separate layer set to *Overlay*, I airbrushed white to bring up the specularity of the curled edges. I kept the selection loaded during the painting to prevent any airbrushing from bleeding outside its edges. I then added another photo image to the heart area of the figure, changed its blending mode, and erased any overlapping pixels that touched the forearms.

3D

CONVENTUM ELEMENTUM

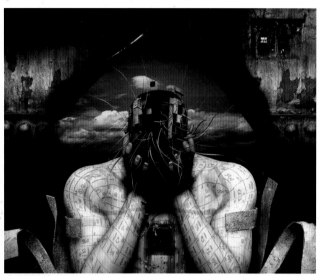

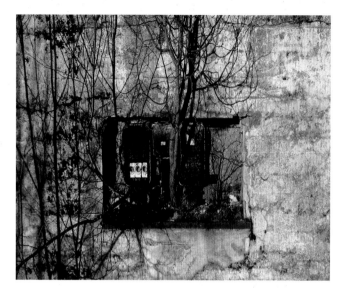

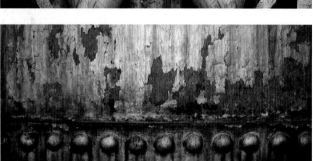

13 Now I noticed the curled rusty panels were too dark and needed more contrast and a stronger texture. I composited another rust texture by using the panels' original mask and erasing some areas to blend them together. At this point I needed to unbalance the symmetry of the image so I did some more research in my texture photo library and composited another image in the upper right panel which brought in more organic elements.

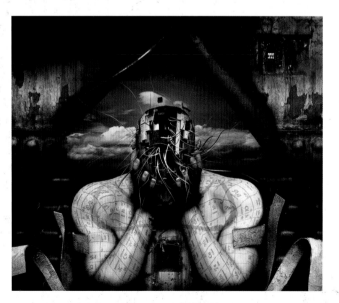

14 The only remaining task was to paint in any details required to fix any inconsistencies in the joints of the figure that were caused from within the 3D render. These were especially visible inside the elbow and shoulder areas. I also made a new layer and airbrushed in shadows that I felt would help bring out contrast between areas in the image, such as the wrapped metal around the arms, and the armpit areas of the figure. This final procedure helps increase the sense of depth in the image.

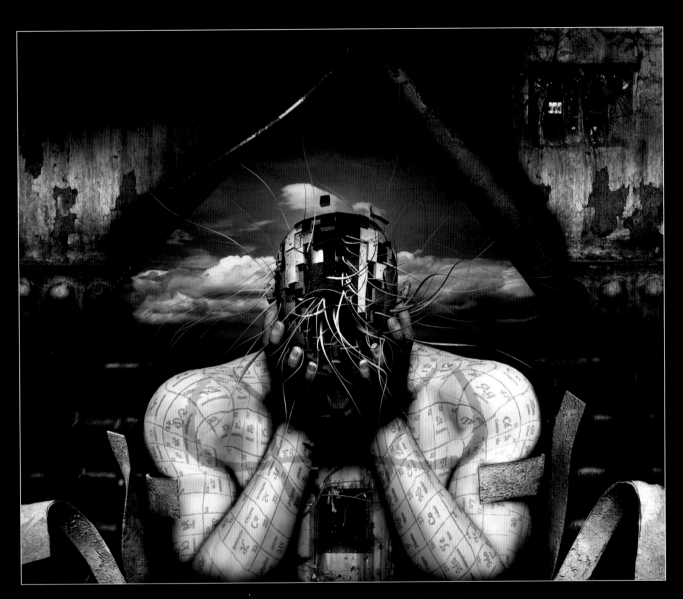

Final Image

The power of 3D packages is
that they make certain effects
simple that would otherwise be
impossibly difficult to achieve,
such as the explosion and
extrusion effects applied to the
head of this figure.

© Frank Picini

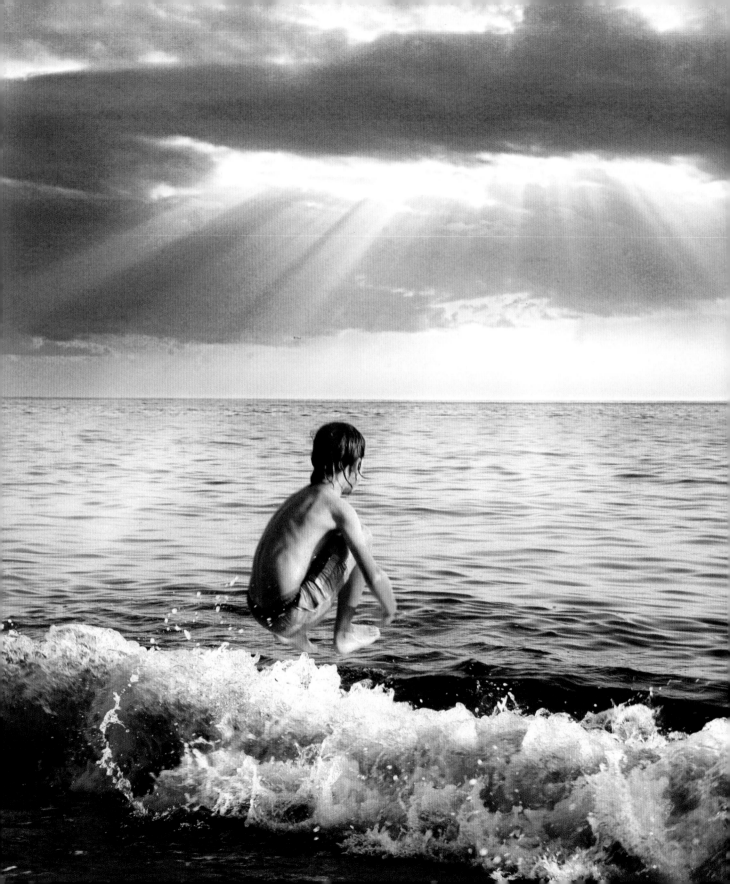

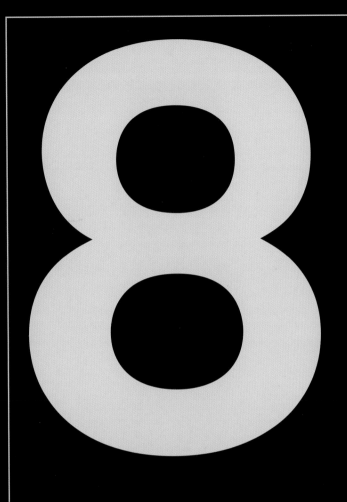

reference

GLOSSARY

Adjustment Layer

A layer that contains no image pixels but affects the appearance of layers below it in the layer "stack." These include changes to levels, contrast, and color, plus gradients and other effects. These changes do not permanently affect the pixels underneath, so by masking or removing the adjustment layer, you can easily remove the effect from part or all of an image with great ease. You can also change an adjustment layer's parameters at a later time, even after restarting Photoshop.

Aliasing

The term describing the jagged appearance of bitmapped images or fonts either when the resolution is insufficient or when they have been enlarged. This is caused by the pixels—which are square with straight sides—making up the image becoming visible.

Alpha Channel

A channel that stores selections in Photoshop.

Ambient

A term used in 3D modeling software to describe a light source with no focus or direction, such as that which results from bouncing off all objects in a scene.

Antialiasing

A technique of optically eliminating the jagged effect of bitmapped images or text reproduced on low-resolution devices such as monitors. This is achieved by adding pixels of an intermediate tone—the edges of the object's color are blended with its background by averaging the density of the range of pixels involved. Antialiasing is also sometimes employed to filter texture maps, such as those used in 3D applications, to prevent moiré patterns.

Artifact

A visible flaw in an electronically prepared image, usually occurring as a result of the imaging technique employed. JPEG compression, for example, reduces image data in square blocks of pixels that can become clearly visible at high levels, particularly when high-contrast or color effects are applied.

Background Color

A color that will be used when an eraser is applied to a background layer in an image or that is used when a piece is cut from a background layer. The background color appears with the foreground color in a box at the foot of Photoshop's Toolbar.

Background Layer

The bottom layer in the *Layers* palette that cannot be moved, made transparent, or have a blending mode or layer style applied to it. It can be converted into a regular layer.

Bitmap

A "map" describing the location and binary state (on, off) of bits. It defines a complete collection of pixels that comprise an image, such as a letter.

Blending Mode

The way in which layers interact and how a layer's pixels and color information affect the underlying layers. This produces a result based on the base color and the blending mode.

Blur Filter

The conventional *Blur* effect filter, designed to detect noise around color transitions and remove it. It does this by detecting pixels close to boundaries and averaging their values, effectively eliminating noise and random color variations. *Blur More* is identical but applies the effect more strongly. Somewhat crude, the Blur filter is now joined in many filter sets with more controllable versions, such as *Gaussian Blur* and *Smart Blur*.

Brightness

The relative lightness or darkness of a color, measured as a percentage from 0% (black) up to 100% (white).

Brush

The digital equivalent of a regular paintbrush that can not only paint onto an image but also be used to erase areas of the image.

Calibration

The process of adjusting a machine or item of hardware to conform to a known scale or standard so that it performs more accurately. In graphic reproduction it is important that the various devices and materials used in the production chain, such as scanners, monitors, imagesetters, and printing presses conform to a consistent set of measures in order to achieve true fidelity, particularly where color is concerned. Calibration of reproduction and display devices is generally carried out with a densitometer.

Capture

The action of "getting" an image, either by taking a digital photograph and transferring it to your computer, or by scanning an image and saving the file on the hard drive.

Channels

In most photo-editing applications, a color image is usually composed of three or four separate single-color images, called *Channels*. In standard *RGB* mode, the *Red*, *Green*, and *Blue* channels will each contain a monochromatic image representing the parts of the image that contain that color. In a *CMYK* image, the channels will be *Cyan*, *Magenta*, *Yellow*, and *Black*. These individual channels can be manipulated in much the same way as the main image.

Clipping

Limiting an image or piece of art to within the bounds of a particular area.

Clipping Group

A stack of image layers that produce an image or effect that is a net composite of the constituents. For example, where the base layer is a selection shape (say, an ellipse), the next layer a translucent texture (such as *Craquelure*), and the top layer a pattern, the clipping group would produce a textured pattern in the shape of an ellipse.

CMYK (Cyan, Magenta, Yellow, and Black)

The four printing-process colors based on the subtractive color model (black is represented by the letter K, which stands for "key plate"). In color reproduction, most of the colors are achieved by mixing cyan, magenta, and yellow; the theory being that when all three are combined, they produce black. However, this is rarely achievable—and would be undesirable because too much ink would be used in the process, causing problems with drying time, and so on. For this reason, black is used to add density to darker areas—while, to compensate, smaller amounts of the other colors are used. This also has cost benefits, because black ink is cheaper than colored inks.

Color

The visual interpretation of the various wavelengths of reflected or refracted light.

Color Cast

A bias in a color image that can be either intentionally introduced or the undesirable consequence of a lighting problem. Intentionally created color casts are usually introduced to enhance an effect (such as accentuating the oranges of a sunset, or applying a sepia tone to imply an aged photo) and can be done via an appropriate command in an image-editing application. Undesirable casts arise from a number of causes but are typically due to an imbalance between the lighting source and the response of the CCD (Charge-coupled Device) in a digital camera.

Color Depth

This is the number of bits required to define the color of each pixel. For example, only one bit is required to display a black and white image, while an 8-bit image can display either 256 grays or 256 colors, and a 24-bit image displays 16.7 million colors—eight bits each for red, green, and blue (256 x 256 x 256 = 16,777,216).

Color Temperature

A measure of the composition of light. This is defined as the temperature—measured in degrees Kelvin—to which a black object would need to be heated to produce a particular color of light. The color temperature is based upon a scale that sets zero as absolute darkness, and increases with an object's brightness. A tungsten lamp, for example, has a color temperature of 2,900K, while the temperature of direct sunlight is around 5,000K and is considered the ideal viewing standard in the graphic arts.

Constrain Proportions

A feature that fixes the ratio between the width and height of an image and used when resizing it to ensure the image remains in proportion and is not stretched or squashed.

Contrast

The degree of difference between adjacent tones in an image (or computer monitor), running from the lightest to the darkest. High contrast describes an image with light highlights and dark shadows but with few shades in between, whereas a low-contrast image is one with mostly even tones, and few dark areas or highlights.

Crop

To trim or mask an image so that it fits a given area or so that unwanted portions can be discarded. In Photoshop, this is done with the *Crop* tool.

Default

The tool or filter settings that will take effect if you do not make a change to them.

Definition

The overall quality—or clarity—of an image, determined by the combined subjective effect of graininess (or resolution in a digital image) and sharpness.

Desaturate

A quick way to make a color image black and white by equalizing the *Red*, *Green*, and *Blue* channel values.

Displacement Map

A bitmap image file, normally grayscale, used for modifying surfaces or applying textures. The gray values in the image are assigned height values, with black representing the troughs and white the peaks. Displacement maps (also sometimes called "bump maps") are used in 3D software packages, too, and in the form of digital elevation models (DEMs) for generating cartographic relief maps.

DPI (Dots Per Inch)

A unit of measurement used to represent the resolution of devices such as printers. The closer and smaller the dots (the more there are to each inch), the better the quality. Also used as a misnomer for PPI (Pixels Per Inch) when describing screen resolution.

GLOSSARY

Drop Shadow

Effect (available as a filter, plugin, or layer feature) that produces a shadow beneath a selection conforming to the selection outline. This shadow (depending on the filter) can be moved relative to the selection, given variable opacity, or even tilted. In the last case, a drop shadow can be applied to a selection (say, a person) and that shadow will mimic a sunlight shadow.

Export

A feature that is provided by many applications to allow you to save a file in an format so that it can be used by another application or on a different operating system. For example, a 3D figure created in the Poser modeling application may be exported as an OBJ file so that it can be used in other 3D-modeling applications.

Eyedropper Tool

A tool available in most photo-manipulation applications that is used to select the foreground or background color from the colors in an image or from a selectable color swatch. Eyedropper tools are also used to sample colors in other Photoshop dialogs, including the *Levels* or *Color Range* dialogs.

Feather

An option used to soften the edge of a selection, in order to hide the seams between adjusted or manipulated elements and neighboring areas.

Filter

A process applied to an image that changes or distorts it. For example, a blur effect removes some of the focus from the image, and a watercolor effect makes the photo look as if it has been painted. Filter effects are generally customizable, so you can alter the amount of the effect that you want to apply to a given image.

Foreground Color

The color that is used by the *Brush* tool to paint with. The foreground and background colors appear in boxes at the foot of the Toolbar. See also *Background color*.

Gaussian Blur Filter

A Photoshop filter that applies a weighted average (based on the bell-shaped curve of Gaussian distribution) when identifying and softening boundaries. It also introduces low-frequency detail and a mild "mistiness" to the image which is ideal for covering (blending out) discrete image information, such as noise and artifacts. A useful tool for applying variable degrees of blur and a more controllable tool than conventional *Blur* filters, it can be accessed through the *Filter > Blur > Gaussian Blur* menu.

Gradient Tool

Allows the creation of a gradual blend between two colors within a selection. Several types exist, including *Linear*, *Radial*, and *Reflected* gradients.

Grayscale

A black-and-white image in which pixel brightness values are recorded on a scale of 0 to 255 for black to white. Unlike RGB or CMYK images, a grayscale image has no color information.

Hard Light

A Photoshop blending mode. Creates an effect similar to directing a bright light at the subject. Depending on the base color, the paint color will be multiplied or screened. The base color is lightened if the paint color is light, and darkened if the paint color is dark. Contrast tends to be emphasized and highlights exaggerated. Somewhat similar to *Overlay* mode but with a more pronounced effect.

High Key

An image comprising predominantly light tones and often imparting an ethereal or romantic appearance.

Histogram

A graphic representation of the distribution of tonal values in an image, normally ranging from black at the left-hand vertex to white at the right. Analysis of the shape of the histogram (either by the user or automatic) can be used to evaluate criteria and establish whether there is enough detail to make corrections.

Hue

Color expressed as a degree between 0° and 360° on the standard color wheel or normally referred to as red, orange, or green, etc. See also *Saturation*.

Image Size

A description of the dimensions of an image. Depending on the type of image being measured, this can be in terms of linear dimensions, resolution, or digital file size.

Import

To bring text, pictures, or other data into a document.

Interpolation

A computer calculation used to estimate unknown values that fall between known ones. One use of this process is to redefine pixels in bitmapped images after they have been modified in some way—for instance, when an image is resized or rotated, or if color corrections have been made. In such cases the program takes estimates from the known values of other pixels lying in the same or similar ranges. Interpolation is also used by some software to enhance the resolution of images that have been scanned at low resolution. Some applications allow you to choose an interpolation method. Photoshop, for example, offers *Nearest Neighbor* (for fast but imprecise results, which may produce jagged effects), *Bilinear* (for medium-quality results), and *Bicubic* (for smooth and precise results, but with slower performance).

Lasso

The freehand selection tool indicated by a lasso icon in the Toolbar. There are many other variations on the basic *Lasso*, such as the *Magnetic Lasso* (that can identify the edges nearest to the selection path, aiding accurate selection of discrete objects) and the *Polygonal Lasso* (that allows straight-edged selections to be made). In the case of the latter, to draw a straight line, the user places the cursor point at the end of the first line and clicks, then place the cursor at the end of the next line and clicks again.

Layer

A common feature in photo-manipulation software for creating composite images by keeping image elements on separate "overlays." Once these layers have been created, they can be reordered, blended, and have their transparency altered.

Layer Effects/Layer Styles

A series of effects, such as *Drop Shadow*, *Inner Glow*, *Emboss*, and *Bevel* that can be applied to the contents of a layer.

Layer Mask

A mask that can be applied to the elements of an image in a particular layer. The layer mask can be modified to create different effects but such changes do not alter the pixels of that layer. As with adjustment layers (of which this is a close relation), a layer mask can be applied to the "host" layer (to make the changes permanent) or removed, along with any other changes.

Marquee

The shape around an object that appears when you Ctrl/Cmd+click on its layer or that you see when you choose one of the two *Marquee* tools. The marquee is often referred to as "marching ants," and shows the area you are working on.

Opacity

In a layered Photoshop document, the percentage of transparency that each layer of an image has in relation to the layer beneath. As the opacity is lowered, the layer beneath shows through.

Pen Tool

A tool used for drawing vector selection paths in applications such as Photoshop and Illustrator.

Pixel

Acronym for "picture element." The smallest component of a digitally generated image, such

as a single dot of light on a computer monitor. In its simplest form, one pixel corresponds to a single bit: 0 = off and 1 = on. In color and grayscale images or monitors, a single pixel may correspond to several bits: an 8-bit pixel, for example, can be displayed in any of 256 colors (the total number of different configurations that can be achieved by eight 0s and 1s).

Plugin

A small program that "plugs in" to an application to extend its features or add support for a particular file format.

PPI (Pixels Per Inch)

The most common unit of resolution, describing how many pixels are contained within a single square inch of image.

Primitive

In 3D programs, a basic geometric element (e.g. a cylinder or cube) from which more complex objects can be built.

Rasterization

The conversion of vector outlines into bitmap dots.

Rendering

The process of creating a 2D image from 3D geometry. 3D models must be rendered before they can be imported to photo-manipulation applications.

Resolution

The degree of quality, definition, or clarity with which an image is reproduced or displayed on screen or the printed page. The higher the resolution, the more pixels are contained within a given area, and the greater the detail captured.

RGB (Red, Green, Blue)

The primary colors of the "additive" color model—used in video technology (including computer monitors) and also for graphics (for the Web and multi-media, for example) that will not ultimately be printed by the four-color (CMYK) process method.

Rotate

To swivel an image around a central axis so edges that were horizontal and vertical are now at an angle.

Saturation

The strength or purity of a color. Saturation is the percentage of gray in proportion to the hue: 100% is fully saturated. On the standard color wheel, saturation increases from the center to the edge. Also called chroma.

Scale

A 3D transformation that shrinks or enlarges an object about its axes.

INDEX

AUTHOR BIOGRAPHIES & ACKNOWLEDGMENTS

Thanks to the following artists for their participation in this book:

Patrik Blomqvist

Heartbroken; Tired Tire
www.patrikland.com
During the day, Patrik Blomqvist works as an art director for an advertising agency in Gothenburg, Sweden, and at night he runs his own business, www.patrikland.com. The core business is creative digital photo manipulations—some commercial, some eye pleasing, and some just plain scary. His alter-ego, hygglobert, also judges Photoshop artwork at www.freakingnews.com.

Andrew Brooks

Falling Man
www.andrewbrooksphotography.com
Andrew Brooks has been a professional digital imagemaker for more than 10 years, working on a wide range of projects, from advertising photography to music videos. He has exhibited his work in many galleries and his photography has featured in *WebPhotoMag* and other online publications. He has also had his video work shown on MTV2, and was awarded a fujifilm professional merit award for his *Falling Man* image. He is rapidly building an international reputation for his breathtakingly different and lovingly labored-over large-scale print images.

Georgia Denby

Muscle Man; Trapped
www.georgiadenby.co.uk
Georgia Denby discovered a love for and fascination with photography after many years of paints, pencils, and various other media, but came to the conclusion that digital photography and computers were where her true talents lie. She is known for her diverse creative abilities, strong composition, and dramatic quality of lighting. She is a fellow of the British Institute of Professional Photography, an Associate of the Royal Photographic Society, and a Qualified European Photographer.

Nela Dunato

Electric Medusa; You Can't Own Me
www.inobscuro.com
Nela Dunato was born in 1985 in Rijeka, Croatia. She is currently a student of electrical engineering, and works as a web designer.

Ben Goossens

The Gate of Eden; Sweet Home
www.photo.net/photos/ben.goossens
Ben Goossens spent most of his working life as an art director for an advertising firm. Since retiring, he began submitting his images to various international photographic contests. In the 10 years he has been entering contests, he has won many accolades, including first prize in the Austrian Super Circuit competition, a gold medal and the Best of Show award at Interimage 2005, and the Grand Prix de Ville de Limours at the Limours 2005 contest.

As well as entering competitions, Ben shares his years of Photoshop experience by doing presentations and lectures in many photo clubs and art schools in his native Belgium.

Jeffrey Harp

The Leonine Hatman
www.hippopotamouse.com
Jeffrey Harp spent 11 years working as a tattoo artist where he developed his interest in photography and his eye for the surreal.

In 2001, he was introduced to the work of photographer Adam Fuss, which led him to experiment with photograms, pinhole photography, and a variety of antique photography techniques. This experimentation ultimately brought him to digital art, a technology that has allowed him to create artwork he had never been able to express on skin, paper, or canvas.

Margot Quan Knight

Cheerio Worm; Spilt Milk
www.margotknight.com
Margot Quan Knight studied photography at Dartmouth College, graduating Summa Cum Laude with a BA in Studio Art. From September 2000 to May 2002 she was a sponsored photographer at Fabrica, the communication arts research center of Benetton in Italy. She is currently an MFA student at Bard College in New York, and is represented by G.A.S. Art Gallery in Turin, Italy.

Margot's photographs have been exhibited internationally, including personal shows in Milan, Paris, Lisbon, and Seattle. In October 2005 her Hospital Triptych won first prize at the Verona Art Fair. Her work has been featured in over 60 international publications, including *PHOTO France*, *EFX Art and Design*, and *Zoom*.

The image "Spilt Milk" was made possible in part by a Special Projects Grant from 4Culture and by a CityArtist Project Grant from the Seattle Mayor's Office of Arts and Cultural Affairs.

Domen Lombergar

Guardian Angel
www.lombergar.com
Domen Lombergar is a contemporary surreal painter and photographer who uses new technologies to find alternative means of

expression. He is currently working on his eighteenth exhibition, which explores the relationship of human and machine through visual media.

Frank Picini

Conventum Elementum

www.frankpicini.com

Frank Picini has been an illustrator for the past 10 years, creating artwork for CD covers as well as books. He was a Digital Art contest winner at Macworld in 2002, 2003, and 2005, and collections of the winning art have been displayed in many digital art galleries across the U.S. His work is also on display in digital galleries across the globe, and on various digital art forums on the Internet. He has won numerous awards for his artwork, and created the box art for Poser 6 SE.

Simon Rudd

Troll; Secrets

www.pompeysworst.co.uk

Simon Rudd graduated in 2001 from the University of Portsmouth, U.K. He has spent his time developing a diverse portfolio of photomanipulations—usually concentrating on horror, the macabre, and fantasy. He has written numerous magazine articles and book tutorials regarding his work.

He would like to thank Nara Vieira, Daniel Drucker, David Notarius, and Ned Horton for the use of their photographs.

Liva Rutmane

Lover; Blind

www.mandragora.ex.lv

Liva Rutmane is an artist and photographer living in Riga, Latvia. She uses a variety of software from Photoshop and Illustrator, to Painter and Cinema4D to create her artwork.

Hampus Samuelsson

Thing in the Woods

www.abacrombie.se

Hampus Samuelsson has been familiar with Photoshop since he was 14, when his father, a photographer, brought home Photoshop 3.0. He learned Photoshop the hard way, teaching himself how to use the application from scratch, and is now, 12 years later, thinking of taking some classes on it.

Thomas Speer

Yankee Rose

Thomas Speer is a self-taught graphic artist who resides in Jacksonville, Florida, USA. He has worked in the graphic arts field for six years, designing images for dozens of commercial and private web sites. He is also an award winning member in several graphic design contest sites such as Worth1000.com (member name: BrownTrout).

Special thanks to Stock Xchng Imagery (www.sxc.hu) and photographer Majoros Attila for the original Yellow Rose image.

Anthony VenGraitis

Bear; Invasion

www.pixelsandwich.com

Anthony VenGraitis is a self-taught Photoshop junkie. He works primarily with digital photographs manipulated in Photoshop, combining them with scans of traditional photographs and occasionally other artifacts. Being able to work in a filmless environment allows him enormous freedom to experiment with his photographs, and he believes the computer has rewritten the rules of artistic photography in the same way that the Internet has revolutionized the way artists can exhibit their work. He has won awards for his art at Adobe's 2001 International Digital Imaging contest, and Bit-by-Bit's 2000 Digital Competition and Exhibit.

Useful Websites

USEFUL WEBSITES

Tutorial & gallery websites

2D Valley
www.2dvalley.com

Absolute Cross
www.absolutecross.com

Artcyclopedia
www.artcyclopedia.com

Artuproar
www.artuproar.com

Artworld
www.artworld.si

Bluesfear
www.bluesfear.com

Concept Art
www.conceptart.org

CreativePro
www.creativepro.com

deviantART
www.deviantart.com

Digital Photography Review
www.dpreview.com

ePHOTOzine
www.ephotozine.com

Epilogue
www.epilogue.net

Flickr
www.flickr.com

HexValue
www.hexvalue.net

National Association of Photoshop Professionals
www.photoshopuser.com

Pixel2Life Tutorials
www.pixel2life.com

Photo.net Resource Site
www.photo.net

Photoshop Today
www.photoshoptoday.com

Planet Photoshop
www.planetphotoshop.com

Photoshop Support
www.photoshopsupport.com

Surreal Art Photo Gallery
www.surrealartists.org

The Complete Guide to Digital Photography
www.completeguidetodigitalphotography.com

The Imaging Resource
www.imaging-resource.com

The Photoshop Roadmap
www.photoshoproadmap.com

The Saatchi Gallery
www.saatchi-gallery.co.uk

Tutorial Outpost
www.tutorialoutpost.com

Tutorialized
www.tutorialized.com

Worth 1000
www.worth1000.com

Software

Adobe
www.adobe.com

Alien Skin
www.alienskin.com

Apple Computer
www.apple.com

Corel
www.corel.com

e frontier
www.e-frontier.com

Extensis
www.extensis.com

GIMP
www.gimp.org

Maxon
www.maxon.net

Microsoft
www.microsoft.com

ABOUT THE EDITOR

Ben Renow-Clarke has written and edited a wide range of books on almost every aspect of digital creativity, from Photoshop image manipulation to 3D modelling, video editing to Flash ActionScripting.

OTHER TITLES OF INTEREST

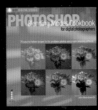
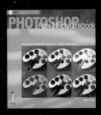
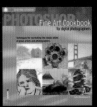

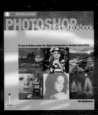
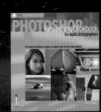

Photoshop Cookbook series

Ilex Digital Studio

Push your Photoshop skills to the limits. Each title is packed with essential techniques in step-by-step format.

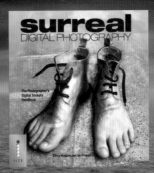

Surreal Digital Photography

ISBN 1-904705-41-3

Step-by-step workthroughs take you behind the scenes with some of the leading exponents of the surreal artform, showing you how to manipulate digital images to produce stunning results.

ILEX

Digital technology has given a new breed of photographers and image-makers the freedom to realize their wildest dreams and strangest fantasies. The best of this surreal output from around the world is collected here in *Surreal Digital Photography 2*.

Each artist provides an in-depth tutorial explaining how their work was created, and supplies expert tips on how you can create spectacular visual effects of your own. All you need is an idea and the right tools, and it won't be long before you are creating your own stunning works of surreal photographic art.

Fully compatible with Adobe Photoshop CS3.

ISBN-10   1-905814-07-0
ISBN-13   978-1-905814-07-7

9 781905 814077

Category 1
Photography: Digital
Category 2
Computers: Digital Photography

£17.99

ILEX
The Old Candlemakers
West Street
Lewes
East Sussex BN7 2NZ
www.ilex-press.com

ILE